GREEK AND ROMAN COLONIZATION

GREEK
AND
ROMAN
COLONIZATION

Origins, Ideologies
and Interactions

Editors

Guy Bradley

and

John-Paul Wilson

Contributors

Edward Bispham, Guy Bradley, Michael Crawford,
David Gill, John R. Patterson, John-Paul Wilson

The Classical Press of Wales

First published in 2006 by
The Classical Press of Wales
15 Rosehill Terrace, Swansea SA1 6JN
Tel: +44 (0)1792 458397
Fax: +44 (0)1792 464067
www.classicalpressofwales.co.uk

Distributor in the United States of America:
The David Brown Book Co.
PO Box 511, Oakville, CT 06779
Tel: +1 (860) 945–9329
Fax: +1 (860) 945–9468

ISBN 1-905125-06-2

A catalogue record for this book is available from the British Library

Typeset by Ernest Buckley, Clunton, Shropshire
Printed and bound in the UK by Gomer Press, Llandysul, Ceredigion, Wales

The Classical Press of Wales, an independent venture, was founded in 1993, initially to support the work of classicists and ancient historians in Wales and their collaborators from further afield. More recently it has published work initiated by scholars internationally. While retaining a special loyalty to Wales and the Celtic countries, the Press welcomes scholarly contributions from all parts of the world.

The symbol of the Press is the Red Kite. This bird, once widespread in Britain, was reduced by 1905 to some five individuals confined to a small area known as 'The Desert of Wales' – the upper Tywi valley. Geneticists report that the stock was saved from terminal inbreeding by the arrival of one stray female bird from Germany. After much careful protection, the Red Kite now thrives – in Wales and beyond.

CONTENTS

PREFACE

The origins of this project lie in a conference organized by the two editors in the Institute of Classical Studies, University of London (12–13th July 1998). The conference was supported by the British Academy, the Institute of Classical Studies, the Graduate School of University College London, and the University of Wales Institute of Classics and Ancient History (UWICAH). We would like to extend our thanks to those institutions for enabling the conference to take place.

Although the conference was lively and well received, most of the papers delivered could not, for various reasons, be published in their original form.* The contributions to this volume are thus mostly new pieces of work, written to respond to the themes stated in our conference prospectus and to themes that emerged over the two days of the conference. The benefits of this long gestation are, we hope, evident in the way that papers explicitly address the themes of the project.

The editors would like to thank Anton Powell, the Director of UWICAH, for his support and guidance in bringing this project to publication, and Ernest Buckley for skilful handling of the production of this book.

---

* The original line-up included, besides the contributors to this volume, Emmanuele Curti, Giovanna Ceserani, John Graham, Irad Malkin and Massimo Osanna.

ABBREVIATIONS

AJA	*American Journal of Archaeology*
AIONArch	*Annali dell'Istituto Universitario Orientale di Napoli. Archeologia e storia antica*
AIIN	*Annali dell'Istituto Italiano di Numismatica*
ANRW	*Aufstieg und Niedergang der römischen Welt*
Arch. Class.	*Archaeologia Classica*
ASNP	*Annali della Scuola Normale Superiore di Pisa, Classe di Lettere e Filosofia*
BCH	*Bulletin de Correspondance Hellénique*
BEFAR	*Bibliothèque des Écoles Françaises d'Athènes et de Rome*
BICS	*Bulletin of the Institute of Classical Studies*
BMI	*The Collection of Ancient Greek Inscriptions in the British Museum*
BSA	*Annual of the British School at Athens*
CAH	*The Cambridge Ancient History*
CIL	*Corpus Inscriptionum Latinarum*
CQ	*Classical Quarterly*
CP	*Classical Philology*
CR	*Classical Review*
CRAI	*Comptes rendus de l'Académie des Inscriptions et Belles-lettres*
DdA	*Dialoghi di Archeologia*
HSCP	*Harvard Studies in Classical Philology*
ILLRP	A. Degrassi (ed.) *Inscriptiones Latinae Liberae Rei Publicae*, Florence, 1957–65
ILS	H. Dessau (ed.) *Inscriptiones Latinae Selectae*, Berlin, 1892–1916
JDAI	*Jahrbuch des deutschen archäologischen Instituts*
JHS	*Journal of Hellenic Studies*
JRA	*Journal of Roman Archaeology*
JRS	*Journal of Roman Studies*
MAAR	*Memoirs of the American Academy in Rome*
MEFRA	*Mélanges d'archéologie et d'histoire de l'Ecole Française de Rome*
MonAL	*Monumenti Antichi pubblicati per cura della Reale Accademia dei Lincei*

Abbreviations

NSA	*Notizie degli scavi di antichità*
PBSR	*Papers of the British School at Rome*
PdP	*La parola del passato*
RA	*Revue archéologique*
RFIC	*Rivista di filologia e di istruzione classica*
RIL	*Rendiconti dell'Istituto Lombardo di scienze e lettere*
RSA	*Rivista storica dell'antichità*
SEG	*Supplementum Epigraphicum Graecum*
SIG	W. Dittenberger, *Sylloge Inscriptionum Graecarum*, 3rd edn., Leipzig, 1915–24
SNG ANS	*Sylloge Nummorum Graecorum. American Numismatic Society*

INTRODUCTION

Background and aims of the project

The original idea for this project developed from a course taught by John-Paul Wilson at University College London, which analysed colonization across the Greek and Roman worlds. Both editors shared an interest in the processes of colonization and in the contribution of archaeological evidence to its study. This interest was in part stimulated by work on archaic Greek history by Snodgrass, Morris, Whitley and others. Appreciation of the complexity of state formation in early Greece has opened up questions about the nature of colonization: what sort of colonies, for instance, were being established by communities themselves undergoing revolutionary change (on Snodgrass's model) in the eighth century? A key element in the vitality of archaic Greek history is the increased availability of archaeological evidence, which has been a means of analysing the nature of colonial settlements, and of comparing them to the cities of the Greek mainland. Many of the same questions have considerable relevance to Roman history, where archaeology is providing a much more rounded picture of Roman colonies within Italy, and where there is vibrant debate over the nature of early Rome. Yet historians of Greek colonization have made greater progress in illuminating the development of colonial activities over time, the great differences between earlier and later colonies, and the divergence of the imagined picture in ancient texts from the evidence of archaeology.

Whilst methodologies from the study of archaic Greece would seem to have much to offer in analysing Roman colonization, it is striking that direct comparisons have rarely been attempted.[1] There is good reason for this, given the obvious differences between Greek and Roman colonial practices. For example, one set of colonizations is undertaken by an ethnic/regional group of disputed boundaries (Greece), the other by a city (Rome). A closer comparison might be between Greece and Italy as a whole, encompassing Etruscan and Italic as well as Roman colonization; that might provide something more akin to the diversity of agents involved in Greek colonization. Also, maritime travel is a critical feature of the Greek experience of colonization but is largely absent from Roman Republican colonization.[2] This means that Greek colonies tend to be open to greater individual mobility, and that there is more difficulty in imposing state control over comings and goings. Again, there is an explicit link between colonization and conquest in Roman history, made plain by Roman sources such as Livy and Velleius. This connection is much more controversial and problematic for Greek colonization, particularly in its earliest phases.

The most productive way to compare the two worlds of colonization has seemed to us to involve comparing ancient views of colonization, and using modern methodological approaches to the available evidence, archaeological as well as literary. Our starting point was that the ancient sources represented colonization in the archaic past in similar ways. What we might call 'ideologies' of colonization developed in both Greece and Rome. Many characteristic features of these ideologies are shared: the emphasis on a particular foundation date and individual founders (whether Roman king/*triumvir* or Greek *oikist*); the dichotomy between colonists and natives; and the role of the mother state.

It is not our intention to sweep away the entire literary tradition as 'invented'.[3] But it seems to us that all of these elements of the colonizing process should be put up for discussion. It is clear that both Greek and Roman colonization were less tightly regulated in their earlier phases than was the case later. We might talk of 'pre-' or 'protocolonial' phases for both worlds, although this begs the question of when and how such phases should be distinguished from 'true' colonization.[4] State control was much more gradually asserted over such enterprises than our literary sources often suggest.[5] Episodes more characteristic of early colonization still show through in later periods, such as the abortive attempt of the Spartan Dorieus to found a colony 'privately' in Libya (Herodotus 5.42, discussed by Wilson in this volume) or the (attempted) seizure of cities such as Capua and Rhegion by their garrisons in the mid-Republic (discussed by Bradley).[6] In fact, much of the modern emphasis on standard colonial procedures derives from over-dependence on ancient ideologies of colonization, and from too restrictive a definition of colonization. This inevitably becomes a standardized process if it is defined to exclude alternative forms such as gentilial colonization in early Rome, or mercantile foundations (*emporia*) in the Greek world.

One other impetus to our project is the influence of modern 'post-colonial' historiography, and the increasing scrutiny of imperialistic assumptions which this encouraged. It was evident to us that the discussion of colonialism had some relevance, particularly given the baggage attached to the word 'colonization'. In an influential article Osborne highlighted the term's overtones of 'political and cultural control' (1998, 252). He drew attention to the origins of the term 'colony' in the Latin *colonia*, with its imperial associations: Roman *coloniae* could be portrayed by Cicero as 'bulwarks of empire' (discussed by Bispham and Bradley below). Osborne's point was that this term brings too many 'statist' associations to the Greek process of colonization, extraneous baggage that is both ancient and modern. But whilst the idea of *coloniae* as a fundamental element of empire predates modern colonialist enterprises, and is evident in Roman sources, the distorting effect of modern overtones is also apparent in the consideration of Roman colonization. Awareness of such tendencies frees us to question how far later Romans understood, and correctly represented, the nature of colonization in earlier periods.

The ultimate aim of this volume is to open up discussion, provoke questions, and suggest new avenues of approach. This does involve problematizing earlier views, and the reader's patience is required if we do not necessarily prescribe answers. Much will be controversial, and the volume is certainly not intended to be a complete reference work on the topic.

Themes of the volume

The first theme, addressed in the majority of papers, is the pervasive influence of ancient historiography on the study of ancient colonization. Colonization processes are inevitably of great interest to ancient authors. Colonization and migration might be said to be fundamental to the Graeco-Roman vision of the origins of ancient peoples, and therefore the key to explaining their identities. Dionysius of Halicarnassus, for instance, states that most peoples of Italy had an ultimate origin outside the peninsular, whether they arrived from abroad or broke off from a group that did.[7] The autochthony of the Etruscans was unusual – and disputed. Many of the studies in this volume show the distorting influence of ancient writers' own *milieux* on their record of earlier colonial enterprises, though (as Patterson notes) this does not necessarily lead to an ahistorical picture. Several of the studies (Bradley, Bispham, Wilson) argue that the vision of past colonizations presented in the ancient sources is 'tidied up', particularly by the over-emphasis placed on the role of the 'mother' state in early foundations, whether Greek polis or the city of Rome.

The second theme is the impact of archaeological evidence. Several studies emphasize the usefulness of archaeological evidence as a corrective to the literary history of colonies. It is often critical to interpret the literary evidence in the light of the archaeological situation, and not the other way round. This point is illustrated in practical fashion by the two case-studies in this volume, Gill's analysis of the evidence for the origins of Euesperides, and Crawford's reassessment of Poseidonia/Paestum. Wilson and Bispham discuss the application of this principle to Greek and Roman colonization respectively.

Closely linked to these two themes is the idea that we should pay particular attention to the diversity of colonies, even when founded by the same city (such as the Roman colonies of the mid Republic examined by Bispham). Bradley's chapter emphasizes the variety of colonization mechanisms in Rome and Latium in the sixth and fifth centuries BC. The variation in the religious topographies of Latin colonies is examined in Bispham's chapter. Crawford and Bradley examine the varied treatments of local populations in different Latin colonies. Crawford's analysis of cultural change in Paestum illustrates the influence of the pre-existing Greek inhabitants. It thus seems important to study colonies in their local contexts and not only as products of their place of origin (see Wilson). Most papers have stressed scepticism about over-standardized pictures of ancient colonies based around colonial 'blueprints'.

Another important theme is the origins and role of colonies. A key idea for early colonization (especially Greek) is individual and group mobility.[8] Horden's and Purcell's recent study of Mediterranean history (2000) shows how a pervasive mobility is promoted by the environment of the Mediterranean. As Wilson demonstrates in this volume, migration and mobility are also characteristic of classical Greek ways of looking at their archaic past. He argues that we should be thinking not in terms of an age, or ages, of Greek colonization, but rather of colonization as being a constant feature of Mediterranean history. This observation might equally be applied to Italy. Bradley's chapter looks at inter-community mobility in the archaic period. Later, in the middle and late Republic, there were massive state-organized transfers of populations and significant levels of private individual migration.[9]

Wilson poses the question in his chapter of why particular eras of Greek colonization have been identified. Modernizing perspectives tend to privilege the treatment of later periods of colonization, when states are thought to have been fully formed. The problematization of different eras of colonization is also pertinent to Roman history. Although Roman colonization is commonly seen in terms of a transition from a more military to a more socio-economic function, Patterson's study in this volume emphasizes the complexity of motives behind colonial foundations in Italy. Both functions were evident in Roman colonial foundations from their early origins. Wilson's point about the arbitrary application of more statist agendas to Greek colonies after the late eighth century BC ('colonization' as opposed to 'migration') is echoed by Bispham's exploration of the limits of the application of statist agendas to Latin colonies in the mid-Republic.

Several of the papers take a similar approach to the role of myth in colonization. Greek historians often ask whether myths of colonization are aetiological or historical. But as Wilson shows, the creation of such hierarchies of types of myth is problematic, given that all were treated alike by the ancients. Mythical elements might appear less significant in Roman colonization, which is usually accorded a much more prosaic treatment, and whose utilitarian purposes are usually emphasized above all.[10] Notices of colonization under the kings and other 'non-standard' types of colonization in early Roman history (for which see Bradley's chapter) are frequently excluded because they are regarded as lacking historical authenticity. Yet the distinction between mythical and historical colonization is often as difficult to justify for Rome as it is for Greece.

Several papers also deal with the role of founders. Wilson argues that the cult of the founders does not extend back into the earliest periods of Greek colonization. Tyrants, particularly in the late seventh century, may be significant as 'pattern-setters', providing a model for conceptions of earlier founders. Kings and the leaders of warrior bands instigate colonial enterprises in early Roman history. Their role is taken over by *triumviri* in the early Republic. The historicity of the named *triumviri* we have for the early Republic is disputed.[11] Nevertheless it is interesting that the role of these Republican officials seems to have evolved from earlier practice: the leader of the triumvirate, usually the primary conqueror of the territory to be distributed, remained a powerful figure. He had the right to reward his soldiers in the same way as kings and the leaders of warrior bands, with a plot of land. A later echo might be found in the way late Republican dynasts directly rewarded their own soldiers with plots carved out of land confiscated from their defeated enemies.

Overall, we hope this volume shows colonization to be a vital and important field of classical study.[12] The term subsumes diverse processes of settlement, and this variety helps lend the subject much of its interest. Approaches to colonization in different areas and periods of the ancient world must benefit if they continue to learn from each other, a trend to which we hope to have given impetus.

Notes

[1] Cf. Hurst 2005, 1. It is notable that there is little direct comparison in Horden and Purcell 2000, even though their work draws on a huge range of cross-cultural Mediterranean parallels, and colonization is a significant topic in their discussion. However, Torelli (1999, 18–19) has drawn stimulating parallels between archaic Roman colonization and the Etruscan colonies of the Po valley and Campania.

[2] Note, however, the reputed Roman attempts to found colonies on Sardinia and Corsica (Diodoros 15.27.4; Theophrastus *HP* 5.8.2) discussed by Bispham in this volume.

[3] For the dangers of such an approach, see Malkin 2003.

[4] For a discussion of the terms (preferring 'protocolonial'), see Malkin 1998, 10–14. Cf. Osborne 1998, 258.

[5] This was questioned at the original conference by Malkin, who argued that colonization is a sign of statehood.

[6] On Dorieus, see also Osborne 1998, 251, 255.

[7] Cf. Wilson on Greek traditions.

[8] Cf. Osborne 1998, 258–9 on the implications of the growth of Pithekoussai in the 8th century; Malkin 2003, 161.

[9] On this see Patterson, this volume; Broadhead 2002; Scheidel 2004.

[10] See, for example, Salmon 1969. Torelli 1999 is the most notable exception.

[11] See Bradley for discussion of the reputed triumvirate at Antium in 467.

[12] Cf. Hurst and Owen 2005, which appeared during the writing of this introduction.

Bibliography

Broadhead, W.
2002   *Internal Migration and the Transformation of Republican Italy*, Ph.D thesis, London.

Horden, P. and Purcell, N.
2000   *The Corrupting Sea. A study of Mediterranean history*, Oxford.

Hurst, H.
2005   'Introduction', in Hurst and Owen (eds.) *Ancient Colonizations*.

Hurst, H. and Owen, S. (eds.)
2005   *Ancient Colonizations: Analogy, similarity and difference,* London.

Malkin, I.
1998   *The Returns of Odysseus: Colonization and ethnicity*, Berkeley.
2003   '"Tradition" in Herodotus: the foundation of Cyrene', in P. Derow and R. Parker (eds.) *Herodotus and his World. Essays from a Conference in memory of George Forrest*, Oxford, 153–70.

Osborne R.
1998   'Early Greek colonization? The nature of Greek settlements in the West', in N. Fisher and H. van Wees (eds.) *Archaic Greece. New approaches and new evidence*, London and Swansea, 251–70.

Salmon, E.T.
1969   *Roman Colonization under the Republic*, London.

Scheidel, W.
2004   'Human mobility in Roman Italy, 1: the free population', *JRS* 94, 1–26.

Torelli, M.
1999   'Religious aspects of early Roman colonization', in *Tota Italia*, Oxford, 14–42.

EARLY COLONIZATION AT EUESPERIDES: ORIGINS AND INTERACTIONS

David Gill

I. Introduction

The cemeteries of Euesperides in Cyrenaica had been explored and widely looted in the nineteenth century by a number of early travellers including George Dennis,[1] although it was not until the early twentieth century, during the Italian survey of the area, that the site of the settlement was recognized.[2] Pottery collection was made on the site in 1947, and in 1950 and 1951 a surface survey was conducted which confirmed occupation in the fifth and fourth centuries BC, though there was no evidence for anything earlier than the 470s.[3]

The Greek colony lies on the northern, that is to say seaward, side of the Sebka Es-Selmani, a lagoon lying to the east of modern Benghazi which was also the site of the relocated ancient city which was renamed Berenice.[4] The original Greek settlement stood on a low hill, the Sidi Abeid, which was subsequently covered by a muslim cemetery.[5] The city extended southwards towards the lagoon, which was clearly drying out during the fifth century BC; indeed the fourth century BC extension to the city was built over the now dry salt marsh. One of the most evocative descriptions of the site of Benghazi was written by George Dennis in 1867:

> The traveller will be struck with the dreary position of the town on a narrow strip of sand between the sea and a salt lagoon, its crumbling castle, a solitary minaret, and a grove of date-palms, being the only distinguishing features that rise above the monotonous line of low red walls which compose the town... Nor is the country around Benghazi more attractive than the town. For some 20 miles inland it is an undulating, arid waste, for the greater part of the year unrefreshed by leaf or blade, shrub or wild flower. It is hard to believe that this dreary, sandy, barren shore can ever have possessed such attractions as to deserve the reputation of a Paradise.[6]

One of the aims of the excavation of the colony in the early 1950s, sponsored by the Ashmolean Museum, Oxford, was to establish the date of the

Fig. 1. Aerial view of Euesperides. The Sidi Abeid is in the foreground, and Benghazi in the distance. Photograph by courtesy of the Ashmolean Museum, Oxford.

Fig. 2. East Greek Hemispherical Bowl fragment from the archaic levels of the southern scarp on the Sidi Abeid, Eusperides (BUS152, 7), © Ashmolean Museum, Oxford.

Fig. 3. Attic black-figured skyphos fragment from the archaic levels of the southern scarp on the Sidi Abeid, Eusperides (BUS152, 7), © Ashmolean Museum, Oxford.

foundation.[7] Further excavations were conducted on the site in 1968 and 1969 by Professor Barri Jones but these were terminated by the changing political situation in Libya.[8] Most of the trenches were in the lower city where the excavated material appears to belong to the fourth and early third centuries BC;[9] a scarp on the Sidi Abeid was also re-explored. Further excavations, supported by the Society for Libyan Studies, have resumed in recent years, initially under John Lloyd and then under Andrew Wilson.[10]

II. The literary evidence for the early colony

The first historical mention of Euesperides is in 515 BC during the revolt of Barca from the Persians, when an expedition reached as far as Euesperides.[11] Early reports that excavations in the lower city had found remains of a Persian destruction level proved to be premature when it was recognized that this in fact was an early fourth-century level.[12]

Euesperides was one of a number of Greek colonies in Cyrenaica which, if Herodotus is to be believed, were settled as a result of the Delphic oracle prompting settlers from Thera.[13] They founded the colony of Cyrene, and Herodotus suggests that a further Delphic oracle during the reign of Battos' grandson, Battos II, prompted a further colonizing movement to Cyrenaica which provoked a response from Egypt, then ruled by the Saite pharaoh Apries.[14] The Egyptian forces were defeated and in the aftermath the philhellenic Amasis seized power.[15]

III. The archaeological evidence for the early colony

The earliest archaeological survey of the city found no clear evidence for an archaic phase of the colony. However, deep trenches on the Sidi Abeid have now found certain archaic levels, and archaic pottery also appears in later contexts. The first survey of archaic pottery was prepared in 1971; this identified the presence of East Greek, Cycladic, Laconian, Corinthian and Attic pottery.[16] There are three key deposits for the archaic city, two first explored by the expedition of the early 1950s, and the third by the more recent excavations.

1. *Square* B7

One of the deepest sections on the Sidi Abeid comes from section B7, the north-west corner of an insula block which adjoins the north-south road running across the Sidi Abeid, and the east-west road which runs down to the so-called house by the city wall.[17] The section, some two metres deep, suggested that there had been four main periods in this part of the city; up to ten archaeological layers were recognized in the course of the excavation. The upper levels contain coins that suggest that periods 3 and 4 should be dated to the third century.[18] Indeed it now seems likely that a phase of building work was taking place in the city immediately prior to its abandonment, in favour of the establishment of the new city of Berenice, which almost certainly took place in the 250s.[19] Although only part of the insula block was excavated, the thick eastern wall at the south end of the trench should probably be considered as the rear wall of a house, measuring approximately 10.2 m by at least 9.4 m; as such this might indicate that it formed one quarter of the block.[20] Along the side of the block adjoining the road was a well-built wall with foundations which went down to bedrock. This probably marked the edge of the block from the archaic period onwards.

The period 2 house (*Fig.* 4) has a number of features which do not continue in later periods. Notably at the north-east corner of the house is a rectangular room, *c.* 4 m x *c.* 3.3 m (internal measurements), with paving stones on the floor. The door is offset to one side which might suggest that it was an *andron*. The room to its south is puzzling as it is of a similar size, *c.* 3.5 m x *c.* 3.3 m (internal measurements), with a door opening to the south, and at the centre is a mudbrick stand and a large jar set in the floor. This may well have been a utility room. Given the access to this pair of rooms, it seems possible that there was a courtyard to their south, with this house taking a strip of the block some 10 m wide, that is to say with two houses per block.

The layout of this archaic house is similar to that found at Lato on Crete.[21] A number of rooms with offset door were entered through a foyer that had a central stand. For example, the so-called house of the Prytaneion seems to be two linear houses. The one on the south side has a rectangular room at the west end, *c.* 3.2 m x *c.* 5.5 m, with a nearly square foyer, *c.* 5 m x *c.* 5.5 m. House D ran approximately north-south. The end room, *c.* 4.1 m x *c.* 4.5 m, gave access at its south end to a rectangular room, *c.* 6.5 m x *c.* 5.5 m, with a central hearth. These rooms placed before the *andron* have been described as a foyer area. The architectural form can be traced back to the Bronze Age, and its function seems to have been to help cool the main room of the house. Given the unusual nature of this house plan, it might suggest that the colonists of this phase of the archaic city came from Crete, or a place that used a Cretan style of architecture.

The internal walls of the Euesperides house consisted of a stone socle with mudbrick walls. The eastern wall of the house, serving as a boundary wall with the adjoining property, is notably thicker than the others. One explanation is that it served as a retaining wall on what was the downslope side of the building. This level is equated by a large number of archaic finds which are described as coming from the hearth layer.[22] These include a number of East Greek cups, East Greek rosette bowls, Middle Corinthian skyphoi, and one skyphos fragment that is possibly Early Corinthian.[23]

Fig. 4. Reconstruction of archaic building on the eastern side of the Sidi Abeid (B7). © Patricia Flecks.

This house, which we can place in the Middle Corinthian horizon, was preceded by earlier occupation, represented by some 1 m of stratification. Although there are no apparent architectural features, it would seem that the wall along the east-west street marked the original line of the house. Within the block are two distinct bands of grey-brown and brown earth which sit on a black layer. Immediately under the hearth was Middle Corinthian material, but in the lowest level the pottery is almost completely dominated by East Greek material.[24]

One further feature which deserves comment is the structure identified on the plan as an 'oven', lying to the east of the archaic house. The internal diameter of this structure is approximately 1.1 m, perhaps large for a domestic oven.[25] This structure might possibly be a pottery kiln. Such kilns were in fact noted in the next insula block to the north during the excavation of the so-called Italian Trench.[26] If this interpretation is correct, then this may well have been the potters' quarter of the colony. An alternative interpretation may be that these structures were linked to dye-works.[27]

2. *Northern Sidi Abeid: House* HI

Recent excavations in the northern part of the Sidi Abeid have discovered the line of the city wall which may have followed the line of a stone and mudbrick defensive construction probably dating to the archaic period.[28] Immediately behind the wall was a building whose orientation seems to have been influenced by the alignment of the wall, and which rested on the bedrock. The earliest pottery identified is a Middle Corinthian skyphos and other associated material.[29] The house appears to have had a linear arrangement, some 2.5 m wide, and the internal length of the main room (room 3) seems to have been *c.* 3.5 m. This seems to be slightly smaller than the complex discovered in square B7, though it is possible that they were of a similar design.

3. *The scarp on the south edge of the Sidi Abeid*

The Ashmolean expedition cut a section through the scarp on the south side of the Sidi Abeid in 1953. The excavators identified four main periods of occupation in a depth of some 3 m of stratigraphy. The key thing to note is the way that the walls of the period 3 house were built on the same alignment as the walls of period 2 which suggests the continuity of the block within the framework of a possible grid system. There are few architectural details from period 1, though a hearth was identified.

One of the earliest pieces of pottery from the Ashmolean section was an East Greek hemispherical bowl (*Fig.* 2).[30] Similar bowls have been found at Cyrene.[31] Other pieces include late Attic black-figured skyphoi decorated with sphinxes (*Fig.* 3),[32] and an Attic black-figured lekythos which is considerably later than the pottery that has been discovered in square B7. The section was recleaned by Barri Jones' excavation in 1968–9.[33] The material contained late Attic black-figured pottery, an early Attic black-glossed Type C cup (contemporary with the black-figured material); the earliest piece was a fragmentary Corinthian skyphos though no precise phase could be ascribed.

4. *Other sections to bed rock*

Other sections within the colony indicate the extent of the archaic city. On the east side of the Sidi Abeid a house was excavated adjoining the city wall.[34] It seems clear that this house was constructed on a levelled site, perhaps in the late fifth century, and there is no evidence of archaic occupation. The road leading from the Sidi Abeid to this house was excavated both in the early 1950s and more recently.[35] The area to the east of the house explored in square B7 does not appear to be any earlier than the late sixth century.

A number of excavations have taken place in the lower city which extends into the lagoon.[36] There is as yet no evidence of any archaic material from this location, and the section to the south of the supposed agora was almost certainly constructed in the early fourth century due to the appearance of Attic black-glossed pottery with rouletting in the earliest layers.[37]

IV. Relative chronology

Sir John Boardman has wisely commented within the context of archaic decorated pottery that 'absolute dating...for pottery has to be taken cautiously since it indicates primarily what appears to be its relevant place in a sequence'.[38] He has also made the important methodological point that 'we should probably trust relative archaeological chronology more than detailed relative chronologies derived from one or more written sources, while acknowledging that absolute chronology must depend ultimately on written sources, but preferably not of a hundred years and more after the event, and preferably not Greek at all'.[39] In archaeological terms the sequence of occupation at a site should be described in terms of the ceramic sequence which can then be compared to a similar sequence at another site irrespective of the absolute chronological dating-scheme used by the excavator. It is therefore important that chronologically sensitive information should be presented in chronologically neutral language, in terms of archaeological horizons.

The earliest pottery from Euesperides may be Early Corinthian,[40] although periods 1 and 2 in the house at B7 appear to belong to the Middle Corinthian horizon; period 1 may have started earlier. One of the best stratified archaic sites for Cyrenaica is Tocra, excavated in the early 1960s, where the excavators identified three deposits.[41] The East Greek rosette bowls from Euesperides are comparable with those found in Tocra Deposits II and III, though one was found in Deposit I.[42] Deposits II and III also provide parallels for the earliest pieces of Attic pottery.[43] One of the earliest Laconian pieces from Euesperides, an aryballos, can be placed in the Middle Corinthian horizon.[44] In the light of material from the deep sections, the main burst of activity at Euesperides can be placed in the same chronological horizon as Tocra Deposit II, though it seems that some pottery from the colony is contemporary with Tocra Deposit I which contained Early Corinthian and some Transitional Corinthian.[45]

Placing Euesperides and Tocra in a wider context, it is possible to reconstruct the relative pottery sequence for the Greek colonization of Cyrenaica. At the possible site of Aziris, the settlement which preceded the colony of Cyrene, Protocorinthian pottery was discovered as well as East Greek pottery.[46] At Cyrene a number of Early Corinthian sherds have been found at the extra-mural sanctuary of Demeter and Kore though none from 'an undisturbed archaic context'.[47] Early Corinthian material seems to have been found at Apollonia (the port for Cyrene) and Ptolemais.[48] One of the earliest pieces of Corinthian pottery to have been found in Cyrenaica is a Middle Protocorinthian conical oinochoe from Tocra which Boardman has interpreted as an 'heirloom'.[49] This is atypical, and most of the Corinthian finds from Tocra start in the Transitional or Early Corinthian horizon.[50]

Although it is important to remember that the earliest pottery might not yet have been found,[51] it does seem as if there is a relative sequence emerging from the colonies of Cyrenaica. There are a small number of pieces of pottery which can be placed in the Middle Protocorinthian horizon from Aziris and Tocra. At Cyrene the earliest pottery is Early Corinthian, and this is found at other sites in Cyrenaica. The Middle Corinthian horizon seems to have been particularly significant at Euesperides, as this is the point when architectural features can first be identified; the same is true for the sanctuary of Demeter and Kore at Cyrene where at this time 'there is an expansion in both the volume and range of [Corinthian] pottery imports'.[52]

This activity in Cyrenaica can be placed in a broader setting. The establishment of Naukratis in the Nile Delta falls into a similar chronological horizon. Three sherds of Transitional Corinthian pottery have been found, but the earliest period of Greek occupation seems to have occurred in the

TABLE 1. Colonies placed in the same ceramic horizon as Euesperides (based on Graham 1982).

	Mother city or cities	Literary foundation date
'*c.* 600'		
Abdera	Klazomenai	654
	Teos	*c.* 545
Apollonia in Illyria	Corinth and Corcyra	*c.* 600
Apollonia in Libya	Thera	–
Casmenae	Syracuse	643
Elaios	Teos	–
Massalia	Phocaia	*c.* 600
Nymphaion	?Miletos	–
Panticapaion	Miletos	–
'*c.* 600–575'		
Akragas	Gela	580
Amisus	Miletos and Phocaia	*c.* 564
Apollonia Pontica	Miletos	*c.* 610
Black Corcyra	Cnidus	?*c.* 625–585
Emporiae	Massalia/Phocaia	–
Hermonassa	?Miletos	–
Myrmekion	Miletos or Panticapaion	–
Odessos	Miletos	–
'*c.* 600–570'		
Camarina	Syracuse	598
'*c.* 600–500'		
Agathe	Massalia	–
Assos	Methymna	–
Tyras	Miletos	–

Early Corinthian phase.[53] The horizon that saw the settlement of Cyrenaica and the establishment of Naukratis coincides with a burst of other colonial activity. Taking the list of Greek colonies founded between 800 and 500 which appears in *The Cambridge Ancient History*, some 20 colonies can be deemed to be roughly contemporary with Euesperides;[54] 8 of these are placed in the precise range defined by the presence of Middle Corinthian pottery. Of the 20 colonies, only 10 seem to have a foundation date derived from literary sources (TABLE 1). These colonies include Massalia,[55] and a series of colonies in the Black Sea including Apollonia Pontica, Odessos, Tyras, Nymphaion, Panticapaion, and Myrmekion.[56]

Middle Corinthian pottery seems to belong to the phase when Old Smyrna was reoccupied after its sack. The siege mound from the city contained 'Early Corinthian of not very late date'.[57] It might be suggested that the capture of Old Smyrna, perhaps as part of a concerted attack on the cities of Ionia, led to emigration of sectors of the community, perhaps with the encouragement of Delphi. Thus the burst of colonies where the earliest apparent activity can be dated to the Middle Corinthian horizon might be interpreted as coming in the wake of such attacks on the Greek world.

V. Absolute chronology

Euesperides would appear to belong to a second phase of colonization in Cyrenaica, an event recorded by Herodotus.[58] Herodotus provides a possible fixed date for this as the Libyans appealed to the Egyptian pharaoh Apries (589–570 BC) who sent an expedition against Libya that was soundly defeated; this disaster resulted in Amasis seizing control in Egypt. This would suggest that this colonizing movement was taking place in the 570s[59] and during the reign of Battos II.[60]

It is not immediately clear how these historical events can be detected in the archaeological record at Euesperides. One of the problems is that some of the excavators have been interpreting the archaeological remains using the orthodox chronology for Greek painted pottery. So for example it has been suggested that 'the knoll was fortified by *c.* 600 BC'[61] when in fact what is meant is that the earliest pottery found in this area is Middle Corinthian which is dated on the orthodox chronology to *c.* 600 BC.[62] Such absolute dates, rather than more relative chronological horizons, are frequently used in discussions of the colonization of Cyrenaica. Osborne, for example, has suggested that the earliest pottery from Aziris can be dated to *c.* 650, whereas the earliest occupation of Cyrene, Tocra and Ptolemais is placed *c.* 620 BC.[63]

Some scholars present their absolute chronologies for archaic pottery as if there are no problems with the present scheme.[64] This would be to ignore the issues raised by, for example, the lack of stratigraphy for Late Geometric pottery at Hama,[65] and the Bocchoris scarab in a grave containing Early Protocorinthian pottery at Pithekoussai.[66]

	Dunbabin[67]	Amyx[68]
MPC I:	*c.* 700–675	690–670
MPC II:	*c.* 675–650	670–650
LPC:	*c.* 650–640	650–630
Trans:	*c.* 640–625	630–620/615
EC:	*c.* 625–600	620/615–595/590
MC:	*c.* 600–575	595/590–570

TABLE 2. 'Orthodox' dating of Corinthian pottery

VI. Pottery and the origins of the colonists

It is now widely accepted that pottery need not identify the origin of the traders. Commercial graffiti especially from the fifth and fourth centuries BC have demonstrated that Attic pottery was moved by Etruscans and Phoenicians as well as a range of Greek traders. Boardman identified three main reasons why pottery moved in the archaic period: first, 'for the supply or use of Greeks overseas who had not their own kilns or could not be satisfied with local non-Greek products'; second, for 'commercial value' either for their contents or as valuable objects in their own right; and third, as 'curios'.[69] Although Greek pottery can no longer be seen as travelling due to its own 'intrinsic merit'[70] pottery may reflect contact with a particular region.[71] East Greeks play a part in the story of the colonization of Cyrenaica. Kolaios the Samian came across the Cretan fisherman Korobios who had been left on the island of Platea by the Theran settlers.[72] The Lindian temple chronicle suggested that a Lindian had been part of the original settlement with Battos.[73] A possible Lakonian element may be reflected in the story, preserved by Pausanias,[74] of the Olympic victor Chionis who apparently took part in the original expedition with Battos.

This East Greek element is also reflected in Herodotus' account of Demonax of Mantinea, who came as a lawgiver to Cyrene during the reign of Battos III.[75] The colony was divided into three Dorian tribes consisting of first the Therans and the *perioikoi*, second the Peloponnesians and the Cretans, and third all the islanders.[76] Either this cosmopolitan mix can be taken as representative of the original colonists, or, as is perhaps more likely, the result of an intake as a result of Delphi's call to colonize Cyrenaica after the initial foundation. It may, therefore, be important to note the presence of East Greek pottery at Euesperides and elsewhere in Cyrenaica especially from early contexts.[77]

The presence of imported pottery at Euesperides needs to be viewed against similar material from the other Greek settlements in Cyrenaica, notably the archaic sanctuary at Tocra, the sanctuary of Demeter and Persephone at Cyrene, and the agora excavations at Cyrene. Although some pottery remains unpublished (or even unpublishable) – in this case less than 10% of the Corinthian pottery from the sanctuary of Demeter and Persephone at Cyrene[78] – it is clear that East Greek pottery was a major component of the pottery finds at the sanctuary with almost equally high levels of Laconian.

This question of identity has been addressed on several occasions by Boardman.[79] Boardman, who helped to conduct excavations at Tocra in the early 1960s as well as discussing the archaic material from Cyrenaica, has presented percentages of the archaic material from Tocra and Cyrene.[80] The combined pottery from both of the *Tocra* volumes suggests that approximately 38% of the archaic pottery is Corinthian, 6% Laconian and 3.2% Chian (CHART 1). Boardman reproduced Stucchi's figures for the material discovered during the excavations in the Agora at Cyrene. However, if one looks at the published pottery from the sanctuary of Demeter and Persephone at Cyrene, it is immediately clear that the Agora material is not representative of the colony as a whole (CHART 3). For example Chian and Laconian each represent just under 7% of the total archaic material. Yet the Demeter sanctuary has published 69 Chian sherds, and 223 Laconian; in other words there is three times as much Laconian as Chian.[81] It is also clear that Laconian forms a substantial proportion of the archaic material,[82] falling only slightly behind East Greek.[83]

The comment that the similarities between Tocra and the Agora material from Cyrene 'are more impressive than not' is potentially misleading.[84] For example Boardman places great emphasis on the amount of Corinthian at Tocra (38%) compared to 10% from Cyrene Agora. Although only a fraction of the Corinthian pottery from the sanctuary of Demeter and Kore has been published, it seems to represent more than 40% of the published archaic sherds (CHART 2).[85] The fact that substantial amounts of Corinthian pottery arrived at Cyrene (via Apollonia) may suggest that Boardman's claim that Tocra was 'at the end of the trading run along the coast' now needs to be revised.[86]

Any attempt to quantify the amount of archaic pottery from Cyrenaica is thwarted by the lack of information on the sum total of sherds that have been found rather than just published. Bald percentages do not give a useful indication about the rate at which pottery arrived in Cyrenaica, though for Tocra it has been possible to chart the changes in percentages through the three main deposits of the archaic period. Most significant is the fact that the presence of Attic pottery in Deposit III is at the expense of East Greek pottery which declines marginally. However Tocra is no longer the sole index

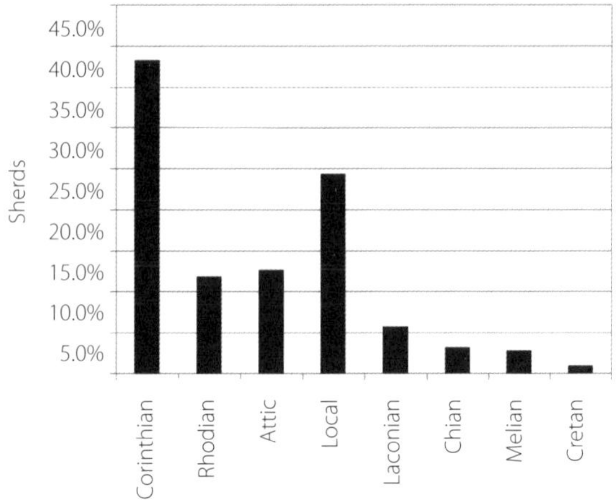

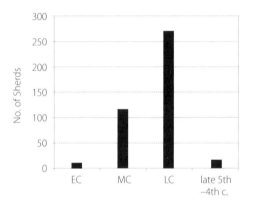

CHART 1. Archaic pottery from Tocra (based on Boardman and Hayes 1966, 1973).

CHART 2. Published Corinthian pottery from the sanctuary of Demeter and Kore, Cyrene (based on Kocybala 1999).

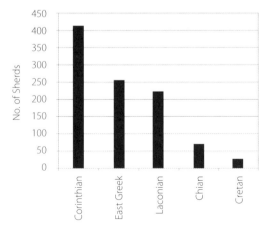

CHART 3. Selected archaic fabrics from the sanctuary of Demeter and Kore, Cyrene (based on Schaus 1985).

for interaction between Cyrenaica and the rest of the Greek world during the archaic period, and a careful analysis of the pottery from Cyrene may reveal a different pattern.

Perhaps there needs to be some comment about links with areas outside Cyrenaica. Venit has argued that the Laconian pottery from Tocra and Cyrene does not compare well with that found at Naukratis, arguing 'against a direct trade route between the two regions'.[87] Perhaps more significantly, the distribution pattern of Laconian pottery has suggested that it was arriving in Egypt via Samos, and Venit has extended this to include pottery movement aboard Samian ships.[88] The presence of imported archaic pottery at Euesperides, Tocra or Cyrene does not necessarily mean that there is direct contact between the regions producing the pottery and Cyrenaica. For example, if Venit is right to suggest that Laconian pottery came via Samos, then Laconian needs to be considered against East Greek material arriving in Cyrenaica.

VII. Conclusion

Excavations by the Ashmolean Museum and the Society for Libyan Studies have helped to plot the extent of the archaic city located on the Sidi Abeid. The northern line is fixed by the line of the city wall around the 9 m datum line. The southern limit is clearly to the south of the excavation on the southern scarp, and it may well have followed the original 8 m datum line. The archaic city does not seem to have gone as far as the later city wall on the eastern side; it must lie to the east of the house excavated in square B7 and the wall should therefore be around the 7 m datum line. The western limit is not at all clear, though it might have been around the 7 or 8 m datum line. However, what is not clear is whether there were any buildings in the lower city, perhaps round the site of the harbour, or if the agora, so far unexcavated, was established in an earlier period.

This would give an area of the archaic city of approximately 2 ha. Clearly parts of the city included kilns, but there may have been some 60 houses of the size discovered in square B7. Using the hearth multiplier of 5,[89] the possible population is likely to have been no higher than 300 people. Such a figure is not unreasonable given the size of the original colony at Cyrene, perhaps in the region of 200 men, or Apollonia in Illyria.[90] One reason why the colony was so compact is probably because of the threat of attack by the local Libyan population.

The pottery found in deep excavations on the Sidi Abeid demonstrates that there was regular contact, either direct or indirect, between the site and the Greek world, notably Corinth but also East Greece, from the Middle Corinthian horizon onwards. Such contact can be mirrored at Tocra and

Cyrene, and it may reflect a small Greek presence in this part of Cyrenaica. The limited amount of Early Corinthian pottery and the lack of any architectural features, at least so far, would suggest an earlier limited settlement, perhaps even seasonal. This Early Corinthian horizon coincides with the development of the main colony of Cyrene, and the main developments at Euesperides come in a later second phase of colonization.

Acknowledgements

I am grateful to Michael Vickers who has been generous with his support and encouragement for the work on the Euesperides material. Two of my research students, David Sturgeon and Patricia Flecks, have provided valued comments on aspects of the city, and the latter has kindly allowed me to reproduce her reconstruction of the archaic building on the Sidi Abeid. Andrew Wilson has made helpful comments about the later excavations. The late John Lloyd and the late Barri Jones also provided access to their material at key points during the project.

Notes

[1] Dennis 1867 [1870]. Much of the pottery discovered by Dennis is now in the British Museum; unfortunately the provenance is usually given as the general 'Cyrenaica'. For example, the fifth-century BC black-glossed stemless cups, London, British Museum 1866.4–15.41–42, or the Lykinic lekanis, 1866.4–15.29. For a find of an archaic terracotta in 1863: Higgins 1954. For details of the career of Dennis: Rhodes 1973. For reports of other early visitors to the site: Lenormant 1848; Vattier de Bourville 1848; 1849; 1850.

[2] Salvadori 1914.

[3] Goodchild 1952. The sherds are now in the British Museum: see Gill forthcoming.

[4] Goodchild 1962.

[5] For a description and view of the site in 2004: Wilson et al. 2004, 186–7, fig. 17.

[6] Rhodes 1973, 83, quoting Dennis 1867 [1870].

[7] Vickers et al. 1994. For further material from the excavations in the 1950s see also Gill 1998; 2004; Gill and Flecks, in press; Hinds 1991; Sturgeon 1996; Treister and Vickers 1996. See also Wright 1995. Some of the material from the Ashmolean excavations appears in Elrashedy 1985; 2002. A final report is in preparation by Gill and Vickers.

[8] Jones and Little 1979; Jones 1983; 1985. See also Vickers and Reynolds 1971–2, 41.

[9] For comments on the mosaics found in the lower city: Dunbabin 1979, 269–70, pl. 37, fig. 4; Joyce 1979, 260. For a discussion of one of the later inscriptions: Fraser 1951; 1953.

[10] Buzaian and Lloyd 1996; Lloyd et al. 1995; 1998; Hayes and Mattingly 1995; Bennett et al. 2000; Wilson et al. 1999; 2001; 2002; 2003; 2004.

[11] Hdt. 4.204. For the date of the introduction of taxation on the cities of Cyrenaica: Mitchell 1966, 107.

[12] For the interpretation of the Persian destruction: Jones 1983: 110–11; Jones and Little 1971, 66. For the observation that the level was in fact later: Vickers and Gill 1986: 97. Full discussion will appear in the final report of 1968–9 excavations.

[13] Hdt. 4.150–1.

[14] Hdt. 4.159. At this time the Cyrenaican constitution was reorganized by Demonax of Mantinea who had been sent at the indication of the Delphic oracle (Hdt. 4.161.2). Herodotus records that the cult site outside Cyrene where the Persian army stopped in 515 BC was the site of Zeus Lykaios (Hdt. 4.203.2). As this sanctuary was in fact that of Zeus Ammon, Herodotus may be recording the influence of Arcadians who had brought their cult of Zeus Lykaios with them. For contacts between Delphi and Cyrenaica under Arkesilas IV: Mitchell 1966, 108.

[15] For a convenient summary of the period: Lloyd 2000.

[16] Vickers and Gill 1986. This is the report predicted by Humphrey 1980, 84. Contextual information concerning the archaic pottery published in 1986 has now been identified and it may be possible to identify the deposits where some of the material was found.

[17] See most recently: Gill 2004, 398–403. See also Gill and Flecks, in press.

[18] Coin E20 [B7/1/0, found *c.* 20 cm down], Magas in revolt, *c.* 282–261 BC; coin E10 [B7/E/3, grey ashy], Magas reconciled with Ptolemy II Philadelphus, *c.* 261–258 BC. On the coinage of Euesperides: Buttrey 1994; 1997, 59–62. See also Bond and Swales 1965. On the significance of coins for dating the third century BC layers at Euesperides: Wilson et al. 2003, 153.

[19] The appearance of Euesperitans in the third-century BC P. Hibeh 91 is significant. There is a funerary stele of the Euesperitan Theudasios from Amathus on Cyprus (*BMI* no. 974). He was probably part of the Ptolemaic garrison on the island.

[20] Lloyd 1985, 53, notes the dimensions of the blocks as *c.* 18 m by *c.* 20 m.

[21] Hadjimichali 1975. For a reconstruction of the house and discussion of the differences between the houses at Euesperides and Lato: Gill and Flecks, in press.

[22] Context B7/GA/7.

[23] cf. Boardman and Hayes 1966, 39, pl. 25, no. 341.

[24] This occupation, period 1, also contained a pyramidal loomweight. For a review of loomweights at Euesperides: E. Tébar Magías, in Wilson et al. 2004, 180–4.

[25] For ancient kilns: Sparkes 1991, 23.

[26] Further kilns were identified to the north of the line of the city wall in area M: Buzian and Lloyd 1996, 134–6. The kiln in the Italian Trench was *c.* 2.5 m across.

[27] See Gill and Flecks, in press. This aspect is discussed in detail by Patricia Flecks in her Swansea M.Phil dissertation (2005). There is clear evidence of processing murex shells at Euesperides; for the most recent discussion see E. Tébar Magías, in Wilson et al. 2004, 168–9.

[28] Buzaian and Lloyd 1996, 144 suggest a date 'as early as the late seventh or early sixth century BC' based on the conventional chronology of pottery found in an adjoining house. For a recent overview of the ceramic finds from area H: Lloyd et al. 1998: 158–60, 'Pottery associated with the first recognized phase of habitation, dating to around 580–570 BC'.

[29] Buzaian and Lloyd 1996, 144, 147 fig. 18.

[30] BUS152.7: Vickers and Gill 1986, 98–9, fig. 1, no. 1.

[31] Schaus 1985, pl. 18, nos. 299 and 306, dated to '600–590' and '600–570' BC. The

type is also common at Naukratis

³² BUS152.1 and 2. BUS152.3 probably comes from the rim of another skyphos. For a similar piece from Tocra: Boardman and Hayes 1973, 48, no. 2171, pl. 29. Another skyphos of this type comes from the Italian Trench to the east of the Sidi Abeid: BUS181.1.

³³ Jones 1985, 32: 'pottery of mid- to late sixth century date from the primary levels'.

³⁴ The most recent discussion is Sturgeon 1996.

³⁵ Buzaian and Lloyd 1996, 146 ('Area J'); Lloyd et al. 1998: 161, 'The ceramic sequence…from the later sixth to late fourth/early third centuries BC'. The excavations in the 1950s designated this as the Italian Trench extension, so-named after using a gun-pit as the starting point of a trench designed to find the east line of the city.

³⁶ For cores in this area: Alette Kattenberg, in Wilson et al. 2004, 169–71.

³⁷ This area was excavated by Barri Jones: Jones 1983. It is clear from his notes that rouletted pottery comes from the burnt layers that he had associated with the Persian destruction of the city. Key contexts: T12, 6; and T20, 11.

³⁸ Boardman 1998, 10. Cf. 'although absolute dates remain somewhat elusive the application of conventional dates to new finds invariably tallies well with other, historical expectations' (pp. 178–9).

³⁹ Boardman 1994, 147.

⁴⁰ In 1986 it was thought that the earliest Corinthian material was Middle Corinthian: Vickers and Gill 1986, 100. Some of the very fragmentary Corinthian sherds from the deepest levels of square B7 may be earlier.

⁴¹ Boardman and Hayes 1966; 1973.

⁴² Vickers and Gill 1986, 98. See also Vickers and Gill 1986, 106: 'the most judicious way to describe the earliest activity on the site [Euesperides] is to say that it seems to be contemporary with Tocra Deposit II'.

⁴³ Vickers and Gill 1986, 103.

⁴⁴ Vickers and Gill 1986, 100.

⁴⁵ Boardman, in Boardman and Hayes 1966, 12.

⁴⁶ Boardman 1966, 150–1. Boardman dates this material to 637–631, the six years (Hdt. 4.158) preceding the traditional founding of Cyrene.

⁴⁷ White 1984, 23; Kocybala 1999, esp. p. 5. See also Boardman 1966, 152.

⁴⁸ Boardman 1966, 152–3.

⁴⁹ Boardman 1966, 153; Boardman, in Boardman and Hayes 1966, 21: 'there is every reason to believe that it was brought to Tocra as a prized possession by one of the early colonists and subsequently offered as a dedication in the sanctuary'.

⁵⁰ Boardman, in Boardman and Hayes 1966, 21: 'The main series of Corinthian scarcely begins before the Early Corinthian period. There are only one or two pieces which might be called Transitional'.

⁵¹ See the cautionary tale of Selinus in Sicily: Snodgrass 1987, 54–6.

⁵² Kocybala 1999, 5.

⁵³ Boardman 1980, 121; Venit 1988, 60–6; Möller 2000, 217 (with additional examples), 217–18 (16 examples of EC pottery); James 2003, 261. Boardman 1994, 141–2, only provides absolute dates.

⁵⁴ Graham 1982, 160–2. Euesperides is dated to '*c.* 600–575': Graham 1982, 161. The chronological horizon '*c.* 600–575' no doubt means that Middle Corinthian pottery was found on the sites concerned. Kocybala (1999, 5) provides a date of '595/90–570 BC'

for Middle Corinthian pottery.
55 Shefton 1994.
56 Tsetskhladze 1994. This is identified as the second stage of Miletos' colonization of the Black Sea (Tsetskhladze 1994, 119).
57 Dunbabin 1953–4, 260. See James 2003, 261–3.
58 Hdt. 4.159. Herodotus also gives an internal chronology for Cyrenaica by indicating that Battos ruled for 40 years and was succeeded by his son Arkesilaos I who ruled for 16 years.
59 Graham 1982, 136 suggests a date of *c.* 580.
60 Graham 1982, 137 takes the Lindian chronicle to refer to the colonizing movement under Battos II. See Chamoux 1953, 124.
61 Buzaian and Lloyd 1996, 150.
62 Cf. Boardman 1980, 15: 'We rely very much on the dating of Corinth's vases in these years, but it is easy to fall into the error of saying that "the earliest imported vases found at x are Corinthian", when all that can fairly be said is "the earliest *datable* vases…are Corinthian'.
63 Osborne 1996, 15.
64 e.g. Boardman 1994, 141 on the chronology of Naukratis. His unreferenced mention of those who argue against the orthodox chronology of Naukratis is presumably to Bowden 1991; and see also Bowden 1996; James 2003. For the chronology of Corinthian pottery: Amyx 1988, 397–434.
65 Francis and Vickers 1985. See most recently Waldbaum and Magness 1997.
66 Gill and Vickers 1996. The most likely dates for Bocchoris' reign are 720–715 (or 719–714). These dates would provide the *terminus post quem* for the pottery. The response by Ridgeway (1999) does not address the central methodological issue of using this scarab for dating Greek pottery. See also Ridgway 2004, 22.
67 Amyx 1988, 399.
68 Amyx 1988, 428. A similar set of dates is used by Kocybala 1999, 5.
69 Boardman 1980, 16–18. For a more sophisticated discussion of pottery in the archaic Greek economy see Osborne 1996b.
70 Boardman, in Boardman and Hayes 1966, 14.
71 For a discussion of the link between imports at Tocra and links outside see Boardman, in Boardman and Hayes 1966, 14–15.
72 Hdt. 4.152.
73 Cf. Boardman, in Boardman and Hayes 1966, 14. Jeffery 1976, 198: 'The Lindians who with Pankis' children founded Kyrene with Battos, to Athena and Herakles a tithe from war-spoils'.
74 Paus. 3.14.3. Chionis' first victory was in 668.
75 Hdt. 4.161.
76 Jeffery (1976, 187) suggested that the three tribes were arranged 'in a descending social scale'. The first group would be the original settlers from Thera along with those original Greeks, the second group would consist of Dorians, and the third group would be Ionians.
77 It is important to be cautious about linking pottery to specific groups of colonists: see Graham 1971, 36.
78 Kocybala 1999, 2.
79 e.g. Boardman 1994.

[80] Boardman has in fact never published absolute figures for Tocra, merely percentages in a series of charts and tables, e.g. Boardman, in Boardman and Hayes 1973, 4 fig. 1 ('Percentages of Archaic wares represented'), 5 fig. 2 ('Proportions of principal Archaic wares in each Deposit'); Boardman 1996, 145 fig. 8.2 ('Proportions of pottery from the Archaic deposits at Tocra'), 147 table 8.1 ('Percentages of Archaic pottery found at Tocra and at Cyrene Agora'). Boardman's presentation includes comments on Stucchi's earlier compilation of archaic material from Cyrene, drawing attention to the fact that there is a 10% discrepancy in Stucchi's figures: Boardman 1994, 146. See also Osborne 1996b, 38.

[81] An analysis of the published sherds suggests that Chian forms 7% of the total, Laconian 22%. See also Lemos 1991, 194–5.

[82] Cf. Boardman 1994, 146: 'an allegedly heavy proportion of Laconian at Cyrene Demeter'. For Laconian pottery from the sanctuary: Schaus 1985.

[83] East Greek Wild Goat represents 20% of the total archaic pottery, Ionian bucchero 2%, Fikellura 2% and Clazomenian 1%, i.e. 25% against 22% Laconian. For the published material see Schaus 1985.

[84] Boardman 1994, 146.

[85] Kocybala 1999, 2, where it is noted that the catalogue publishes less than 8% of the pottery from the sanctuary (394 catalogue items out of 5100 pieces).

[86] Boardman 1994, 146, based on Boardman 1968. See also Boardman 1979.

[87] Venit 1985, 393.

[88] Venit 1985, 394; see also Venit 1988, 113–16. The argument lies in the observation that Laconian pots attributed to the Boreads painter were found in large numbers on Samos. For links between Sparta and Tocra: Boardman, in Boardman and Hayes 1966, 14. For Sparta and Cyrene: Schaus 1985, 98–102.

[89] De Angelis (1994, 98) uses this multiplier for Megara Hyblaia. For the problem applied to the Southern Argolid survey: van Andel and Runnels 1987, 173, 198–9 (5 people as a 'hearth-multiplier'; suggesting 150 people per ha). De Angelis (1994) also suggested that each household would need some 3–4 ha. for cultivation at Selinous.

[90] For the numbers in early colonies: Graham 1982, 146.

Bibliography

Amyx, D.A.
  1988   *Corinthian Vase-painting of the Archaic Period*, Berkeley, Calif.
Barker, G., Lloyd, J. and Reynolds, J.
  1985   *Cyrenaica in Antiquity*, Society for Libyan Studies Occasional Papers 1, BAR International Series 236, Oxford.
Bennett, P., Wilson, A.I., Buzaian, A., Hamilton, K., Thorpe, D., Robertson, D. and White, K.
  2000   'Euesperides (Benghazi): preliminary report on the spring 2000 season', *Libyan Studies* 31, 121–43.
Boardman, J.
  1966   'Evidence for the dating of Greek settlements in Cyrenaica', *Annual of the British School at Athens* 61, 149–56.
  1968   'Reflections on the Greek pottery trade with Tocra', in F.F. Gadallah (ed.) *Libya in History*, Tripoli, 89–91.

1979   'The Athenian pottery trade: the classical period', *Expedition* 21, 4, 33–9.

1980   *The Greeks Overseas: Their early colonies and trade*, 2nd edn, London.

1994   'Settlement for trade and land in North Africa: problems of identity', in Tsetskhladze and De Angelis (eds.) *The Archaeology of Greek Colonisation*, 137–49.

1998   *Early Greek Vase Painting 11th–6th Centuries BC: A handbook*, London.

Boardman, J. and Hayes, J.W.

1966   *Excavations at Tocra 1963–5: The archaic deposits I*, British School at Athens Suppl. vol. 4, London.

1973   *Excavations at Tocra 1963–5: The archaic deposits II and Later Deposits*, British School at Athens Suppl. vol. 10, London.

Bond, R.C. and Swales, J.M.

1965   'Surface finds of coins from the city of Euhesperides', *Libya Antiqua* 2, 91–101.

Bowden, H.

1991   'The chronology of Greek painted pottery: some observations', *Hephaistos* 10, 49–59.

1996   'The Greek settlement and sanctuaries at Naukratis: Herodotus and archae-ology', in M.H. Hansen and K. Raaflaub (eds.) *More Studies in the Ancient Greek Polis*, Stuttgart, 17–38.

Buttrey, T.V.

1994   'Coins and coinage at Euesperides', *Libyan Studies* 25, 137–45.

1997   'Part I: the coins', in *The Extramural Sanctuary of Demeter and Persephone at Cyrene, Libya: Final reports*, Philadelphia, 1–66.

Buzaian, A. and Lloyd, J.A.

1996   'Early urbanism in Cyrenaica: new evidence from Euesperides (Benghazi)', *Libyan Studies* 27, 129–52.

Chamoux, F.

1953   *Cyrène sous la monarchie des Battiades*, Paris.

De Angelis, F.

1994   'The foundation of Selinous: overpopulation or opportunities?', in Tset-skhladze and De Angelis (eds.) *The Archaeology of Greek Colonisation*, 87–110.

Dennis, G.

1867 [1870]   'On recent excavations in the Greek cemeteries of the Cyrenaica', *Transactions of the Royal Society of Literature* 9, 135–82. [Reprinted as pamphlet, pp. 1–48.]

Dunbabin, K.M.D.

1979   'Technique and materials of Hellenistic mosaics', *American Journal of Archae-ology* 83, no. 3, 265–77.

Dunbabin, T.J.

1953/4 'The chronology of Protocorinthian vases', *Archaiologike Ephemeris*, 247–62.

Elrashedy, F.M.

1985   'Attic imported pottery in classical Cyrenaica', in Barker et al., *Cyrenaica in Antiquity*, 205–17.

2002   *Imports of Post-Archaic Greek Pottery into Cyrenaica from the End of the*

Archaic to the Beginning of the Hellenistic Period, BAR International Series 1022, Oxford.

Francis, E.D. and Vickers, M.

1985 'Greek geometric pottery at Hama and its implications for Near Eastern chronology', *Levant* 17, 131–8.

Unpublished 'New wine from Old Smyrna: Corinthian pottery and the Greeks overseas'.

Fraser, P.M.

1951 'An inscription from Euesperides', *Bulletin de la Societé d'Archéologie d'Alexandrie* 39, 132–43.

1953 'Corrigendum', *Bulletin de la Societé d'Archéologie d'Alexandrie* 40, 62.

Gill, D.W.J.

1998 'A Greek price inscription from Euesperides, Cyrenaica', *Libyan Studies* 29, 83–8.

2004 'Euesperides: Cyrenaica and its contacts with the outside world', in K. Lomas (ed.) *Greek Identity in the Western Mediterranean: Papers in honour of Brian Shefton*, Mnemosyne Supplement 246, Leiden, 391–409.

Forthcoming 'Euesperides: the surface-survey', in preparation.

Gill, D.W.J. and Flecks, P.

Forthcoming 'Defining domestic space at Euesperides, Cyrenaica: archaic structures on the Sidi Abeid', in R. Westgate, N. Fisher and J. Whitley (eds.) *Building communities: House, settlement and society in the Aegean and beyond*, London.

Gill, D.W.J. and Vickers, M.

1996 'Bocchoris the wise and absolute chronology', *Römische Mitteilungen* 103, 1–9.

Goodchild, R.G.

1952 'Euesperides: a devastated city site', *Antiquity* 26, 208–12.

1962 *Benghazi, the story of a city*, 2nd edn, Benghazi.

Graham, A.J.

1971 'Patterns in early Greek colonisation', *Journal of Hellenic Studies* 91, 35–47.

1982 'The colonial expansion of Greece', in *CAH*² III 3, 83–162.

Hadjimichali, V.

1971 'Recherches à Latô III. Maisons', *BCH* 95, 167–222.

Hayes, P.P. and Mattingly, D.J.

1995 'Preliminary report on fieldwork at Euesperides (Benghazi) in October 1994', *Libyan Studies* 26, 83–96.

Higgins, R.A.

1954 'Two archaic terracottas', *Journal of Hellenic Studies* 74, 177.

Hinds, S.

1991 *Euesperides: A devastated city site*, unpublished MA thesis, Leicester University.

Humphrey, J.H.

1980 'North African news letter 2', *American Journal of Archaeology* 84, no. 1, 75–87.

James, P.

2003 'Naukratis revisited', *Hyperboreus. Studia classica* 9, 235–64.

Jeffery, L.H.
  1976   *Archaic Greece: The city-states, c. 700–500 BC,* London.
Jones, G.D.B.
  1983   'Excavations at Tocra and Euhesperides, Cyrenaica 1968–9', *Libyan Studies* 14, 109–21.
  1985   'Beginnings and endings in Cyrenaican cities', in Barker et al. *Cyrenaica in Antiquity*, 27–41.
Jones, G.D.B., and Little, J.H.
  1971   'Coastal settlement in Cyrenaica', *Journal of Roman Studies* 61, 64–79.
Joyce, H.
  1979   'Form, function and technique in the pavements of Delos and Pompeii', *American Journal of Archaeology* 83, no. 3, 253–63.
Kocybala, A.
  1999   *The Corinthian pottery, The Extramural Sanctuary of Demeter and Persephone at Cyrene, Libya: Final reports*, vol. 7, Philadelphia.
Lemos, A.A.
  1991   *Archaic Pottery of Chios: The decorated styles*, Oxford University Committee for Archaeology Monograph 30, Oxford.
Lenormant, C.
  1848   'Note sur un vase panathénaïque récemment découvert à Bengazi', *RA* 5, 230–41.
Lloyd, A.B.
  2000   'The late period (664–332 BC)', in I. Shaw (ed.) *The Oxford History of Ancient Egypt*, Oxford, 364–87.
Lloyd, J.
  1985   'Some aspects of urban development at Euesperides/Berenice', in Barker et al. *Cyrenaica in Antiquity*, 49–66.
Lloyd, J.A., Buzaian, A. and Coulton, J.J.
  1995   'Excavations at Euesperides (Benghazi), 1995', *Libyan Studies* 26, 97–100.
Lloyd, J.A., Bennett, P., Buttrey, T.V., Buzaian, A., El Amin, H., Fell, V., Kashbar, G., Morgan, G., Ben Nasser, Y., Roberts, P.C., Wilson, A.I., and Zimi, E.
  1998   'Excavations at Euesperides (Benghazi): an interim report on the 1998 season', *Libyan Studies* 26, 145–68.
Mitchell, B.M.
  1966   'Cyrene and Persia', *Journal of Hellenic Studies* 86, 99–113.
Möller, A.
  2000   *Naukratis: Trade in Archaic Greece*, Oxford Monographs on Classical Archaeology, Oxford.
Osborne, R.
  1996a   *Greece in the Making 1200–479 BC,* London.
  1996b   'Pots, trade and the archaic Greek economy', *Antiquity* 70, 31–44.
Rhodes, D.E.
  1973   *Dennis of Etruria: The life of George Dennis*, London.
Ridgway, D.
  1999   'The rehabilitation of Bocchoris: notes and queries from Italy', *Journal of Egyptian Archaeology* 85, 143–52.

2004   'Euboeans and others along the Tyrrhenian seaboard in the 8th century BC', in K. Lomas (ed.) *Greek Identity in the Western Mediterranean: Papers in Honour of Brian Shefton, Mnemosyne Supplement* vol. 246, Leiden, 15–33.

Salvadori, A.
1914   *La Cirenaica ed i suoi servizi civili,* Rome.

Schaus, G.P.
1985   *The East Greek, Island, and Laconian pottery. The Extramural Sanctuary of Demeter and Persephone at Cyrene: Libya Final reports II, University Museum Monograph* 56, Philadelphia.

Shefton, B.B.
1994   'Massalia and colonisation in the north-western Mediterranean', in Tsetskhladze and De Angelis (eds.) *The Archaeology of Greek Colonisation,* 61–86.

Snodgrass, A.M.
1987   *An Archaeology of Greece: The present state and future scope of a discipline,* Berkeley.

Sparkes, B.A.
1991   *Greek Pottery: An introduction,* Manchester.

Sturgeon, D.
1996   *The House by the City Wall and the Use of Fine Pottery from Domestic Contexts at Euesperides, Cyrenaica,* unpublished M.Phil. thesis, University of Wales, Swansea.

Treister, M. and Vickers, M.
1996   'Stone matrices with griffins from Nymphaeum and Euesperides', *Colloquia Pontica* 1, 135–41.

Tsetskhladze, G.R.
1994   'Greek penetration of the Black Sea', in Tsetskhladze and De Angelis (eds.) *The Archaeology of Greek Colonisation,* 111–35.

Tsetskhladze, G.R. and De Angelis F. (eds.)
1994   *The Archaeology of Greek Colonisation: Essays dedicated to Sir John Boardman,* Oxford University Committee for Archaeology Monograph 40, Oxford.

van Andel, Tj.H. and Runnels, C.
1987   *Beyond the Acropolis: A rural Greek past,* Stanford, Calif.

Vattier de Bourville, J.
1848   'Lettre de M. Vattier de Bourville à M. Letronne sur les premiers résultants de son voyage à Cyrène', *Revue Archéologique* 5.1, 150–4.

1849   'Lettre à M. Lenormant sur les antiquités de Cyrénaïque', *Revue Archéologique* 6, 56–8.

1850   'Rapport adressé à M. le Ministre de l'instruction publique et des cultes, par M. J. Vattier de Bourville, chargé d'une mission dans la Cyrénaïque', *Archives des Missions scientifique*s 1, 580–6.

Venit, M.S.
1985   'Laconian black figure in Egypt', *American Journal of Archaeology* 89, 391–8.

1988   *Greek Painted Pottery from Naukratis in Egyptian Museums,* American Research Center in Egypt Catalogs vol. 7, Winona Lake.

Vickers, M. and Gill, D.W.J.
   1986   'Archaic Greek pottery from Euesperides, Cyrenaica', *Libyan Studies* 17, 97–108.

Vickers, M., Gill, D.W.J. and Economou, M.
   1994   'Euesperides: the rescue of an excavation', *Libyan Studies* 25, 125–36.

Vickers, M. and Reynolds, J.M.
   1971–2 'Cyrenaica, 1962–72', *Archaeological Reports* 18, 27–47.

Waldbaum, J.C. and Magness, J.
   1997   'The chronology of early Greek pottery: new evidence from seventh-century BC destruction levels in Israel', *American Journal of Archaeology* 101, no. 1, 23–40.

White, D.
   1984   *Background and Introduction to the Excavations*, The Extramural Sanctuary of Demeter and Persephone at Cyrene, Libya Final Reports 1, University Museum Monograph 52, Philadelphia.

Wilson, A.I., Bennett, P., Buzaian, A., Ebbinghaus, S., Hamilton, K., Kattenberg, A. and Zimi, E.
   1999   'Urbanism and economy at Euesperides (Benghazi): preliminary report on the 1999 season', *Libyan Studies* 30, 147–68.

Wilson, A., Bennett, P., Buzaian, A., Buttrey, T.V., Fell, V., Göransson, K., Green, C., Hall, C., Helm, R., Kattenberg, A., Swift, K. and Zimi, E.
   2001   'Euesperides: preliminary report on the Spring 2001 season', *Libyan Studies* 32, 155–77.

Wilson, A., Bennett, P., Buzaian, A., Buttrey, T.V., Göransson, K., Hall, C., Kattenberg, A., Scott, R. Swift, K. and Zimi, E.
   2002   'Euesperides (Benghazi): preliminary report on the Spring 2002 season', *Libyan Studies* 33, 85–123.

Wilson, A., Bennett, P., Buzaian, A., Buttrey, T.V., Fell, V., Found, B., Göransson, K., Guinness, A., Hardy, J., Harris, K., Helm, R., Kattenberg, A., Morley, G., Swift, K., Wootton, W. and Zimi, E.
   2003   'Euesperides (Benghazi): preliminary report on the spring 2003 season', *Libyan Studies* 34, 191–228.

Wilson, A., Bennett, P., Buzaian, A., Fell, V., Found, B., Göransson, K., Guinness, A., Hardy, J., Harris, K., Helm, R., Kattenberg, A., Megías, E.T., Morley, G., Murphy, A., Swift, K., Twyman, J., Wootton, W. and Zimi, E.
   2004   'Euesperides (Benghazi): preliminary report on the spring 2004 season', *Libyan Studies* 35, 149–90.

Wright, G.R.H.
   1995   'A funeral offering near Euesperides', *Libyan Studies* 26, 21–6.

2

'IDEOLOGIES' OF GREEK COLONIZATION

John-Paul Wilson

Anyone who studies Greek colonization in the archaic period is met by a series of long-established certainties. Views on the duties of the *oikist*, the role of the Delphic oracle, the relationship between colony and mother-city and between colonist and 'native', and so on, are well entrenched and subject to only minor disagreement. First, it is generally accepted that *most* colonies were founded by a *polis*, or on rare occasions by two or more *poleis*;[1] that a decision was made within the community to send out a group of colonists, normally men, to settle elsewhere.[2] Second, these colonists were generally led by a single individual, the *oikist*, who was responsible for the political, social and religious organization of the new colony, and who was worshipped as a hero upon his death. Third, before the colony was founded, the Delphic Oracle was consulted: either to gain Apollo's blessing for the enterprise; or to seek advice, sometimes geographical, about the foundation. Fourth, the colony was in most instances politically independent from the outset but maintained cultural and particularly religious ties with the *metropolis*, ties which could be invoked by both the colony and the mother-city in times of crisis.[3] Fifth, colonization, when it took place on virgin territory, involved the violent expulsion of the indigenous population.

One is thus faced with a clear sense that the *nature* of archaic Greek colonization is well understood and not open to serious debate. The only intensely contested issue has concerned the motives for Greek colonization in the archaic period. On the one side are those who favour commercial motives, the search for new resources and new markets, as the driving force.[4] On the other are those who see land hunger as the key factor: either absolute land-hunger, reflective of rising population in the homeland placing too great a strain on Greece's limited agricultural resources;[5] land-hunger resulting from long-term drought and famine;[6] or relative land-hunger, caused by one group restricting the access of another group to land and, by extension, to political power.[7]

Recent scholarship, however, has sought to challenge some of the certainties that have underpinned this traditional model of archaic Greek colonization. The impetus for this challenge has in part come from our post-colonial perspective. In other words, a shift in contemporary ideologies allows, even encourages, one to look afresh on Greek colonization, freed of the distorting lens of European colonialism and imperialism, and, at the same time, increasingly aware of the impact of this distortion. So, for example, De Angelis (1998) shows how nineteenth- and twentieth-century discussions of the Greek colonial experience have been fundamentally shaped by contemporary European experiences. Meanwhile, Osborne (1998) has demonstrated that the very application of the term colonization to the Greek overseas settlement of this period originates from the mistaken assimilation of the Greek term *apoikia* with the Latin term *colonia*, which at once imbued the Greek movement with an imperialistic character it never had. The other important impetus has been, if not an abandonment, then a re-assessment of the value of the literary tradition in relation to the archaeological evidence; an increased desire to treat the material culture on its own terms, not to force its evidence into a historical framework built upon the less-than-secure foundations of the literary evidence. More and more colonies are being examined within their immediate geographical and cultural context rather than within the confines of an overarching model of Greek colonization.

The debate consequently no longer focuses on the well-worn question of motives for colonization, which explicitly draws upon the analogy of western imperialism, but rather on the now re-opened issue of the nature of early Greek colonization. So, for example, Osborne (1998) presents a picture of early Greek colonization in the West that suggests that rather than the product of organized expeditions, Greek overseas settlements were in many instances opportunist settlements, incorporated into or incorporating indigenous communities, some of which flourished and became formal cities, Greek *poleis*, but others of which failed to do so, either being destroyed or simply fading away. This organic model of settlement is in striking contrast to the traditional model of colonization with its emphasis on the formal role of mother-city and *oikist*, and on the Delphic oracle. Osborne correctly emphasizes that the 'traditional model' of colonization comes to some extent from the inappropriate retrojection of classical (that is fifth and fourth century BC) models into the archaic period, models that have much more in common with both the Roman colonial experience *and* the modern imperialist experience. In other words the 'traditional model' is a product of the interplay between ancient and modern ideologies of colonization. It is the former that is of particular interest here. Thus we will explore the development of ideologies of colonization in the archaic period, examining the historical and cultural contexts within which the 'ideal' of Greek colonization may have emerged.

We will begin by demonstrating that the treatment of archaic colonization as a unity – the desire to see this period as an 'age of colonization' – was an ancient as much as a modern impulse. It will be argued, however, that this impulse hides the diverse nature of settlement within this period. The recognition that the nature of archaic Greek settlement changed dramatically within this period is key to understanding the Greek 'colonial' experience but also to understanding the manner in which ancient ideologies of colonization emerged.

We will then explore the earliest evidence for ancient colonial ideologies, i.e. Homer. It will be argued that rather than pointing towards the realities of colonization in the poet's own time (the late eight century BC), the colonial stories to be found within the Homeric epics were in part a product of the Greek experiences of pre-colonial exploration in the West and in part reflective of an existing body of settlement myths which might be associated with Dark Age 'colonization' in the Aegean. Nevertheless these stories acted as models for subsequent accounts of the archaic colonial experience, in particular poetic accounts of colonization as seen in Pindar. The role of the *oikist* will then be explored in relationship to this discussion.

Finally, we will consider how, when and why two key elements of the traditional view of colonization may have been incorporated into this 'model': that is, the cult of the founder and Delphic consultation.

In essence, then, this paper is another attempt to present a revisionist view of archaic Greek colonization, by emphasizing the impact that shifting ancient ideologies have had both on ancient perceptions of this experience and on our own perceptions.

An 'age of colonization'?

In modern scholarship, the period of Greek history from *c.* 730 BC to *c.* 550 BC is often fashioned, sometimes explicitly, sometimes implicitly, as an 'age of colonization'.[8] The force of this classification is clear enough, not least because it encourages one to draw parallels with other so-called 'ages' of colonization. This, so it is inferred, is a period marked out from previous and subsequent eras not only by the relative intensity of settlement, but also by the geographical scope of this settlement. There is, of course, some truth in such inferences. No one questions that during these centuries the Greeks populated some areas they had never reached before and others that had perhaps been settled in the Late Bronze Age, but never with equivalent voracity. The problem arises, however, first, when drawing clear distinctions between the *nature* of Greek settlement in this period and Greek settlement in the preceding centuries, and, second, when treating overseas settlement in the archaic period as a single movement.

The Greeks of the classical period and later perceived their past as marked by an almost continuous series of population movements, both within Greece itself, and beyond into Asia Minor and the western Mediterranean. Most often heroes led these movements, founding cities in their wake. Before the Trojan War, for example, Dardanos and Iapyx, among others, were said to have led Cretans to Italy, while Herakles founded cities across much of the Mediterranean. The heroes of the Trojan War were themselves remembered as great city-founders, settling parts of North Africa, Sicily and southern Italy, as they attempted to make their way home. In the period after the Trojan War, the descendants of Herakles led the Dorians into the Peloponnese where they would re-found the great cities of Argos, Sparta, Messene and Corinth, a process that led in turn to the driving out and resettlement of the Achaians, Ionians and Aiolians, some within Greece, others in the Aegean and Asia Minor. Subsequently the Spartans would create further settlements within the Peloponnese, and across the Aegean, for example, on Melos and Thera. Within the Greek imagination, all this occurred in the centuries before the overseas settlement of the late eighth to mid-sixth centuries BC. From this mythical perspective the archaic period seems unremarkable: it is just another age of population movements and overseas settlement.

Strikingly, it seems that the Greeks used the same language, the same terminology of settlement, to describe all these experiences. The term *apoikia* – most often translated as 'colony' but literally meaning something like 'home away from home' – is used as readily to describe the various activities of Dardanos, Herakles, the Homeric heroes, the Dorians, the Ionians, and so on, as it is to describe the activities of the archaic Greek settlers. A few examples will suffice.

Skylettion (Scolacium) in southern Italy, normally identified as a dependent 'colony' of Kroton, founded in the sixth century BC, is mentioned by Strabo (6.1.10), Solinus (2.10) and Pliny (*NH* 3.95) as having been settled by Athenians led by Menestheus, their leader at Troy. Strabo calls it explicitly an *apoikos Athenaiōn*, a 'colony of the Athenians'.

The Melians, Herodotus (8.48) notes in passing, were of Lakedaimonian stock. Thucydides (5.112.2) expands on this considerably in the course of the 'Melian Dialogue': the Melians claimed their city to be 700 years old, a chronology that would place its foundation shortly after the Dorian invasion, a 'fact' emphasized by Conon (*Narrationes* 36), where the name of the *oikist*, Philonomos, is also added. The key point for this discussion, however, is Thucydides' (5.84.2) denomination of the Melians as *apoikoi*, 'colonists' of the Lakedaimonians.

Strabo (8.7.2), in explaining the Ionian departure from the mainland as a function of Achaian aggression after the return of the Herakleidai to the

Peloponnese, describes the Ionian settlements in the Aegean and Asia Minor as *Iōnikēs apoikias*; while Sparta is described simply as the *apoikia* of the Dorians by Pindar (*Isthmian* 7.12–15).

Further examples could be added but it should be clear that the Greeks of the classical period and later were happy to describe, using the same language, experiences that have been treated very differently in the modern scholarship. It might be argued, however, that the term *apoikia* was never a technical term for the Greeks in the way in which *colonia* was a technical term for the Romans.[9] Rather that it is simply a generic term used to describe any overseas settlement, whatever its origins or its nature. Another example, however, will demonstrate how a more clearly technical term was applied in the same manner.

There is a whole series of stories concerning the origins of Brundisium (Greek Brentesion). One, found in Stephanos of Byzantium, describes it as being founded by Brentus, son of Herakles. Another, found in Justinian (12.2.7) and Isidorus (*Origines* 14.4.23), recognizes Aetolians led by Diomedes as the founders. Cretans, however, are prominent in four other variant foundation myths. One has Iapyx, son of the Cretan Lykaon, leading the Messapians to found the city.[10] Another has Dicte leading Cretan exiles sailing on Athenian ships to settle the colony.[11] The third and fourth variants are found in Strabo (6.3.6):

Βρεντέσιον δ’ ἐποικῆσαι μὲν λέγονται Κρῆτες οἱ μετὰ Θησέως ἐπελθόντες ἐκ Κνωσσοῦ, εἶθ’ οἱ ἐκ τῆς Σικελίας ἀπηρκότες μετὰ τοῦ Ἰάπυγος (λέγεται γὰρ ἀμφοτέρως)·

Brentesion, they say, was further colonized by the Cretans, whether by those who came over with Theseus from Knossos, or by those who set sail from Sicily with Iapyx.

The use of ἐποικέω is interesting. It can simply mean 'to settle' or 'to colonize' but it also has a more technical sense. This is evident perhaps in a fifth century BC inscription detailing the Athenian settlement of Brea.[12] It differentiates between *apoikoi*, the initial colonists, and *epoikoi*, those who join the colony at a later date. An *epoikos* then is an 'additional colonist', and ἐποικέω implies a process of secondary colonization. In the case of Brentesion, it is probable that Strabo sees the Cretan colonization as secondary to the prior Messapic colonization, the existence of which he implies earlier in Book 6.

The language of colonization thus suggests that the Greeks did not draw clear distinctions between these 'population movements'. It is only within modern scholarship that any such distinctions of terminology have been made. For the most part those foundation myths that pre-date the Trojan War are treated as purely mythical. The Cretan myths are most often classified as aetiological: for example the Iapygians, the Italic peoples who inhabited the heel of Italy, are seen as descendants of the Cretan Iapyx and his followers.[13] Herakles' city-foundations are also sometimes recognized as aetiological,[14] but also function more generally to provide divine origins for a community. The so-called *nostoi* foundations, although sometimes seen as memories of either Mycenaean settlement, or of the activities of the 'Sea Peoples', often seem to act primarily as charter myths for later 'historical' colonization.[15] So, the settlement of 'historical' Achaians at Kroton might be seen as justified through Strabo's account of Homeric Achaians being forced to land in the area and subsequently being joined by like-minded Greeks.[16]

Foundation myths that concern the period after the Trojan War, that is those describing the activities of the Dorians, Ionians, Aiolians and Achaians, have traditionally been treated in a different fashion, as describing actual historical movements of peoples. These 'movements', however, have been classified as 'invasions' or 'migrations' and are therefore clearly differentiated from the 'colonization' of the archaic period.[17] For example, the movement of Greeks from the mainland into Asia Minor during the Dark Ages is described by modern scholars as the Ionian 'migration'. On the other hand, the movement of Greeks from Kolophon to found the *polis* of Poleion in Italy in the mid-seventh century is portrayed as an act of 'colonization'.[18] Yet the ancient sources attribute both the Ionian movement and the Kolophonian 'colonization' to outside aggression and use very much the same language in doing so: in the former case Dorian and Achaian aggression forces the Ionians to flee from mainland Greece; in the latter case it is Lydian aggression that forces the Kolophonian hand.[19] The terms 'invasion' and 'migration', however, conjure up images of tribal movements, of disjointed and disorganized actions, in stark contrast to the images of carefully planned and organized settlement invoked by the word 'colonization'.

What seems to underpin this clear differentiation is the belief that during the so-called Dark Ages, i.e. from the twelfth through to the first half of the eighth century, these population movements are the product of a pre- or at best proto-state society. Archaic population movements, on the other hand, as already noted, are deemed to have been driven by the *polis*. It is thus the emergence of the *polis* in the latter part of the eighth century BC that is the key to understanding this classification. The term 'colonization' carries with it 'statist' connotations and can thus only be appropriately applied to the period after the emergence of the *polis*. This raises a whole series of questions about the impact of modern ideologies of colonization on the study of the ancient experience. This paper's focus, however, is primarily the impact of ancient ideologies and although we have seen so far that the ancient sources do not in their use of terminology make the clear distinctions between experiences found in modern scholarship, this does not mean that other distinctions were not drawn in the ancient sources.

One important passage in particular reveals the manner in which stories about settlement and population movements could be readily manipulated to make an ideological point. This passage, Thucydides 1.12, comes at the heart of his *archaeologia* within which he provides a rapid trawl through early Greek history (and indeed proto- and pre-history). Thucydides has a clear agenda in this section: primarily to demonstrate why the Peloponnesian War was the greatest of all wars to that date, by emphasizing the gradual development of Greek sea-power and economic vigour across the centuries, coupled with increased political stability.[20]

The passage we are concerned with here describes the situation in Greece in the period from the Trojan War down to eighth century BC:

ἐπεὶ καὶ μετὰ τὰ Τρωϊκὰ ἡ Ἑλλὰς ἔτι μετανίστατό τε καὶ κατῳκίζετο, ὥστε μὴ ἡσυχάσασαν αὐξηθῆναι. ἥ τε γὰρ ἀναχώρησις τῶν Ἑλλήνων ἐξ Ἰλίου χρονία γενομένη πολλὰ ἐνεόχμωσε, καὶ στάσεις ἐν ταῖς πόλεσιν ὡς ἐπὶ πολὺ ἐγίγνοντο, ἀφ' ὧν ἐκπίπτοντες τὰς πόλεις ἔκτιζον…Δωριῆς τε ὀγδοηκοστῷ ἔτει ξὺν Ἡρακλείδαις Πελοπόννησον ἔσχον. μόλις τε ἐν πολλῷ χρόνῳ ἡσυχάσασα ἡ Ἑλλὰς βεβαίως καὶ οὐκέτι ἀνισταμένη ἀποικίας ἐξέπεμψε, καὶ Ἴωνας μὲν Ἀθηναῖοι καὶ νησιωτῶν τοὺς πολλοὺς ᾤκισαν, Ἰταλίας δὲ καὶ Σικελίας τὸ πλεῖστον Πελοποννήσιοι τῆς τε ἄλλης Ἑλλάδος ἔστιν ἃ χωρία.

Even after the Trojan War, Greece was still subject to upheaval and settlement, such that it could not become peaceful and grow stronger. For the return of the Greeks from Ilion, after such a long time, led to many changes. Factions generally began to emerge in the cities, and, in consequence of these, men were driven into exile and founded new cities… The Dorians, too, in the eightieth year after the war, together with the Herakleidai occupied the Peloponnese. After a long period of time, Greece, having finally become permanently settled, and being no longer subject to population movements, began to send out *apoikiai*. The Athenians settled Ionia and most of the Islands. The Peloponnesians settled the greater part of Italy and Sicily and some parts of the rest of Greece.

Here Thucydides compresses five hundred years of population movements into a single chapter. The vocabulary he adopts to describe these movements is diverse. It is clear that he is not using this vocabulary in any technical sense. He does, however, seem to draw a structural distinction between cities 'founded' during the long period of disruption and *apoikiai* 'sent out' when Greece became settled: the former were an unavoidable product of civil strife, *stasis*; the latter an apparently conscious, unforced decision, a product of stability.[21] One could reasonably argue that this is a false distinction given the timbre of many 'archaic' foundation myths. Civil strife is very much at the heart of the foundation of, for example, Taras.[22] One assumes that Thucydides must have been aware of such stories. This is one potential example, then, of how these fluid categories could be manipulated. More striking, however, is Thucydides' treatment of the Athenian 'colonization' of Ionia and the so-called Peloponnesian 'colonization' of the West and 'some parts of the rest of Greece' as analogous. He must have known that, according to most ancient chronologies, the settlement of Ionia and the islands pre-dated the 'colonization' of Italy and Sicily by several centuries, if not necessarily the settlement of 'some parts of the rest of Greece'.[23] He must also have been aware that for some the settlement of Ionia and the islands was ultimately a response to the Dorian 'settlement' of the Peloponnese, and was thus a part of the general disorder that enveloped Greece in the wake of the Trojan War, rather than a product of the order that, Thucydides himself argues, eventually emerged from this chaos.

Thucydides' political motive, or at least the political context in which he was writing, is plain enough to see. The Athenians were making great play with their position as mother-city of the Ionians in the second half of the fifth century BC, primarily because this conception of the past legitimized their current position as head of the Delian League. There were, however, alternative stories about the origins of the Ionians linking them with Messenian Pylos and with the Achaians of the north-west Peloponnese.[24] In the archaic period, it seems that Athens had actually regarded itself as an Ionian city: Pseudo-Aristotle (*Ath. Pol.* 5) says that Solon called Attika 'the oldest land of Ionia'. The developing notion of Athenian autochthony that appears in the fifth-century sources was, however, incompatible with the idea of an Ionian Athens.[25] Athens clearly wished to retain its Ionian connections, given its political position at the head of a primarily Ionian Empire, but no longer wished to connect itself with the Peloponnesian origins that an Ionian identity implied. Hence the apparently fifth-century development of the myth of the Ionian cities as Athenian 'colonies' which one sees here in Thucydides.[26]

Thucydides, in equating the Ionian 'migration' and archaic colonization, in presenting them as part of the same process, was, as we have seen, doing nothing unusual. The language used to describe these two experiences in the ancient sources was more or less identical. What makes Thucydides' account interesting is that he clearly differentiates these two experiences from the population movements that had come before; and the nature of this differentiation to some extent mirrors that which we have observed within modern scholarship. Thucydides' desire to present the 'sending out of colonies' as the product of a stable political environment is very similar to the desire in modern scholarship to present 'colonization' as the product of a state society, the *polis*. In both Thucydides' account and within modern scholarship, it is

argued that colonization cannot take place within a world of political instability, or rather that such settlement which occurs within this politically
unstable world is fundamentally different from that which took place in the
politically stable world of the eighth century BC.

Both Thucydides and modern scholars have thus been driven by ideological views about the nature of colonization to posit either implicitly or
explicitly the existence of an 'age of colonization' – a product for Thucydides
of political stability and for modern scholars of the emergence of the *polis*
– that is distinct from the population movements and settlement, whether
mythical or historical, of the previous period.

One can easily question Thucydides' reasoning. As already noted, political
instability is often cast as the explanation for many archaic colonial expeditions. There is also little question that Greece throughout the archaic period
was wracked by political conflict both within the aristocracy but also between
the aristocracy and other groups demanding political power.

One can as easily cast doubt on the ideological underpinnings of the traditional view in modern scholarship. This is not the place to enter fully into
the debate about the nature of the *polis* and the question of whether it was
a product of a long evolution or whether it was the product of a 'big bang',
but some general points can be made. Firstly, most would accept that the *polis*
was a geographically and perhaps culturally delimited phenomenon within
the Greek world. The *ethnos* dominated not only in much of northern and
north-western Greece, but also in the north-western and central Peloponn-
nese.[27] Yet colonization was not limited to the *polis*. The *ethnos* of Achaia,
for example, is presented in our ancient sources as a major player in colonization. Yet, as Morgan and Hall (1996) have amply demonstrated, the region
cannot even be seen as a cultural unity in the early archaic period, let alone
as a political one. Nor can one reasonably identify communities within
Achaia that could be called *poleis*. Secondly, the most striking evidence for
the emergence of the *polis* in the early archaic period is that which suggests
the development of a strong communal identity.[28] In contrast, there is little
evidence in the late eighth or early seventh century BC for the centralization
of political power. Indeed the ability of a community to send out a colony
has been seen as one of the best indicators of centralization, but one need
hardly point out the circularity of this argument.[29] To sum up this brief
assessment of the evidence: it was not only *poleis* that sent out colonies in the
early archaic period; and such evidence as there is for the *polis* does not show
that there was the level of centralized power one might assume necessary to
plan a state-sponsored colony. To take this to its conclusion: whether or not
one might wish to differentiate between archaic colonization and settlement
during the Dark Ages, the emergence of the *polis* is not the differentiating

factor.

I turn now to the question of whether archaic colonization can be usefully treated as a single movement, as classifying it as an 'age of colonization' would seem to imply. I will not dwell too long on this point since the answer is unequivocally 'no'. It is clear that a series of experiences, distinct in nature and also intention, can be identified within the archaic period.

First, there is Euboian overseas settlement, focused primarily on the northern Aegean and on Sicily and southern Italy. Broadly speaking, the Euboians seemed to have been more interested in seeking out new resources and securing trade routes than in territorial control, than in creating *apoikiai*, 'homes away from home'. This did not, however, stop them from creating genuine communities. Pithekoussai is the extreme example of the Euboian settlement model. Although there is patent evidence of social organization at the site, reflected most clearly by the careful adherence to family plots in the cemetery and the demarcation of a 'manufacturing zone' from the habitation areas, the ethnically diverse population, and the community's apparent reliance on trade and manufacture, have led many to classify the site as an *emporion* rather than an *apoikia*, i.e. as a trading community rather than a 'proper' colony, and to distance it from the colonization movement which began in earnest a generation or so later.[30] More recently, new evidence for agricultural activity and settlement on the south side of the island, perhaps implying, at the very least, agricultural motives for the settlers, but maybe also control of the *chōra*, has encouraged some to reclaim the community as an *apoikia* and to see it as the beginning of the archaic colonial movement.[31] In my opinion, this new evidence helps to align Pithekoussai more fully with Euboian settlement patterns rather than with the archaic colonial movement in general.

Next, there is the more territorially aggressive colonization of, for example, the Corinthians and the Achaians in the western Mediterranean. Generally, this movement is marked by the expulsion or destruction of the native population and the rapid marking out of a territory. Nevertheless it is worth pointing out that the aggressive model has been subject to some recent attempts at modification; and that the distance between the Euboian model and the aggressive model may not be so great after all.[32]

Third, there is the Greek colonization of the Black Sea. Obvious parallels can be drawn with colonization in the West, but it is nevertheless dangerous to see it automatically in the same terms.

Fourth, there is what has been described as 'secondary colonization' in the West. This is colonization undertaken by communities which were themselves 'colonies'. So, for example, Megara Hyblaia, a colony of Nisaean Megara according to the sources, is presented as the mother city of Selinous.

And Sybaris, an Achaian *apoikia*, is identified as the founding city of Poseidonia. The relationship between these colonies and their mother-city is potentially very different, primarily because in many instances the distance between the two is minimal. The possibility that some form of control was exerted is much greater in these instances, not only because of the issue of distance, but also because the communities who sent out these colonies are more recognisably *poleis*. Both literary and archaeological evidence places the earliest secondary colonies no earlier than the mid-seventh century BC, and many from in the early sixth, a time when there is much stronger evidence for political centralization within the *polis*. This is reflected not least by the growing evidence for town planning in the primary colonies in the second and third generations of settlement.[33]

Finally, there is the colonization associated with the Greek tyrants of Corinth and Athens. Graham (1964, 30–4) has shown that these were colonies in the fuller sense of the world, dependent communities, founded by sons or other relatives of the tyrant on his behalf, with imperial ambitions.

The modern conception of an 'age of colonization' has undoubtedly played a role in masking the variety of archaic colonial experiences in the same way that it has forced the drawing of very clear distinctions between archaic colonization and earlier settlement. It is inevitable that the application of a single model to these diverse experiences has concealed the very different motives for, and the very different nature of, Greek *apoikiai* in this period. At the same time, the tendency in the ancient sources, Thucydides notwithstanding, to bracket together an even broader range of experiences has further obscured the diversity of the archaic colonial experience.

Yet there is still a clear desire in the scholarship to trace the ancient evidence for the traditional model, as laid out in the introduction of this paper, back to the beginning of the archaic period. Essentially, it has been argued that many of the key elements of the ancient colonial ideology are to be seen already in Homer.[34] If one accepts this argument, then it undermines the possibility that this model was formed over a long period of time in response to the very distinct experiences laid out above. It is important, then, to consider what evidence there is for 'colonial ideologies' in Homer.

Homeric ideologies

The consensus view on the composition of the Homeric epics suggests that they were written down towards the end of the eighth century BC; synchronous, that is, with the early decades of the archaic colonization movement. Morris (1986) has argued that the nature of oral composition is such that the social and cultural background of an oral poem changes to replicate the poet's own society. According to his argument, Homeric society must be reflective of Greek society in the late eighth century BC. If one accepts Morris' position, and it is a position that has become something of a consensus, then one might expect to see reflections of the colonization movement, of the realities of the colonial experience and the ideologies underpinning it, in the Homeric epics. The *Odyssey* as a whole, a story of maritime exploration, of encounters with foreign peoples, might be seen as a general commentary on this experience; while there are a small number of specific passages in Homer, which might be taken as more direct commentaries on colonization, and a few further that might be recognized as the earliest examples of a foundation myth. Such an interpretation of the *Odyssey* and of these specific passages acts as support for Morris' dating of Homeric society (and, by extension, of the consensus view for the date of composition): hence, for example, Crielaard (1995) argues that Homer's awareness of colonization makes a late-eighth-century date highly probable both for the poem's composition, and for the society described in the poems. Yet there is a danger of circularity in such an argument: the epics were written down in the late eighth century; the poems therefore, following Morris, are reflective of late-eighth-century Greek society and since colonization was a part of this society the poems must reflect on colonization in some way; several passages in the epics can be interpreted in such a fashion, i.e. as descriptive of the colonial experience; and since colonization begins in the late eighth century then the society described by Homer cannot be dated any earlier than the late eighth century. If, however, one starts from the position that Homeric society is descriptive of an earlier society, then this enforces a reconsideration of these passages. Finley (1956) famously argued that the poems described a Dark Age Greek society of the tenth and ninth centuries BC, a position now largely rejected. More recently, Malkin (1998) has pushed back the composition and by extension the dating of Homeric society to the ninth century BC, and has argued at length that the *Odyssey* describes a pre-colonial world. Raaflaub (1998), who is not explicitly interested in colonization, has argued that the poet, although writing in the late eighth century, deliberately sets the events of the poem in a society of the near past rather than in the present; a society still recognizable to his audience but also a society definitively not of the immediate present. He thus suggests a date of *c.* 800 BC. If one accepts any one of these positions it raises questions about how the 'colonial' passages should be treated, and about how the *Odyssey* as a whole might be read. Here I broadly accept Raaflaub's dating. With this in mind, I will look now first at three specific passages, before turning to consider the *Odyssey* as a whole.

The first passage to consider is *Odyssey* 6.2–11:

αὐτὰρ Ἀθήνη
βῆ ῥ' ἐς Φαιήκων ἀνδρῶν δῆμόν τε πόλιν τε·

οἳ πρὶν μέν ποτ' ἔναιον ἐν εὐρυχόρῳ Ὑπερείῃ,
ἀγχοῦ Κυκλώπων ἀνδρῶν ὑπερηνορεόντων,
οἵ σφεας σινέσκοντο, βίηφι δὲ φέρτεροι ἦσαν.
ἔνθεν ἀναστήσας ἄγε Ναυσίθοος θεοειδής,
εἷσεν δὲ Σχερίῃ, ἑκὰς ἀνδρῶν ἀλφηστάων,
ἀμφὶ δὲ τεῖχος ἔλασσε πόλει καὶ ἐδείματο οἴκους
καὶ νηοὺς ποίησε θεῶν καὶ ἐδάσσατ' ἀρούρας.

Athena went to the land and city of the Phaeacians. These dwelt of old in spacious Hypereia beside the Cyclopes, men overweening in pride who plundered them continually and were mightier than they. From thence Nausithous, the godlike, had removed them, and led and settled them in Scheria far from men that eat grain. About the city he had drawn a wall, he had built houses and made temples for the gods, and divided the ploughlands.

A number of scholars have treated this passage as a direct reflection of the archaic colonization movement: as, indeed, descriptive of the nature and the practice of this movement. Dougherty (2000, 128), for example, describes it as a 'colonial history' of the Phaeacians. In particular, they have seen in the narration of Nausithous' actions the definitive portrait of the colonial founder. So Graham, for example, in his *Colony and Mother-City in Ancient Greece* (1964, 29) places the latter part of this passage (ll. 7–11) at the head of his chapter 3, 'The Role of *Oikist*', emphasizing the importance of this passage to his understanding of the founder's duties. Meanwhile Dougherty (2000, 129) states that 'the description…captures the essential activities of a colonial founder'.

Demand (1990, 28), however, is surely correct to point out that this passage does not describe colonization at all, but 'urban relocation'. Demand (1986, 28–33) argues that this account of a whole people driven from their homeland by the aggression of their neighbours to settle elsewhere is based on the experience of the east Greeks in the first half of the seventh century BC. She suggests that the Cimmerian offensive in Asia Minor is a possible model for the Cyclopes' treatment of the Phaeacians, and that the 'happy and successful life attributed to the Phaeacians perhaps bespeaks the hope that preceded actual experience – the immigrant's anticipation of "streets paved with gold" '.[35] This is not chronologically impossible. It does, however, enforce a downwards dating by some fifty years or so of the generally accepted late-eighth-century date for the composition of the poems, i.e. it requires one to accept a date of *c.* 650 BC for the composition. More problematically it requires one to see the whole Phaeacian episode as a late development in the epic cycle, since the whole story as we have it seems to rest on the opposition drawn between the Phaeacians and the Cyclopes, not just in this passage but also elsewhere in book 6 and book 9. If one argues that the story of the Phaeacian origins is incorporated into the tradition in the mid-seventh century BC, just at the moment the *Odyssey* is written down, then we must either assume that the whole episode was developed at that same point, or ask difficult questions about how this section worked before the inclusion of the passage.

There are, however, other possible models for this passage. The story seems to have much in common with the myths of 'migration' from the Greek mainland in the wake of Dorian aggression. Indeed, in the brutish, powerful Cyclopes one might even recognize a negative portrait of the Dorians. It is possible, then, that an archaic audience on hearing this story was drawn to think of mythical episodes such as the Ionian migration much more readily than any contemporary colonization movement. It is also worth noting that such myths may have some basis in reality. Although a wholesale 'migration' from the mainland to Asia Minor and the Aegean islands during the Dark Age is not supported by the archaeological evidence, there is some indication of Greek settlement in Ionia in the tenth and ninth centuries BC.[36] It is thus feasible that the 'historical' model for this story is not the contemporary experience but that of Dark Age settlement in Ionia. One might reasonably ask why in constructing this episode the poet would look beyond contemporary events for inspiration. If one accepts Raaflaub's argument that the poet sought to set the poem in some recent past, then the answer might be that a story that recalled the myths of Ionian migration provided the requisite distance. To take this argument to its conclusion, this passage, so frequently brought forward as a guide to the practice of the archaic colonial founder, may in fact reflect more directly on an earlier period of population movements.

We turn now to *Odyssey* 9.116–41:

νῆσος ἔπειτα λάχεια παρὲκ λιμένος τετάνυσται,
γαίης Κυκλώπων οὔτε σχεδὸν οὔτ' ἀποτηλοῦ,
ὑλήεσσ'· ἐν δ' αἶγες ἀπειρέσιαι γεγάασιν
ἄγριαι· οὐ μὲν γὰρ πάτος ἀνθρώπων ἀπερύκει,
οὐδέ μιν εἰσοιχνεῦσι κυνηγέται, οἵ τε καθ' ὕλην
ἄλγεα πάσχουσιν κορυφὰς ὀρέων ἐφέποντες.
οὔτ' ἄρα ποίμνῃσιν καταΐσχεται οὔτ' ἀρότοισιν,
ἀλλ' ἥ γ' ἄσπαρτος καὶ ἀνήροτος ἤματα πάντα
ἀνδρῶν χηρεύει, βόσκει δέ τε μηκάδας αἶγας.
οὐ γὰρ Κυκλώπεσσι νέες πάρα μιλτοπάρῃοι,
οὐδ' ἄνδρες νηῶν ἔνι τέκτονες, οἵ κε κάμοιεν
νῆας ἐϋσσέλμους, αἵ κεν τελέοιεν ἕκαστα
ἄστε' ἐπ' ἀνθρώπων ἱκνεύμεναι, οἷά τε πολλὰ
ἄνδρες ἐπ' ἀλλήλους νηυσὶν περόωσι θάλασσαν·
οἵ κέ σφιν καὶ νῆσον ἐϋκτιμένην ἐκάμοντο.

οὐ μὲν γάρ τι κακή γε, φέροι δέ κεν ὥρια πάντα·
ἐν μὲν γὰρ λειμῶνες ἁλὸς πολιοῖο παρ' ὄχθας
ὑδρηλοὶ μαλακοί· μάλα κ' ἄφθιτοι ἄμπελοι εἶεν·
ἐν δ' ἄροσις λείη· μάλα κεν βαθὺ λήιον αἰεὶ
εἰς ὥρας ἀμόῳεν, ἐπεὶ μάλα πῖαρ ὑπ' οὖδας.
ἐν δὲ λιμὴν εὔορμος, ἵν' οὐ χρεὼ πείσματός ἐστιν,
οὔτ' εὐνὰς βαλέειν οὔτε πρυμνήσι' ἀνάψαι,
ἀλλ' ἐπικέλσαντας μεῖναι χρόνον, εἰς ὅ κε ναυτέων
θυμὸς ἐποτρύνῃ καὶ ἐπιπνεύσωσιν ἆται.
αὐτὰρ ἐπὶ κρατὸς λιμένος ῥέει ἀγλαὸν ὕδωρ,
κρήνη ὑπὸ σπείους· περὶ δ' αἴγειροι πεφύασιν.

Across the wide bay from the mainland there lies a deserted island, not far out, but still not close inshore. Wild goats in hundreds breed here; and no human beings come upon the island to startle them – no hunter of all who ever tracked with hounds through forests or had rough going over mountain trails. The isle, unplanted and untilled, a wilderness, pastures goats alone. And this is why: good ships like ours with cheek-paint at the bows are far beyond the Cyclopes. No shipwright toils among them, shaping and building up symmetrical hulls to cross the sea and visit all the seaboard towns as men do who go and come across the water. This isle – seagoing folk would have annexed it and built their home-steads on it: all good land, fertile for every crop in season: lush well-watered meadows along the shores, vines in profusion, meadowland, clear for the plough, where grain would grow chin-high by harvest time, and rich sub-soil. The island cove is land-locked, so you need no hawsers out astern, bow-stones or mooring: run in and ride there till the day your crews chafe to be under sail, and a fair wind blows.

This passage is often presented as some kind of colonial 'fantasy island'. Agriculturally rich, blessed with a fine harbour and protected from the aggressive locals, Dougherty (2000, 129) states 'this is an island that embodies all the possibilities of the new world of colonization'. Certainly, Odysseus recognizes the potential of the island as an ideal place for settlement: 'seagoing folk would have annexed it and built their homesteads on it' he says. But Odysseus is no colonist and to suggest, as Dougherty (2000, 129) does, that his arrival on the island is 'like the "surprised *oikist*" of colonial legend' is to overemphasize the 'colonial undertones'. Much more likely parallels can be found, as Malkin (1998) would suggest, with a pre-colonial world of exploration. It might be overstating the case to argue that the western Mediterranean of the late eighth century, particularly the coastlines of eastern Sicily and southern Italy, was already extremely well-known but Phoenicians, Euboeans and other Greeks had been travelling the route to Pithekoussai and beyond for several generations. Although some surprises must still have awaited Greek settlers arriving in the West in the late eighth century, the kind of discovery Odysseus makes in this passage perhaps fits more comfortably into a late-ninth- or early-eighth-century world when the western Mediterranean must have still been very much a mystery. This passage, then, invokes in the audience not images of a colonial 'promised land' but of a recent past when the wider world was being slowly uncovered by intrepid Greek adventurers; when discoveries of this kind were still being made, discoveries which would later be capitalized on by Greek settlers.

The last passages to be examined may be classified as foundation myth and as such the earliest example of the kind.[37] The passage, *Iliad* 2.653–69, describes the origins of the three Greek cities on Rhodes:

Τληπόλεμος δ' Ἡρακλεΐδης ἠΰς τε μέγας τε
ἐκ Ῥόδου ἐννέα νῆας ἄγεν Ῥοδίων ἀγερώχων,
οἳ Ῥόδον ἀμφενέμοντο διὰ τρίχα κοσμηθέντες
Λίνδον Ἰηλυσόν τε καὶ ἀργινόεντα Κάμειρον.
τῶν μὲν Τληπόλεμος δουρὶ κλυτὸς ἡγεμόνευεν,
ὃν τέκεν Ἀστυόχεια βίῃ Ἡρακληείῃ,
τὴν ἄγετ' ἐξ Ἐφύρης ποταμοῦ ἄπο Σελλήεντος
πέρσας ἄστεα πολλὰ διοτρεφέων αἰζηῶν.
Τληπόλεμος δ' ἐπεὶ οὖν τράφ' ἐνὶ μεγάρῳ εὐπήκτῳ,
αὐτίκα πατρὸς ἑοῖο φίλον μήτρωα κατέκτα
ἤδη γηράσκοντα Λικύμνιον ὄζον Ἄρηος·
αἶψα δὲ νῆας ἔπηξε, πολὺν δ' ὅ γε λαὸν ἀγείρας
βῆ φεύγων ἐπὶ πόντον· ἀπείλησαν γάρ οἱ ἄλλοι
υἱέες υἱωνοί τε βίης Ἡρακληείης.
αὐτὰρ ὅ γ' ἐς Ῥόδον ἷξεν ἀλώμενος ἄλγεα πάσχων·
τριχθὰ δὲ ᾤκηθεν καταφυλαδόν, ἠδὲ φίληθεν
ἐκ Διός, ὅς τε θεοῖσι καὶ ἀνθρώποισιν ἀνάσσει.

Tlepolemos, son of Herakles, a man both brave and large of stature, brought nine ships of lordly warriors from Rhodes. These dwelt in Rhodes which is divided among the three cities of Lindos, Ialysos, and Kameiros, that lies upon the chalk. These were commanded by Tlepolemos, son of mighty Herakles and born of Astyochea, whom he had carried off from Ephyra, on the river Selleis, after sacking many cities of valiant warriors. When Tlepolemos grew up, he killed his father's uncle Likymnios, who had been a famous warrior in his time, but was then grown old. So he built himself a fleet, gathered a great following, and fled beyond the sea, for he was menaced by the other sons and grandsons of Herakles. After a voyage, during which he suffered great hardship, he came to Rhodes, where the people divided into three communities, according to their tribes, and were dearly loved by Zeus, the lord, of gods and men.

As it is presented here the myth seems to be a relatively brief synopsis of a more detailed account of Tlepolemos' adventures. One might speculate, for example, whether there was a myth in circulation that described the 'great hardship' that befell the hero on his voyage to Rhodes. Certainly aspects of the story are elaborated in a later version of the myth told by Pindar in

Olympian 7. There we are given more information about Tlepolemos' killing of Likymnios, with the possible implication that Tlepolemos was driven to kill his great uncle by that man's incestuous relationship with Midea, Likymnios' own mother, but with the more straightforward statement – 'disturbances of the mind lead astray even the wise man' – that he did so in a fit of madness.[38] In the *Iliad* no explanation for his actions is proffered. More strikingly Pindar tells us that Tlepolemos consulted the oracle of Apollo, which ordered him to sail to Rhodes.[39] In the *Iliad*, his relatives drive him out.

The key question here is, what is the relationship of this myth to those associated with the archaic colonization movement? Does it fit into the same category? Does it have a similar structure? One might argue, for example, that myths about the origins of the cities of the Greek mainland and the Aegean, in many instances communities long established by the eighth century BC, only developed in response to the archaic colonization movement; that as Greeks settled overseas and were forced to think hard about their origins and to develop stories explaining their presence, so the Greeks of the homeland were encouraged to think about their own origins in the same terms. Thus this myth about Rhodian origins would have developed alongside myths about colonial cities and one might expect it to be similar in form and function. On the other hand, as noted above, there is archaeological evidence for movement from Greece to the coast of Asia Minor in the Dark Ages. Is it not possible that these settlers would have had the same impulse to fashion stories about their origins, and such myths could just as readily have functioned as models for foundation myths about the cities of the Greek homeland and Aegean? If this Rhodian foundation myth did develop in response to the archaic colonization movement then it did so very swiftly. As already noted, there are elements of the Tlepolemos story which imply that it is a much abbreviated version of a longer and perhaps well-established myth.

This story clearly has some elements in common with later foundation myths. The theme of the founder as murderer is one that recurs in such myths. Dougherty (1993) sees, in the murder committed by the founder in the homeland, an analogy for the death and violence inherent in the colonial experience: for her, embedded in the image of the murderous *oikist* is a recognition of the unavoidable slaughter of indigenous peoples that colonization involves. When seen in this light, the passage suggests that the Greeks had a very clear ideological view of the nature of overseas settlement in the late eighth century, as a violent experience involving conquest and control of the native peoples; a colonialist experience in the full sense of the word. The Homeric version of the Rhodian foundation myth does not, however, comply with several other elements within Dougherty's schema. She argues that foundation myths adhere to a general pattern along the following lines: a crisis within a community is caused by some form of pollution; the Delphic oracle is consulted and advises the sending out of a colony to be led by the individual responsible for the pollution; once the colony is sent out the pollution is cleansed and the crisis is resolved. In this passage, however, there is no crisis, no indication of pollution and no consultation of the oracle. Tlepolemos is driven out by vengeful relatives; he does not leave on the advice of Apollo. Whether or not one accepts Dougherty's overall argument, it seems doubtful to me that this myth can be slotted neatly into her schema. Tlepolemos' story in fact has more in common with one of Odysseus' many tall tales. In *Odyssey* 13.256–76, pretending to be a Cretan exile, Odysseus recounts how he murdered the Cretan king Idomeneus' son who was attempting to deprive him of the booty he had won in the Trojan War. The deed done – 'the man's blood fresh on my hands' – he fled on a Phoenician ship. In this instance he is not driven out – in fact, nobody knows he is the murderer – but leaves of his own accord. Murder here leads to exile and a life wandering around Greece, not to colonization.

This myth is as well read in relation to other stories of exile and wandering found within the Homeric epics, such as Odysseus' Cretan story, as it is in relation to archaic foundation myths, a point which Dougherty (1993, 124) allows for. Insofar as this is a foundation myth, I believe that it did not develop in the period of archaic colonization but in relation to earlier periods of population movements.[40]

So where has this discussion led us so far? I have tried to argue that scholars who see evidence of the ideologies and of the practice of the archaic colonization movement in Homer are mistaken. I have argued that the three passages most frequently brought forward as reflections of archaic colonization are in fact reflective of earlier experiences. In the first instance, the foundation of Scheria, the story recalls more readily Dark Age settlement in Asia Minor. In the second instance, 'goat island' is a pre-colonial rather than a colonial fantasy. In the third instance, the Rhodian foundation myth must be read in relation to myths of exile and wandering within the Homeric epics and perhaps in relation to Dark Age settlement myths. More generally I accept Malkin's (1998) view that the *Odyssey* as a whole is best read as a comment on a pre-colonial rather than a colonial society and is therefore not reflective of colonial ideologies.

Rather than a reflection of the practices and ideologies of the archaic colonial experience, these Homeric 'ideologies' played an important part in the construction of the Greek memory of this experience; to some extent they acted as a literary model for later foundation myths. We next examine the role of the *oikist*, as it is represented in modern scholarship and in the ancient sources, in order to demonstrate how this process may have worked.

The role of the *oikist*

Although it is generally accepted that the full role played by the *oikist* in the foundation of a colony is lost to us – no ancient source discusses it in any great detail – most recognize in *Odyssey* 6.7–11 a 'minimum list' of his duties. So the *oikist* is seen by Graham (1964, 29–30), Malkin (1987) and others, as responsible for the urban and territorial organization of the new community: for marking out the urban boundaries of the settlement by building a wall; for organizing the building of houses; for establishing temples; and for allocating plots of land for the settlers. As Malkin (1987, 68) would have it, he is responsible for 'creating a *polis ex novo*'. Graham (1964, 39), however, has posited a development in the role of the *oikist* such that this image of him as 'all-responsible, even monarchical' only applies to the early period of colonization. The *oikists* sent out by tyrants, Graham argues, fell under the immediate sway of the ruler of the mother-city and thus their power was to some extent delimited; while in the classical period the *oikist* became purely a figurehead who in some instances did not even join the expedition.

Graham's model of the early *oikist* as a monarchical figure does not depend solely on the Homeric passages, although the fact that both Nausithous and Tlepolemos are described as *basileis* must have some impact on his position. Also significant to this model is the various later evidence associated with Battos, *oikist* of Cyrene. In Pindar (*Pythian* 5.85–93) the *oikist* is shown performing some of the duties assigned to Nausithous, essentially the establishment of sanctuaries for the gods. It is also clear from Pindar, and from Herodotus' account of the foundation, that Battos led the expedition and became the independent king of the new colony, ruling for forty years and founding the Battiad dynasty.[41] Battos, then, is presented as *both* founder and king, a point made even more explicit in the fourth century BC copy of an alleged seventh century foundation decree for Cyrene which refers to him as '*archageta[n t]e kai basilēa*'.[42] Battos' status is unusual. Very few *oikists* are presented explicitly as rulers of the colony they founded. One wonders how far the images of Nausithous, who is not as we have seen really an *oikist* at all, and Battos, who uniquely becomes king of Cyrene, may have given a false impression, perpetuated in both the ancient *and* the modern literature, of the nature of the *oikist* as a hands-on, all powerful leader of the expedition.

It is worth considering for a moment how stories about the founder would have circulated in the ancient world. Much of the information about individual *oikists* is transmitted to us through the prose accounts of writers such as Herodotus, Thucydides, Strabo and Diodorus Siculus. It is sometimes argued that many of these later prose accounts were drawn from a body of archaic and classical 'ktistic' poetry that would have recorded details about the founder and the settlement.[43] Such poetry, it has been argued, would have been performed annually in connection with celebrations of the city's foundation.[44] This implies that there was an 'authentic' tradition in circulation within the colony itself from quite an early date: authentic in the sense that it reflected the beliefs of the settlers themselves with regard to their founder and founding city.

Dougherty (1994), however, has argued persuasively that there was no corpus of specifically 'ktistic' poetry until the Hellenistic period. She holds that there is no early evidence for an annual celebration of a city's foundation, and therefore no obvious context for the performance of such poetry. Rather, she argues that foundation stories would have been a part of other poetic genres, such as the *epinikean* poetry of Pindar, where frequently we find the civic role of the victor being equated to that of the founder.

Pindar's general relationship with Homer is fairly easy to establish. His relationship with at least one of the Homeric 'foundation myths', that of Tlepolemos and Rhodes, seems clear: at *ll.* 20–1 of *Olympian* 7, Pindar promises 'to correct the common account'.[45] The probable reference here is to the Homeric account since, as we have seen, Pindar offers a distinctly different version, which places the emphasis on the Delphic oracle as the driving force behind the colonization of Rhodes, not Tlepolemos' vengeful relatives. One sees here how Pindar engages with a specific passage in Homer, changing and manipulating it to reflect his own historical and literary context. One might wonder how far Pindar may have drawn more generally on the image of the founder as seen in Homer. Having said this, there are clearly elements in Pindar's model which are not reflected in the Homeric model: the worship of the founder as a hero; and the role of the Delphic oracle. We will now examine these elements considering how and when they may have been incorporated into the 'ideology' of Greek colonization.

Founder-cult

In *Pythian* 5 Pindar states that at his death Battos was buried at the edge of the agora and worshipped as a hero by the Cyreneians.[46] This is the earliest piece of literary evidence for the phenomenon of the Greek founder-cult but it is widely accepted that the observance of such cults goes back to the early days of colonization and that the actual tomb of the founder would have been the focus for cultic rites.[47] The more general growth of both hero- and tomb-cult in the late eighth and seventh century BC provides an obvious historical context in which founder cult could have developed.[48] If one begins, however, from the position that many of the earliest 'colonies' were not so much founded as evolved organically, then by extension both the notion of a founder and of a founder-cult must be later developments. When one examines the scant literary and archaeological evidence for founder-cult then one finds support for the idea that it is a later development, an example of 'invented tradition'.[49]

A key literary passage in the debate is Herodotus 6.38 which describes how Miltiades of Athens, after his death, was offered sacrifices by the people of the Chersonese, of whom he was king, which were '*hōs nomos oikistēi*' – 'customary for a founder' – in addition to which athletic and equestrian games were inaugurated.[50] The key point here is that since Herodotus feels no need to discuss the nature of these sacrifices, one might reasonably assume, as Malkin does, that the audience knew exactly what sacrifices were customary: 'Herodotus firmly believed in the existence of a generally established norm for founder cults'.[51] It is worth pointing out, however, that Miltiades was not strictly speaking a founder at all: he had been invited to become ruler of a people called the Dolonkoi on the advice of the Delphic oracle and had agreed, bringing with him such Athenians as wished to follow him.[52]

Similarly, Thucydides (5.11) tells us that Brasidas was worshipped as founder at Amphipolis after his death in 423 BC, although it was the Athenian Hagnon who was the technical founder:[53]

μετὰ δὲ ταῦτα τὸν Βρασίδαν οἱ ξύμμαχοι πάντες ξὺν ὅπλοις ἐπισπόμενοι δημοσίᾳ ἔθαψαν ἐν τῇ πόλει πρὸ τῆς νῦν ἀγορᾶς οὔσης· καὶ τὸ λοιπὸν οἱ Ἀμφιπολῖται, περιείρξαντες αὐτοῦ τὸ μνημεῖον, ὡς ἥρωί τε ἐντέμνουσι καὶ τιμὰς δεδώκασιν ἀγῶνας καὶ ἐτησίους θυσίας, καὶ τὴν ἀποικίαν ὡς οἰκιστῇ προσέθεσαν.

After this, all the allies parading fully armoured buried Brasidas in the city [Amphipolis] at public expense in front of what is now the agora. From then on, the Amphipolitans, enclosing his grave, sacrificed to him as a hero and honoured him with games and annual sacrifices, and they made him founder of the colony.

What does the evidence of these two passages, coupled with that of Pindar, tell us definitively about the nature of founder cult? First, it tells us that by the second half of the sixth century BC the title *oikistēs* could be assigned to individuals who were not strictly speaking founders at all. Second, it tells us that this was a substantial honour, but one which could be expanded on by the addition of games. Third, it tells us that by the middle of the fifth century BC the practices associated with founder-cult were well established: both Pindar and Herodotus seem to have a clear vision of what founder-cult involved, even if they do not tell us. One cannot, however, assume that these sacrifices were recognized as customary at the time of Miltiades. Fourth, by the second half of the fifth century BC, founders were celebrated at an annual festival. These earliest scraps of information about founder-cult tell us no more and no less than this.[54]

Turning now to the archaeological evidence, one finds that here also there is little or nothing to suggest that hero-cult was a phenomenon to be associated with the early days of colonization, and indeed some evidence to suggest that the importance of such cult was only emerging in the latter part of the sixth century BC.

The so-called grave of Lamis at Thapsos dated to the eighth century BC shows no evidence of any associated cult activity so is hardly evidence of founder cult.[55] A building on the edge of the agora at Megara Hyblaia dating to the mid-seventh century BC has been identified as a *herōon*, and because of its position it has been associated with the colony's founder.[56] It is not immediately clear, however, that this is a *herōon*, although there is strong evidence that it is some sort of sacred area.

Evidence from Cyrene is intriguing. A tomb dating to *c.* 600 BC, that is around the time of Battos' death, was found at the edge of the agora in a position compatible topographically with Pindar's account.[57] When the agora was re-organized at the end of the fifth and again in the later fourth century BC, the tomb was in the first instance marked by a new mound and cenotaph, and in the second by the building of a wall around it.[58] One might reasonably identify this as the tomb of Battos, or at least as the tomb associated with Battos by the Cyreneians. There is, however, no clear evidence for cult activity associated with the tomb in any period.

Perhaps the best, but still by no means unproblematic, archaeological evidence for founder-cult comes from Poseidonia, a notional secondary foundation of Sybaris. An underground chamber, a *hypogaion*, was found to the south of the so-called temple of Athena.[59] It contained five iron spits laid on an elevated platform in the centre of the chamber, eight bronze vessels, six *hydriai* and two *amphorae*, each containing a sticky substance, perhaps honey, and an Attic Black Figure *amphora*, repaired before being deposited, which dates the deposit and probably the chamber to *c.* 500 BC. There was no evidence of a body. The function of the chamber is possibly suggested by the iconography on the Attic vase, which shows the *apotheosis* of Hercules, the implication being that this might be a *herōon*. The spits and the honey might also be seen as the accoutrements of heroic feasting. This could then be the cenotaph of a hero.

Zancani-Montuoro (1954) long ago suggested that this might in fact be the tomb of the founder, not however of Poseidonia, which has a traditional foundation date in the mid-seventh century BC, but of Sybaris, which was destroyed in 510 BC. In other words, she proposes that, along with some of the

Sybarites, the tomb of Sybaris' founder, Is of Helike, was transferred to Posei-donia. Malkin (1987, 214) sees Zancani-Montuoro's hypothesis as no more than a conjecture that 'avoids the difficulty of the late date (i.e. this cannot be a cenotaph for the founder of Poseidonia itself) by positing an unparalleled practice'. If, however, one starts from the position that founder-cult is an 'invented tradition', then it is certainly possible that the cult of Poseidonia's 'founder' was only formally introduced at the end of the sixth century BC. The impetus for this introduction could well have been Sybaris' destruction: one might, for example, see Sybarite refugees, wishing to highlight the connection between the two cities, as the initiators of such a cult.

To my mind, the location of the *hypogaion* supports its identification as a shrine of the founder. The exact location of the Greek agora at Poseidonia is open to question. Some have favoured the idea that it lies beneath the later Roman forum. The position of the *ekklesiastērion* (or *bouleutērion*) as well as the orientation of the so-called sacred way favours the idea that the agora lies to the north of the Roman forum. The *ekklesiastērion* would have sat on the eastern boundary of the agora with the sacred way forming the western boundary. In this scenario, the *hypogaion* would have sat at the north eastern corner of the agora, a highly likely location for a notional tomb of the founder.

There is nothing in the archaeological evidence that allows us to associate founder-cult with the earliest stages of colonization, with the possible exception of the 'tomb of Battos' at Cyrene. Cyrene, however, is a relatively late colony and Battos, as we have seen, is not a standard example of an *oikist*. The evidence from Poseidonia, on the other hand, supports the idea that founder cult could be inaugurated long after the 'foundation' of a community.

The question of when and why founder-cult became important is ulti-mately a matter of conjecture given the state of the evidence. This paper rejects the position that it can be dated to the very early days of Greek colonization. One possible context I would suggest for its emergence as a significant institution is the colonization of the Corinthian tyrants in the latter part of the seventh century BC. We have seen how the Amphipolitans claimed Brasidas as their founder on his death after the Battle of Amphipolis. This was clearly a political act that stated that Amphipolis was aligning itself with Sparta and rejecting Athens, a fact made all the more clear by their treatment of Hagnon's memory. What better way for the colonists of Leukas, Anaktorion, Ambracia, Apollonia, and Epidamnus to celebrate their connec-tion with the Corinthian tyrant than by celebrating as founder heroes the sons and relatives of the tyrant. There is no explicit evidence to support this picture but one incident recorded in our sources and relating to Apollonia may offer some corroboration for this scenario. We are told by Stephanus of Byzantium that Apollonia was formally named, after its founder Gylax, Gylakeia. Malkin (1987, 87) suggests convincingly that the context for this change was the downfall of the Kypselid dynasty, which had sent out Gylax, some eighteen years after the city's foundation. If a city could be named for its mortal founder, as would be so often the case in the Hellenistic period, then it is not difficult to imagine founder-cult emerging in this context as a suitable honour to be given to the powerful representative of the tyrant.

The role of the Delphic Oracle

The absolute centrality of Delphi to the process of colonization is clearly established in the classical period. Thus when Sparta decides to establish a colony at Herakleia in Trachis an essential part of the process as presented by Thucydides (3.92) was the consultation of the oracle:

πρῶτον μὲν οὖν ἐν Δελφοῖς τὸν θεὸν ἐπήροντο, κελεύοντος δὲ ἐξέπεμψαν τοὺς οἰκήτορας αὑτῶν τε καὶ τῶν περιοίκων, καὶ τῶν ἄλλων Ἑλλήνων τὸν βουλόμενον ἐκέλευον ἕπεσθαι πλὴν Ἰώνων καὶ Ἀχαιῶν καὶ ἔστιν ὧν ἄλλων ἐθνῶν. οἰκισταὶ δὲ τρεῖς Λακεδαιμονίων ἡγήσαντο, Λέων καὶ Ἀλκίδας καὶ Δαμάγων. καταστάντες δὲ ἐτείχισαν τὴν πόλιν ἐκ καινῆς, ἣ νῦν Ἡράκλεια καλεῖται.

First, then, they consulted the god at Delphi, and when they had received a favourable reply they sent out settlers from among themselves and from the *perioikoi*. They also called for anyone from the rest of Greece who wished to come forward apart from the Ionians, the Achaians and some other peoples. Three Spartan *oikists* led the expedition: Leon, Alkidas and Damagon. So they established and fortified as new what is now called Herakleia.

Meanwhile, the failure of the former Spartan king, Dorieus, to consult the oracle before attempting to found a colony explains, in Herodotus' version of the story, why the expedition failed:[60]

Ὁ μὲν δὴ Κλεομένης, ὡς λέγεται, ἦν τε οὐ φρενήρης ἀκρομανής τε, ὁ δὲ Δωριεὺς ἦν τῶν ἡλίκων πάντων πρῶτος, εὖ τε ἠπίστατο κατ᾽ ἀνδραγαθίην αὐτὸς σχήσων τὴν βασιληίην. ὥστε ὦν οὕτω φρονέων, ἐπειδὴ ὅ τε Ἀναξανδρίδης ἀπέθανε καὶ οἱ Λακεδαιμόνιοι χρεώμενοι τῷ νόμῳ ἐστήσαντο βασιλέα τὸν πρεσβύτατον Κλεομένεα, ὁ Δωριεὺς δεινόν τε ποιεύμενος καὶ οὐκ ἀξιῶν ὑπὸ Κλεομένεος βασιλεύεσθαι, αἰτήσας λεὼν Σπαρτιήτας ἦγε ἐς ἀποικίην, οὔτε τῷ ἐν Δελφοῖσι χρηστηρίῳ χρησάμενος ἐς ἥντινα γῆν κτίσων ἴῃ, οὔτε ποιήσας οὐδὲν τῶν νομιζομένων· οἷα δὲ βαρέως φέρων, ἀπίει ἐς τὴν Λιβύην τὰ πλοῖα· κατηγέοντο δέ οἱ ἄνδρες Θηραῖοι. ἀπικόμενος δὲ ἐς τὴν Κίνυπα οἴκισε χῶρον κάλλιστον τῶν Λιβύων παρὰ ποταμόν. ἐξελασθεὶς δὲ ἐνθεῦτεν τῷ τρίτῳ ἔτει ὑπὸ Μακέων τε [καὶ] Λιβύων καὶ Καρχηδονίων ἀπίκετο ἐς Πελοπόννησον.

Now Cleomenes, as the story goes, was not in his right mind and really quite mad, while Dorieus was first among all of his peers and fully believed that he would be made king for his manly worth. Since he was of this opinion, Dorieus was very angry when at Anaxandrides' death the Lacedaemonians followed their custom and made Cleomenes king by right of age. Since he would not tolerate being made subject to Cleomenes, he asked the Spartans for a group of people whom he took away as colonists. He neither inquired of the oracle at Delphi in what land he should establish his settlement, nor did anything else that was customary but set sail in great anger for Libya, with men of Thera to guide him. When he arrived there, he settled by the Cinyps river in the fairest part of Libya, but in the third year he was driven out by the Macae, the Libyans and the Carchedonians and returned to the Peloponnese.

The later sources also make it clear that Delphi had played a central role from the outset of the archaic colonization movement. Many foundation myths associated with this movement depict the founder consulting Delphi. In some instances, a consultation is made on matters unrelated to colonization and Apollo orders the sending out of a colony as a solution to the unrelated problem.[61] In others, Delphi is consulted explicitly concerning if or where a colony should be founded.[62] It is reasonable to ask, however, whether the role assigned to Delphi in these myths reflects the role that the oracle played in reality or whether these myths are a product of the retrojection of later experience. There are really two connected questions at stake here. One, is it feasible historically that Delphi was of sufficient pan-Hellenic significance to have been consulted as a matter of course by any and every would-be colonizer? Two, how likely are the Delphic oracles recorded in these myths to be authentic?

Both questions have been the subject of extensive debate.[63] It is worth noting that there has long been scepticism with regard to the role allotted to Delphi in the myths. The most important example of this scepticism is Defradas' 1954 work, *Les thèmes de la propagande delphique*, which puts forward the position that Delphi only established itself as a sanctuary of international importance in the sixth century BC and that the role assigned to the oracle in the myths was a product of the sanctuary's own subsequent propaganda. This is a position that fits well with the arguments of this paper since it casts further doubt on the traditional model of colonization, in particular implying that the information contained within foundation myths is spurious. Defradas, however, has been widely criticized for underestimating the importance of Delphi in the early archaic period.

From a literary perspective, the evidence for Delphi's status in this period is slight. The few Homeric references are dismissed by Defradas as later interpolations.[64] There are no particular internal reasons to support this, but these brief references to the oracle at Pytho hardly demonstrate that the site was of pan-Hellenic importance, so much as they reflect a passing awareness of its existence. In any case, it is the contention of this paper that Homeric society is reflective of late ninth/early eighth century Greek society and as such the position of Delphi within this society is not immediately significant to this debate. The absence of Delphi from the Homeric 'foundation myths' is also not a direct reflection of its colonial role at the time of the poet, i.e. the late eighth century. Some role may be attested for Pythian Apollo in the seventh century poet Kallinos' account of the foundation of Kolophon, but I am less convinced than Malkin (1987, 19) by Gierth's (1971, 85) thesis. Beyond this there is no contemporary literary evidence that demonstrates Delphi's status in the late eighth and seventh centuries. Malkin (1986), however, has made great play with Thucydides' contention that an altar of *Apollo Archēgetēs* was set up in Sicily by the founder of the first Sicilian colony of Naxos, i.e. in 734 BC.[65] It functioned, Thucydides goes on to tell us, as a pan-Sikeliot sanctuary, at which all Sicilian Greeks would sacrifice before attending the great pan-Hellenic games in Old Greece. If taken at face value, this passage would support the idea that Delphi had played a role in the archaic colonization movement from the outset. On the other hand, attributing the initiation of this cult in Sicily to the oldest Sicilian colony seems to me to be explicable as later Delphic propaganda or as *post eventum* legitimization of Greek settlement on Sicily.

From an archaeological point of view, the evidence for Delphi's position in the early archaic period is less than clear-cut. Forrest (1957) argued that the material record supported his general contention that Delphi rose to prominence in the late eighth century in part *because of* the role it played in colonization – that is, the colonial movement was the catalyst for the growth in the sanctuary's 'international' standing – and in part because the Greek colonists were seeking divine sanction and legitimation. Others, however, have traced its importance back into the Dark Ages.[66] Yet others have argued that it only became a pan-Hellenic sanctuary in any meaningful sense in the latter part of the seventh century.[67] To me the archaeological evidence suggests that Delphi was of some local importance, that is within central Greece west of the Corinthian isthmus, in the later eighth and early seventh centuries – Corinthian ware is particularly well represented in the dedications – but only truly came to international prominence, as Morgan (1993) argues, in the middle of the seventh century. The archaeological evidence, then, while it does not entirely argue against Delphi having played some role in the colonial activity of Corinth or Achaia, for example, does not fully support the picture presented by the ancient sources.

On the question of the authenticity of the oracles recorded in the sources, the most recent detailed discussion is that of Malkin (1987, 17–91). He assesses the legitimacy of the oracular responses on a case-by-case basis, rejecting as false those that contain 'folkloristic elements and aetiologies' and generally accepting those that present 'straightforward' geographical information. For the most part, Malkin shows more credence in these oracles than many earlier scholars, such as Pease (1917) and Parke and Wormell (1956). Since many of these oracles are presented in the wider context of what is clearly a foundation *myth*, the question of authenticity seems to me a little misdirected. While one might not dispute that many settlers sought divine sanction before going overseas, or that the Delphic oracle played a role of growing importance in providing this sanction for individuals and for community ventures, I find it difficult to accept that any detailed or accurate reflection of the actual process of consultation and response at the time of settlement is embedded in these myths.

In summary, Delphi did not play the extensive role attributed to it from the outset of the archaic colonial movement by the ancient sources. Rather its importance grew in the course of the seventh century BC. It is difficult to explain exactly how or why Delphi's significance in overseas settlement came to grow. As to the how, perhaps to some extent it was symbiotic (as Forrest (1957) suggests but for an earlier period): as Delphi's role in colonization grew then so its importance grew, but also as it grew in importance so it became more important for would-be colonists to gain its sanction. Within this scenario it is easy to see why existing overseas settlements may have desired to create their own history of Delphic consultation, and why Delphi would have desired to be a part of this process since it further added to the sanctuary's prestige if growing cities such as Sybaris and Syracuse connected themselves to Delphi.

It has been the aim of this paper to present a further challenge to the traditional model of archaic colonization. Following recent scholarship it has been argued firstly that this model is a product of the application of modern colonial ideologies; and secondly that the ancient model upon which the traditional model is fundamentally based was itself a product of colonial ideologies which shifted and changed across the archaic period. *A priori* this position makes a lot of sense since it is clear that Greek overseas settlement became increasingly imperialistic, increasingly colonialist, in the modern sense of the word, as the archaic period progressed, and indeed became more so in the classical period. It was in this context that the Greek memories of earlier colonization were being developed and it should be no surprise that these memories reflect the 'increasingly colonialist' ideologies of the world that created them.

Notes

¹ An example of a joint colonization: Sybaris according to Arist. *Pol.* 1303a29 was settled by Achaians and Troezenians with the latter being expelled shortly after the foundation.

² Graham's comment (1964, 8) that 'both state and private enterprise existed throughout the historical colonizing period' has, for the most part, not been taken on board in subsequent scholarship, as Osborne (1998, 251) observes.

³ A good example of how these ties could be invoked comes from the fourth century BC when the Syracusans, wracked by civil war, called upon Corinth to send assistance (Diod. Sic. 16.69). Help was sent in the form of the general Timoleon with a small fleet. At the time, it must have seemed a rather hollow gesture since Timoleon was hardly proven and the force attached to him was hardly significant, which suggests that Corinth was doing the bare minimum.

⁴ See Blakeway 1933 for an early example of an explicit argument in favour of this view.

⁵ See Gwynn 1918 for an early statement of this view and more recently Cawkwell 1992.

⁶ See Camp 1979.

⁷ See Malkin 1994.

⁸ A few examples: Murray (1993, 102) implicitly describes the period as an age of colonization: 'Two great periods of Greek expansion provided the material basis for the diffusion of Greek culture... in the century and a half between 734 and 580 the number of new cities established there is at least comparable to the number of cities already existing in the Aegean before the colonizing movement began'; while Vidal-Naquet (1986, 26) is explicit in the following passage discussing the status of the Homeric Phaeacaians: 'Phaeacia contains all the characteristic elements of a Greek settlement in the age of colonization'.

⁹ See Casevitz 1985 for a fuller discussion of the language of colonization.

¹⁰ Anton. Lib. *Meta.* 31.

¹¹ Lucan. 2.610–12.

¹² Tod no. 44.

¹³ Anton. Lib. *Meta.* 31 describes how the Cretan Lykaon had three sons, Daunius, Iapyx and Peucetius, who settled in Italy, and after whom the Daunians, Iapygians and Peucetians were named.

¹⁴ One thinks immediately of the various Herakleias – Italian, Sicilian, Trachinian, Pontic, etc. – but a number of communities were, according to the foundation myths, named after a hero that Herakles accidentally killed, e.g. according to Diod. Sic. 4.24.7 and Iamb. *Pythian* 5.50, Herakles founded Kroton in honour of the eponymous hero he killed in error (see also Ovid *Meta.* 15.19–57 for a variation on this story). A similar story is told for Italian Locris by Conon *Nar.* 3.

¹⁵ On the *nostoi* foundations as reflections of Mycenaean colonization see Immerwahr 1960 and Cline 1995. On the *nostoi* foundations as reflections of the activities of the Sea-Peoples see Sandars 1978.

¹⁶ Strabo 6.1.12.

¹⁷ See Snodgrass 1971, 296–323 and 373–8, for good discussions of the Dorian invasion and Ionian migration respectively.

¹⁸ But note that Demand (1990, 31–3) describes it as an act of 'urban relocation'.

¹⁹ See Athen. 12.523 and Strabo 6.1.14, who refers to Ionians rather than specifically Kolophonians.

²⁰ For discussion of the *archaiologia* see Gomme 1959, 85–102, and Hornblower 1991, 3–59.

²¹ Hornblower (1991, 37–8) suggests that the use of the term *stasis* is inappropriate here and that Thucydides is 'extrapolating' from his own experiences of *stasis*. Perhaps at a technical and historical level this is correct, but the events that followed the return of the heroes from the Trojan War, in certain instances the replacement of one dynasty by another, seem well-described by the term *stasis*.

²² See Strabo 6.3.2, Paus. 10.10.6–8 and Diod. Sic. 8.21 for the most detailed versions of the Tarentine foundation myth.

²³ It is not clear what Thucydides has in mind when he talks about the colonization of 'some parts of the rest of Greece'. It may be that he is thinking about, for example, Sparta's 'colonization' of Lakonia, which according to the ancient sources occurred in the middle of the eighth century, and would therefore be more or less synchronous with the western settlements. On the other hand he might have in mind Spartan colonization of the Greek islands, of Thera, Melos and Crete which would be closer in time to the traditional dates for the Ionian migration. Thucydides himself gives us the date for the Spartan foundation of Melos as a little before 1100 BC (5.112).

²⁴ For Ionian origins see Huxley 1977, 23–35.

²⁵ On autochthony see Rosivach 1987.

²⁶ On Ionian cities as Athenian colonies see Saxonhouse 1986.

²⁷ See Morgan 2003 for a full discussion of the *ethnos* in early archaic Greece.

²⁸ On this see especially Morris 1987, 1996.

²⁹ See Snodgrass 1977, 33, for a strong expression of this view. See Malkin 1994 for a variation on this position: he argues that colonization forced the Greeks to assess what a *polis* was.

³⁰ See Ridgway 1992, 107–9, for a discussion of the *emporion-apoikia* debate. Ridgway casts some doubt on the validity of this debate, doubt taken up by Wilson 1997 and 2001.

³¹ See De Caro 1994, Gialanella 1994 and d'Agostino 1999 for presentation and discussion of this new evidence.

³² See Wilson 2000.

³³ See Fischer-Hansen 1996.

³⁴ See most recently Dougherty 2000.

³⁵ Demand 1990, 30.

³⁶ See Huxley 1977.

³⁷ See also *Iliad* 2.678–9 for a much briefer account of the foundation of Kos.

³⁸ Pindar, *Olympian* 7.27–32.

³⁹ Pindar, *Olympian* 7.32 ff.

⁴⁰ Schmid (1947, 5) regards the Tlepolemos story as evidence of the existence, prior to settlement in the West, of a body of ktistic poetry connected with the 'colonization' of the mother-country.

⁴¹ Hdt. 4.156–9.

⁴² *SEG* 9.3, 26–7.

⁴³ See Schmid 1947, 3–52, and Bowie 1986.

⁴⁴ Giangulio 1981, 15–18.

[45] This is Dougherty's translation (1994, 123).

[46] Pindar, *Pythian* 5.92–5.

[47] See Malkin 1987 for the most detailed recent espousal of this position.

[48] See Antonaccio 1995.

[49] For the definitive discussion of 'invented tradition' see Hobsbawm and Ranger 1983.

[50] Similar games were held for Tlepolemos. See Pindar, *Olympian* 7.77–82.

[51] Malkin 1987, 190.

[52] Hdt. 6.34–7.

[53] Thucydides goes on to describe how the memorials of Hagnon were torn down.

[54] Later sources fill out this picture considerably. See Malkin 1987, 190–203.

[55] Boardman (1980, 174) makes a positive identification, which Malkin (1987, 213) rejects.

[56] Vallet, Villard and Auberson 1976, 209–11.

[57] Büsing 1978, 71.

[58] Büsing 1978, 73.

[59] See Kron 1971.

[60] Hdt. 5.42–4.

[61] A classic example is that of Myskellos of Rhypes who approaches the oracle to inquire about his failure to produce any offspring (see Diod. Sic. 8.17).

[62] In the continuation of Herodotus' account of Dorieus' enterprises, we are told (4.45–6) that he was advised to found a colony at Herakleia on Sicily. This time, however, he did consult the Oracle as to the suitability of the site and the legitimacy of his venture.

[63] See Malkin 1987, 17–22, for a brief but thorough discussion of the bibliography on his subject.

[64] Defradas 1954.

[65] Thucydides 6.3.1.

[66] Desborough 1972, 304.

[67] Rolley 1983, Morgan 1993.

Bibliography

Antonaccio, C.
  1995 *An Archaeology of Ancestors: Tomb cult and hero cult in Early Greece*, Lanham, Md.
Blakeway, A.
  1933 'Prolegomena to the study of Greek commerce with Italy, Sicily and France in the eighth and seventh centuries BC', *BSA* 33, 170–208.
Boardman, J.
  1980 *The Greeks Overseas*, 3rd edn, London.
Bowie, E.
  1986 'Early Greek elegy, symposium and public festival', *JHS* 106, 13–35.
Büsing, H.
  1978 'Battos', in T. Lorenz (ed.) *Thiasos*, 51–79.
Camp, J.
  1979 'A drought in the late eighth century BC', *Hesperia* 48, 397–411.

Casevitz, M.
    1985   *Le vocabulaire de la colonisation en Grèce ancienne*, Paris.

Cawkwell, G.
    1992   'Early colonisation', *CQ* 42, 289–303.

Cline, E.H.
    1995   'Tinker, tailor, soldier, sailor: Minoans and Mycenaeans abroad', in R. Laffineur and W.-D. Niemeier (eds.) *Politeia: Society and state in the Aegean Bronze Age*, 265–87.

Crielaard, J.P.
    1995   'Homer, history and archaeology. Some remarks on the date of the Homeric world' in J.P. Crielaard (ed.) *Homeric Questions*, Amsterdam, 201–88.

d'Agostino, B.
    1999   'Euboean colonisation in the Gulf of Naples', in G.R. Tsetskhladze (ed.) *Ancient Greeks West and East*, Leiden, 207–28.

d'Agostino, B. and Ridgway, D. (eds.)
    1994   *Apoikia: Scritti in onore di Girogio Buchner* (AION, n.s. 1), Naples.

De Angelis, F.
    1998   'Ancient past, imperial present: the British Empire', in T.J. Dunbabin, *The Western Greeks, Antiquity* 72, 539–49.

De Caro, S.
    1994   'Appunti per la topografia della *chora* di Pithekoussai nella prima età coloniale', in d'Agostino and Ridgway (eds.) *Apoikia*, 37–45.

Defradas, J.
    1954   *Les thèmes de la propagande delphique*, Paris.

Demand, N.
    1990   *Urban Relocation in Archaic and Classical Greece*, Bristol.

Desborough, V.R.d'A.
    1972   *The Greek Dark Ages*, London.

Dougherty, C.
    1993   *The Poetics of Colonization: From city to text in archaic Greece*, New York.
    1994   'Archaic Greek foundation poetry: questions of genre and occasion', *JHS* 114, 35–46.
    2000   *The Raft of Odysseus: The ethnographic imagination of Homer's Odyssey*, Oxford.

Finley, M.I.
    1956   *The World of Odysseus*, London.

Fischer-Hansen, T.
    1996   'The earliest town planning of the Western Greek colonies. With special regard to Sicily', in M.H. Hansen (ed.) *Introduction to an Inventory of Poleis*, 317–73.

Fisher, N. and van Wees, H. (eds.)
    1998   *Archaic Greece: New approaches and new evidence*, London and Swansea.

Forrest, W.G.
    1957   'Colonization and the rise of Delphi', *Historia* 6, 160–75.

Gialanella, C.
    1994   'Pithecusa: gli insediamenti di Punta Chiarito. Relazione preliminare', in d'Agostino and Ridgway (eds.) *Apoikia*, 169–204.

Giangulio, M.
   1981   'Deformità eroiche e tradizioni de fondazione. Batto, Miscello e l'oracolo delfico', *ASNP* ser. 3, 11.1, 1–24.

Gierth, L.
   1971   *Griechische Gründungsgeschichten als Zeugnisse historischen Denkens vor dem Einsetzen der Geschichtsschreibung*, Diss. Freiburg.

Gomme, A.W.
   1959   *A Historical Commentary on Thucydides, vol.1*, Oxford.

Graham, A.J.
   1964   *Colony and Mother-City in Ancient Greece*, Manchester.

Gwynn, A.
   1918   'The character of Greek colonisation', *JHS* 38, 88–123.

Hobsbawm, E and Ranger, T. (eds.)
   1983   *The Invention of Tradition*, Cambridge.

Hornblower, S.
   1991   *A Commentary on Thucydides, vol.1: Books I–III*, Oxford.

Immerwahr, S.
   1960   'Mycenaean trade and colonization', *Archaeology* 13, 4–13.

Kron, U.
   1971   'Zum Hypogäum von Paestum', *JDAI* 86, 117–48.

Malkin, I.
   1986   'Apollo Archegetes and Sicily', *ASNP* ser. 3, 16, 61–74.
   1987   *Religion and Colonization in Ancient Greece*, Leiden.
   1994   'Inside and outside: colonisation and the formation of the mother city', in d'Agostino and Ridgway, *Apoikia*, 1–9.
   1998   *The Returns of Odysseus: Colonization and ethnicity*, Berkeley.

Morgan, C.
   1993   'The origins of Pan-Hellenism', in N. Marinatos and R. Hägg (eds.) *Greek Sanctuaries*, London, 18–44.
   2003   *Early Greek States Beyond the Polis*, London.

Morgan, C. and Hall, J.
   1996   'Achaian *poleis* and Achaian colonisation', in M.H. Hansen (ed.) *Introduction to an Inventory of Poleis*, 164–232.

Morris, I.
   1986   'The use and abuse of Homer', *Classical Antiquity* 5, 81–138.

Murray, O.
   1993   *Early Greece*, 2nd edn, London.

Osborne, R.
   1998   'Early Greek colonization? The nature of Greek settlement in the West', in Fisher and Van Wees (eds.) *Archaic Greece*, 251–70.

Parke, H.W. and Wormell, D.E.W.
   1956   *The Delphic Oracle*, 2 vols, Oxford.

Pease, A.S.
   1917   'Notes on the Delphic Oracle and Greek colonization', *CP* 12, 1–20.

Raaflaub, K.
   1998   'A historian's headache: how to read "Homeric society"?' in Fisher and Van Wees (eds.) *Archaic Greece*, 169–94.

Ridgway, D.
    1992   *The First Western Greeks*, Cambridge.

Rolley, C.
    1983   'Les grands sanctuaires panhelléniques' in R. Hägg (ed.) *The Greek Renais-sance of the Eighth Century BC*, Stockholm, 109–14.

Rose, P.
    1992   *Sons of the Gods, Children of the Earth*, Ithaca.

Rosivach, V.J.
    1987   'Autochthony and the Athenians', *CQ* 37, 294–306.

Sandars, N.K.
    1978   *Sea Peoples: Warriors of the Ancient Mediterranean 1250–1150 BC*.

Saxonhouse, A.W.
    1986   'Autochthony and the beginnings of cities in Euripides' *Ion*', in J.P. Euben (ed.) *Political Theory and Classical Drama*, Berkeley, 253–73.

Schmid, P.B.
    1947   *Studien zu Griechischen Ktisissagen*, Freiburg.

Snodgrass, A.M.
    1971   *The Dark Age of Greece*, Edinburgh.
    1977   *Archaeology and the Rise of the Greek State*, Cambridge.

Vallet, G., Villard, F. and Auberson, P.
    1976   *Megara Hyblaea I, le quartier de l'agora archaique*, Paris.

Vidal-Naquet, P.
    1986   'Land and sacrifice in the Odyssey', in P. Vidal-Naquet, *The Black Hunter*, Baltimore, 15–38.

Wilson, J.-P.
    1997   'The nature of Greek overseas settlements in the Archaic period: *emporion* or *apoikia?*', in L. Mitchell and P. Rhodes (eds.) *The Development of the Polis in Archaic Greece*, London, 199–207.
    2000   'Ethnicity in the Greek settlements of S. Italy in the early archaic period', in E. Herring and K. Lomas (eds.) *Ethnic and State Identities in First Millennium BC Italy*, London, 31–43.

Zancani-Montuoro, P.
    1954   'Il Poseidon di Poseidonia', *Archivio storico per la Calabria e la Lucania* 23, 165–85.

3

FROM POSEIDONIA TO PAESTUM
VIA THE LUCANIANS

Michael Crawford

Take a Greek city 'barbarized', a Lucanian city as its successor, a colony of
Latin status placed there by Rome in 273 BC; add a campaign of modern
excavation, documenting major changes in the urban framework over the
centuries; mix and stir thoroughly. The result is a series of equations between
political change and urban transformation, with a sub-text that the nice
Lucanians did not change things very much, while the nasty Romans changed
things a lot. But the arguments used do not stand examination: it is no more
plausible to link the filling-in of the *ekklēsiastērion* of the Greek and Lucanian
city with the arrival of the colony than it is to link the supersession of the
comitium or the Italic temple of the Latin colony with an invasion by some
unknown people in the second century BC. The processes of negotiation, first
between Greeks and Lucanians, then between the two and the colonists will
have been complex;[1] and the links with urban change are unlikely to have
been simple. I shall try, first for the city in the Greek and Lucanian periods,
then for the Latin colony, to give an account of what can be known of the
institutional changes that took place; I shall then argue that any impact that
these changes had on the urban framework was slow and indirect.

Barbarization
The story begins with one of the most notorious puzzle passages of the
history of early Italy (Athenaeus XIV, 632a = Aristoxenus, fr. 124 Wehrli):

...διόπερ Ἀριστόξενος, ἐν τοῖς Συμμίκτοις συμποτικοῖς, ὅμοιον, φησί, ποιοῦμεν
Ποσειδωνιάταις τοῖς ἐν τῷ Τυρρηνικῷ κόλπῳ κατοικοῦσιν, οἷς συνέβη τὰ μὲν
ἐξ ἀρχῆς Ἕλλησιν ἐκβεβαρβαρῶσθαι Τυρρηνοῖς ἢ Ῥωμαίοις γεγονόσι, καὶ τήν
τε φωνὴν μεταβεβληκέναι τά τε λοιπὰ τῶν ἐπιτηδευμάτων, ἄγειν δὲ μίαν τινὰ
αὐτοὺς τῶν ἑορτῶν Ἑλληνικῶν ἔτι καὶ νῦν, ἐν ᾗ συνιόντες ἀναμιμνήσκονται
τῶν ἀρχαίων ἐκείνων ὀνομάτων τε καὶ νομίμων...

...so Aristoxenus, in the *Summikta Sumpotika*, says 'We are behaving like the
people of Poseidonia who live on the Tyrrhenian Gulf, to whom it has befallen
that although they were Greeks at the outset they have been barbarized by

59

becoming Tyrrhenians or Romans, changing their language and the rest of their customs, but still observing one Greek festival, in which coming together they recall their original names and practices...

Since Aristoxenus certainly lived and wrote before the Roman foundation of the colony at Paestum, what did he mean by Tyrrhenians or Romans?[2] Both Strabo (6.1.3 (254)) and modern scholars of course describe the people who controlled Poseidonia in the fourth century as Lucanians; but there is no particular reason why Aristoxenus should not have alluded to them vaguely as Tyrrhenians or Romans.[3] The principal concern of Aristoxenus was to find a striking simile for a decline in musical taste,[4] not to analyse the ethnicity of Italy. The Etruscans had long been a major presence between Capua and Salerno, the Romans had had a history intertwined with that of the Etruscans since the sixth century.[5] The Lucanians for Aristoxenus, rather than being people the other side of the peninsula, were surely above all the close neighbours of Taras, who appear in an anti-clockwise ring of – with one possible exception – other close neighbours in another fragment (Porphyry, *de vita Pythag.* 21 = Aristoxenus, fr. 17 Wehrli):

προσῆλθον δ᾿ αὐτῷ, ὥς φησιν Ἀριστόξενος, καὶ Λευκανοὶ καὶ Μεσσάπιοι καὶ Πευκέτιοι καὶ Ῥωμαῖοι...

And there came to him (Pythagoras), as Aristoxenus says, both Lucanians and Messapians and Peucetians and Romans...

The possible exception are of course the Romans, but I suspect that they are present in the list because Aristoxenus has anachronistically retrojected the existence of the Roman-created colony of Luceria, founded in 314 BC.

For the Lucanian presence at Poseidonia there is a small amount of excellent institutional evidence, beginning with the dedication in Oscan in the 'edificio circolare' or *ekklēsiastērion*.[6] The Lucanian period at Poseidonia also sees the arrival of coins of Samnite Campania and the deployment of a die already used for the silver didrachms of the Oscan city of Hyria in Campania;[7] and it *may* be that contact between Lucanians and Campanians is the cause. The pattern of production of silver coinage at Poseidonia, however, is puzzling: silver staters continued to be struck only until *c.* 380 BC, with an isolated issue in *c.* 350 BC; the production of silver fractions was more continuous, but also came to an end; issues in bronze, on the other hand, continued until *c.* 290 BC, some twenty years before the foundation of the colony. The issue of *c.* 350 BC is interesting, bearing as it does the Latin or Oscan name ΔΟΣΣΕΝΝΟΥ.[8] But it is clutching at straws to suggest that the typology of the coinage of Poseidonia becomes 'Lucanian'.[9]

After that, things get even stickier. The evidence of burials is slippery, to say the least: the prominence of scattered burials in the *chōra* between 360 and 320 BC is part of a general pattern of dispersal of settlement into the countryside in Magna Graecia in the fourth century BC;[10] and I should be very hesitant about supposing that groups of warrior burials of 450–400 BC in the Contrada Gaudo (600 m away from the city) are those of Lucanians preparing the way for the take-over.[11] Obviously, given that we (think we) know that there were Lucanians in control of Paestum after 400 BC, we can say that we have a lot of representations in tomb paintings of members of the Lucanian elite, perhaps sometimes as magistrates. And it is obvious that the painted tombs of Paestum are a phenomenon that largely corresponds with the Lucanian period of the city. But it is not at all obvious that there is anything specifically Lucanian about interest in military prestige, ostentatious display of wealth, or eschatological belief systems.[12] Otherwise? There is one Oscan name on a tomb painting, in Greek form, marginal and inconspicuous, and perhaps the signature of the painter.[13] And there has just been published the graffito μιυνηιο, on a black-slip plate, of about 300 BC.[14]

There are indeed apparently far more Greek than Oscan inscriptions from Poseidonia after 400 BC.[15] And at least one rural sanctuary, that of San Nicola di Albanella, seems to provide evidence of continuity: the votive deposit goes from 450 to 300 BC, the cult being that of Demeter and Kore, with no change in the nature of the offerings, consisting of statuettes and other terracottas, normal and miniature pots, as well as two silver coins, a stater (as *SNG* ANS 651–3 = *Historia Numorum. Italy* [n. 8], no. 1114) and a fraction (as *SNG* ANS 706 = no. 1121). The whole deposit was deliberately and carefully sealed *c.* 300 BC.[16]

When we get to the other end of the Lucanian period, a problem is posed by the dumps of votives, similar to each other, from the fill of the 'edificio circolare', from near the Basilica (the so-called Curia), and from the 'Giardino Romano', and a number of other isolated locations. Mario Torelli does not prove against Emmanuele Greco that the votive statuettes of children are colonial, rather than Lucanian, but only that they are earlier than the second floor of the area round the 'Tempio italico' (see below).[17] Stylistic comparison with the finds of 'bambini in fasce' from the Koreion on Lipari, produced in abundance in the half-century before the sack by Rome in 252/1, would suggest that the similar votives at Paestum began to be produced *c.* 300, before the foundation of the colony.[18] Votives of undoubted central Italian type come from the Temple of Hera or Apollo (the so-called Temple of 'Neptune'), and presumably belong to the period of the colony.[19] Remaining with artistic production, I see no way of resolving the disagreement between Mario Denti and Mario Torelli over the statue of Marsyas, found near the south-west corner of the Forum: made in the fourth century BC, but remaining on display in the colony;[20] or made for the colony.[21]

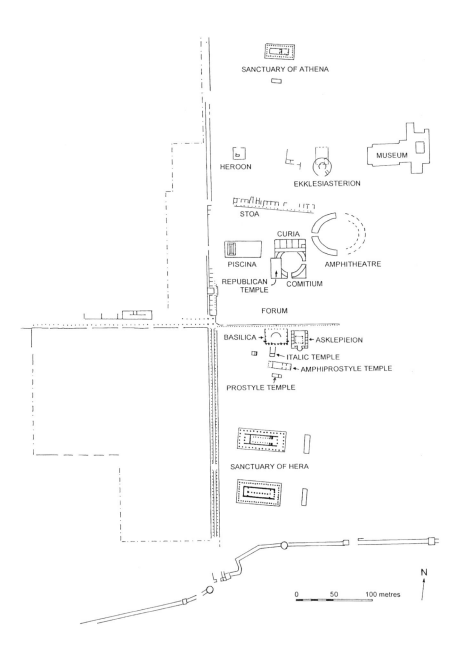

Fig. 1. Paestum. Drawn by Howard Mason, after E. Greco et al., *Poseidonia-Paestum* (Taranto, 1996).

Let us turn to the history of the urban framework of the city.

The Greek and Lucanian city

The layout of the city seems to date to *c.* 500 BC, including the main north–south and east–west streets, that cross at what was to become the south-west corner of the Forum; the Agora is the whole area between the temple of Athena in the north (traditionally 'Temple of Ceres') and the two temples of Hera in the south (traditionally 'Temple of Neptune' and 'Basilica').[22] In particular, the area within the Agora that was to become the Forum was levelled *c.* 500 BC.[23] On the western edge of the Agora lies the Heroon.[24]

What is striking above all, however, is the sheer scale of building activity in the late archaic and classical periods. Apart from the three great temples, the small temple beside the Temple of Athena is of *c.* 500 BC, as is the late archaic 'tempietto' near the 'edificio circolare'. Towards the end of the sixth century BC, a temple was built on the site that was later to be occupied by the Basilica of the Latin colony; it lay just south of the main east–west street, and it was aligned with this, not with the three great temples and their associated smaller structures: I describe it as the 'east–west temple'.[25] The 'sala da banchetto' is of the same period, and – even if precise chronological indications are lacking – most of the small temples in the southern sanctuary must also be buildings of the archaic and classical city. The closing of the archaic votive deposit of the temple of Athena about 500 BC is presumably to be related to the restructuring of the urban centre at that date.[26] The 'edificio circolare', or *ekklēsiastērion*, was built from 450 BC onwards, where the altar with the dedication in Oscan was in due course placed; and a cult area east of the Museum, probably of Demeter, also belongs to the Greek city.[27]

Building activity continued in the Lucanian period, some of which will have markedly altered the appearance of the city centre: in particular, a wall and stoa that divided off the southern from the northern half of the Agora,[28] and a stoa along the south of the main east–west street. In addition, the 'east–west temple' was truncated, and an amphiprostyle temple was built further south, above an archaic altar and perhaps for this reason aligned not with the street, but with the two southern temples. (The prostyle temple to its south cannot be dated.) The late archaic 'tempietto' west of the *ekklēsiastērion* was restored. A kiln between the 'east–west temple' and the amphiprostyle temple, of *c.* 350 BC, presumably serviced much of this activity.[29] The Asklepieion is probably of somewhere between 350 and 300 BC;[30] a wall was also built to the west of the southern half of the southern sanctuary *c.* 300 BC. Nothing in the architectural record would reveal that the city had been taken over by Lucanians.

A similar picture emerges at the Heraion at the Foce del Sele, where an archaic temple with metopes had been built *c.* 550 BC; a classical temple was then built on the same site *c.* 500 BC, with the metopes being re-used; the classical temple perhaps suffered from fire (there are traces on the metopes), and was perhaps ruinous before the Lucanian period.[31] It is extremely hazardous to attribute the dump of debris going down to the fifth century BC to deliberate destruction, by the Lucanians or anyone else.[32] To the Lucanian period, in any case, belongs the so-called 'edificio quadrato', of *c.* 350 BC, perhaps a building for the weaving of cloth for ritual purposes.[33]

At Santa Venera, just outside the city to the south, on the other hand, a shrine in the form of an *oikos*, with an annex attached on the south, was constructed after 500 BC, along with a hall for dining.[34] There appears to be no building activity in the Lucanian period, but once again in the Roman period.

The Latin colony

At least one institutional consequence of the foundation of the colony is readily identifiable: the issue of bronze coinage, similar in style and fabric to the coinage of Neapolis and other cities of Campania, but with the legend in the Latin alphabet, PAISTANO, which means that the issue cannot be Lucanian.[35] The issue encapsulates the fusion of traditions that is character-istic of Latin colonies, in this case a fusion between the Greek institution of coinage and the Greek types on the one hand and the Latin legend and the presence of Roman names on the other; the theme of fusion of traditions is one to which I shall return at the end. The nomenclature of the colony contains a mix of Latin, Oscan, and Etruscan names, though it is of course impossible in most cases to tell whether their owners were part of the colony of 273 BC, and if so whether they formed part of the existing population, or whether they were later arrivals.[36] In the case of the Etruscan names, the parallels are all in Etruria proper, and it seems perverse to suggest a local origin. The earliest colonists seem in any case to have brought with them some cast bronze coinage from Rome, alien to local traditions: two pieces of the heavy Dioscuri/Mercury series, one of the heavy Apollo/Apollo series, with no cast bronze coinage thereafter till the Prow series of 225 BC and later.[37] The epigraphy of the colony also seems to have become wholly Latin overnight. R. Wachter claims that there is virtually no Latin epigraphy at Paestum till *c.* 200 BC, and that it is then archaising;[38] but there is in fact a fair amount of Latin material that certainly falls between the foundation of the colony and the middle of the third century BC: the graffiti *P. Nuom* and *M. Nu* on cups of the early third century BC;[39] a dolium with [*M*]*eneru*[*e*] engraved on the lip before firing, a bronze tablet with *Iue*, a dedication to Hercules.[40]

On the other hand, it is now perfectly clear that the elite of Paestum continued to commission painted tombs for a generation or so after the foundation of the colony.[41] The numismatic evidence, which I have discussed elsewhere, is decisive,[42] and the only argument to the contrary is the quite bizarre *a priori* assumption that such commissions would not have been possible. If refutation were needed, it would be provided by the Mesagne tomb, a burial in every respect typically Messapian, in the territory of Brundisium, a generation and a half after the foundation of the colony.[43]

There seem to have been land measurement and division to the north of the city, with one '*decumanus*' formed by a road dated between *c.* 300 BC and AD 79;[44] but it is not encouraging that, in Roman feet, the '*decumani*' are between 7 and 8 *actus* apart;[45] and in fact the distance between '*decumani*' of *c.* 270 metres is almost exactly 1,000 Oscan feet. At the same time, some sites in the area seem to end *c.* 300 BC; but there was also some new settlement at the edge of the *chōra* of Paestum in the third century BC, and the picture is not so far one of massive convulsions.[46]

The votive deposit at the rural sanctuary of Capodifiume, including both pots and statuettes, seems to run from *c.* 400 to 250 BC, with monumental building taking place at the site *c.* 250 BC, a quarter of a century after the foundation of the colony.[47] The dedication to Minerva, mentioned above, from the area of the temple of Athena, shows continuity of cult there.

The colonial city

We do not know where the Latin colonists of 273 BC were housed; the area of the city east of the modern road is almost unexcavated (see above); but even accepting that the cult area east of the Museum was inside the Greek and Lucanian city (see above), it is possible to hold that there was much empty space in that (or any) part of the city for the colonists, and that no great upheaval was caused. The eastern edge of the Agora was certainly used.[48] Nor would I myself suppose that the displacement of the area of pottery manufacture from within the walls of the city was an 'effetto traumatico causato dalla colonia';[49] I expect everyone was glad that it had been moved. It is in any case clear that the circuit of walls that we see now round the whole city was in place before 273 BC.[50]

The central problem, however, is posed by the 'edificio circolare' or *ekklēsiastērion*, on one view brutally slighted and filled in on the morrow of the foundation of the colony.[51] But the contents of the fill make it clear that it was not filled in until *c.* 200 BC.[52] It is of course obvious that the colony in due course created, as one would expect, a Forum and the other physical appurtenances of a city founded by Rome; and there is no way of knowing whether the 'edificio circolare' was *used* between 273 and *c.* 200 BC. But there is no reason to doubt that it formed part of the urban landscape for a couple of generations after 273 BC; and the altar with the dedication in Oscan was left in place. A temple was eventually built on the spot.[53]

As for the Forum, it of course included, on its north side, a Comitium and Curia.[54] (The four rooms behind the Curia in their present form are the result of a later modification: see below.) The building to the east has been seen as an *aerarium* or *carcer*.[55] The Forum has always been hypothesized as symmetrical, with 12 *tabernae* to the east of the Comitium;[56] and the east end has been found where it should be.[57] A Capitolium probably lay at this east end.[58] The orientation of the Forum clearly respects the layout of the Greek city; and although it is true that the main north–south street was partially blocked by the west end of the Forum, it was presumably actually rather convenient for those using this road to pass through the Forum instead.

With the laying out of the Forum, the stoa on its south side was partly demolished to create an opening to the south; beyond the opening lies an Italic temple, oriented at right angles to the great temples, for whose dating there is no archaeological evidence;[59] but it seems not unreasonable to link the construction of an Italic temple on a wholly unprecedented orientation with the opening-up of the stoa, and both with the colony. But even if one supposes the naiskos nearby, in the area of the so-called 'Giardino Romano', also to be a building of the early colony,[60] the effect on the southern sanctuary will have been minimal. It is hard to see the building of either temple or the demolition of part of the stoa as involving a particularly radical transformation; what remained of the 'east–west temple' (see above) was left untouched until early in the first century AD it was demolished to make way for the Basilica (the so-called 'Curia').[61]

In addition, the Asclepieion was taken over by the colony: a road behind the *tabernae* on the south side of the Forum carefully avoids it.[62] The *heroon* to the west of the *agora* was carefully and reverently surrounded by a protective wall. The north wall of the southern sanctuary was rebuilt between 100 and 50 BC and at the turn of the eras.[63] One may compare in general the repair of the temples of Thurii by the Latin colony of Copia.[64] The area south of the stoa laid diagonally across the agora in the Lucanian period, perhaps a gymnasium, was in part preserved in the Roman period.[65] Perhaps the most prominent monument of the early colony was the so-called 'Piscina', to the north-west of the Forum, on the west of the old Agora, built in the third century BC, perhaps a sanctuary of Fortuna.[66] But one should not forget the role of water in the Lucanian sanctuaries at Rossano di Vaglio and Roccagloriosa.

So much for the first couple of generations of the colony. At a later date, perhaps in the second half of the second century BC, the Comitium was partly covered by a Doric/Corinthian temple.[67] It has been suggested that it is a temple of the Dioscuri.[68] At the same time as the building of the temple, the rooms at the back of the Curia were extended and steps at the back were added.[69] And a temple, perhaps of Mercury, was inserted in the northern half of the west end of the Forum.[70] The Italic temple, probably built after the foundation of the colony, was suppressed, along with a round temple nearby, whose date and attribution are wholly mysterious.[71] The amphitheatre was built between 100 and 75 BC. Needless to say, none of these changes is to be related to a change of population.

At the Foce del Sele, we see continuity between the building activity of the Latin colony and the earlier sanctuary: in about 250 BC, the 'thesauros', perhaps a shrine to replace the classical temple, if this was indeed by then ruinous (see above), was built next to it and aligned with its foundations.[72] Nor is there any reason to suppose that the use of the so-called 'edificio quadrato' came to an end with the end of the Lucanian period; rather, it was probably not covered over until the second century BC.[73]

At Santa Venera, the hall for dining (see above) was equipped with a portico during the third century BC (a portico renovated in the first century AD); and there is a dedication of *c.* 200 BC:[74]

> [---i]us f. Cn Venerei
> [d]onauit

Conclusion

The picture, then, is one of slow evolution of the urban fabric, without institutional or social change having any close causal relationship with architectural developments. In any case, did Latin Paestum ever wholly forget its Greek roots? Perhaps not.[75] It is well known that, along with Greek Velia, with which Paestum formed a single circulation area, and Greek Heraclea, Paestum continued to coin into the late Republic, and, unlike Velia and Heraclea, beyond.[76] During the Second Punic War, it is two hoards of victoriati, equivalent to the Greek drachma, not denarii, that appear at Paestum.[77] And, in the same period, along with Greek Neapolis, Paestum is attested as holding some of its communal wealth in the form of plate in temples, a characteristically Greek practice (Livy 22.32.4–9; 36.9).[78]

Notes

[1] See my comments on the Samnites in Cumae, *CR* 1983, 107–8, reviewing N.K. Rutter, *Campanian Coinages* (Edinburgh, 1979).

[2] Wilamowitz notoriously removed the problem by excising the Romans from the text; M. Torelli, *Tota Italia* (Oxford, 1999), 77–8, casually dates Aristoxenus to after the foundation of the colony, with extreme implausibility.

[3] A. Fraschetti, *AIONArch* 3, 1981, 97–115, 'Aristosseno, i Romani e la barbarizzazione di Poseidonia', rightly holds that the passage is not about economic decline, but fails to explain how Tyrrhenians or Romans might have been responsible for the barbarization of Poseidonia.

[4] See A. Visconti, *Aristosseno di Taranto. Biografia e formazione spirituale* (Naples, 1999), 144–51.

[5] Fausto Zevi, in conversation, has drawn my attention to the presence of Roman *cives sine suffragio* in Campania; but I do not see Aristoxenus as concerned with such technicalities.

[6] H. Rix, *Sabellische Texte* (Heidelberg 2002), Lu 14.

[7] R. Cantilena et al., *AIIN* 46, 1999, 9–154, 'Monete da Posidonia-Paestum. Trasformazioni e continuità tra Greci, Lucani e Romani', at 140–1.

[8] N.K. Rutter, *Historia Numorum. Italy* (London, 2001), no. 1142. G. Manganaro suggested, *RFIC* 87, n.s. 37, 1959, 395–402, 'La *sophia* di Dossennus', that, because Dossennus is a character in Atellan farce, Atellan farce originated at Paestum: far-fetched.

[9] See the account of M. Taliercio Mensitieri, in *Poseidonia-Paestum. Atti del XXVII Convegno di Studi sulla Magna Grecia, Taranto, 1987* (Taranto, 1988), 133–83, 'Aspetti e problemi della monetazione di Poseidonia', at 165–83, emphasizing 'la volontà di richiamarsi alle origini greche'.

[10] E. Greco and D. Theodorescu, in M. Cipriani et al. (eds.) *Poseidonia e i Lucani* (Naples, 1996), 192.

[11] *Contra* M. Cipriani, in *Poseidonia i Lucani* (n. 10), 119–39, 'Prime presenze italiche organizzate alle porte di Poseidonia', at 138–9: '...mercenari chiamati a prestare la loro opera per la *polis* e cooptati in città in funzione marginale, a differenza di altri elementi allogeni, isolati, la cui diversità culturale ed ideologica viene invece assorbita all'interno dei sepolcreti urbani...' (i.e., just outside the city) = M. Cipriani, in E. Greco and F. Longo (eds.) *Paestum. Scavi, studi, ricerche. Bilancio di un decennio(1988–1998)* (Paestum, 2000), 197–212, 'Italici a Poseidonia nella seconda metà del V sec. a.C. Nuove ricerche nella necropoli del Gaudo', at 211.

[12] For the last, see A. Pontrandolfo and A. Rouveret, *Le tombe dipinte di Paestum* (Modena, 1992), 464; and, in general, A. Pontrandolfo, in *Poseidonia-Paestum* (n. 9), 225–65, 'Le necropoli dalla città greca alla colonia latina'; A. Rouveret, ibid., 267–315, 'Les langages figuratifs de la peinture funéraire paestane'.

[13] *Poseidonia e i Lucani* (n. 10), p. 203, no. 96: πλασος, the Greek form of the Oscan name *plasis*.

[14] M. Torelli, *Ostraka* 12, 1, 2003, 103–6, 'Un avo della *domi nobilis* Mineia M.f. in una nuova iscrizione lucana di Paestum'.

[15] See *Poseidonia-Paestum. II. L'agora* (Rome 1983), 133–4; *Poseidonia e i Lucani* (n. 10), 205 (no. 111 is printed as a mirror image); *Poseidonia-Paestum. IV. Forum ouest-sud-ouest* (Rome 1999), 67; M. Torelli, *Tota Italia* (n. 2), 77, nn. 218–19; M. Torelli (n. 14), 103, nn. 7–8; E. Greco (n. 30 below), 73–4.

[16] M. Cipriani, *San Nicola di Albanella* (Rome, 1989), rev. by A. Mastrocinque, *DdA*, ser. 3, 8.2, 1990, 85–6.

[17] M. Torelli, *Tota Italia* (n. 2), 49, n. 47; Torelli in any case holds, 61–2, n. 112, that the colonists continued to use moulds, for statuettes of a goddess holding a child, from the fourth century BC, which rather undercuts the rest of his argument. The claim,

74–5, that the colonists were in large measure freedmen, starting from the belief that the statuettes of 'bambini in fasce' belong to the colonial period, is in any case a model of how not to use evidence: not only is the statuette in Plate 17 not wearing the single *bulla*, but it is clear from Cicero, *II in Verrem* 1, 152, that the *toga praetexta* is the mark of free birth, the *bulla* rather of wealth.

[18] The material from Lipari is to be published by O. de Cazanove, but is on display in the museum on Lipari. For the export of Paestan pottery to Lipari, see A.D. Trendall, *The Red-Figured Vases of Paestum* (London, 1987), 398.

[19] M. Torelli, *Tota Italia* (n. 2), 60; for the identification see below.

[20] M. Denti, in *Poseidonia-Paestum* IV (n. 15), 106–53.

[21] M. Torelli, *Tota Italia* (n. 2), 73–4.

[22] See E. Greco, in A. Vauchez (ed.) *Lieux sacrés* (Rome, 2000), 81–94, 'Poseidonia-Paestum'; and in id. and F. Longo (eds.) *Paestum, Scavi, studi, ricerche* (Paestum, 2000), 85–90. Mario Torelli speculates that the 'Temple of Neptune' was a temple of Apollo, rather than Hera: *Tota Italia* (n. 2), 58–9.

[23] E. Greco originally argued, *Poseidonia-Paestum* II (n. 15), 83, that 'il foro viene edificato altrove (than in the Agora) (a danno di uno spazio di cui ignoriamo ancora le funzioni precedenti)', a view now abandoned; in fact already when Greco was writing, a stoa to the south of the site of the Forum suggested a public space in existence there before the foundation of the colony.

[24] M. Bertarelli-Sestieri, *MEFRA* 97, 2, 1985, 647–91, 'Nuove ricerche sull'ipogeo di Paestum'.

[25] *Poseidonia-Paestum* IV (n. 15), 6.

[26] Information from M. Cipriani.

[27] See L. Jannelli, in *Paestum* (n. 22), 91; I. d'Ambrosio and L. Jannelli, ibid., 103; I. d'Ambrosio and R. de Bonis, ibid., 109; an off-the-cuff remark to the contrary by M. Torelli, *Tota Italia* (n. 2), 65, n. 140.

[28] *Poseidonia-Paestum. III. Forum nord* (Rome, 1987), 25.

[29] For kilns in sanctuary areas, compare, e.g., F. Castegnoli, *Archeologia Laziale* III (1980), 164–7, 'Santuari e culti del Lazio arcaico' (Lavinium).

[30] E. Greco, in S. Adamo Muscettola and G. Greco (eds.) *I culti della Campania antica* (Rome, 1998), 71–9, 'L' Asklepieion di Paestum'.

[31] J. de la Genière, in O. de Cazanove and J. Scheid (eds.) *Sanctuaires et sources* (Collection du Centre Jean Bérard 22, Naples, 2003), 97–102, 'A la recherche du "temple des métopes archaïques" du Sele'.

[32] *Contra* J. de la Genière and G. Greco, in *I culti della Campania antica* (Rome, 1998), 37–43, 'Beaucoup de questions et quelques réponses au sanctuaire de Héra à Foce del Sele', at 42–3.

[33] G. Greco and B. Ferrara, in *Sanctuaires* (n. 27), 103–35, 'Heraion all foce della Sele: nuove letture'.

[34] J.G. Pedley and M. Torelli, *The Sanctuary of Santa Venera at Paestum. I.* (Rome, 1993), chaps. 3–4.

[35] The significance of the Latin alphabet is not emphasized by M.H. Crawford in *La monetazione in bronzo di Poseidonia-Paestum* (*AIIN*, Supp. 18–19, 1973), 47–103, 'Paestum and Rome: the form and function of a subsidiary coinage': see M. Talercio Mensitieri, in *Poseidonia e i Lucani* (n. 10), 210–14, though the legend is wrongly in the Greek alphabet in the 'Schede'.

[36] F. Arcuri, *Bollettino Storico di Salerno e Principato Citra* 4, 1 (1986), 5–15 'In margine ad alcune epigrafi romane di Paestum', for Oscan names among the quaestors of Paestum, marred by prosopographical speculation; M. Torelli, *Tota Italia* (n. 2), 76, for Etruscan names.

[37] R. Cantilena et al. (n. 7), 58.

[38] *Altlateinische Inschriften* (Bern, 1987), 424–6.

[39] *Poseidonia-Paestum* II (n. 15), 109–10.

[40] M. Torelli, *Tota Italia* (n. 2), 53, 64.

[41] *Contra* A. Pontrandolfo, in *Poseidonia e i Lucani* (n. 10), 292; A. Pontrandolfo Greco, in *Atti del XVI Convegno di Studi sulla Magna Grecia, Taranto, 1976* (1977), 800. There is no reason to suppose that either the cremation enclosures in the Santa Venera necropolis (A. Pontrandolfo Greco, ibid., 801–4) or the monumental tombs of the second century BC (M. Torelli, *Tota Italia* (n. 2), 83, n. 255) were deliberately placed in succession to the chamber tombs above which they find themselves.

[42] See A. Burnett and M.H. Crawford, in R. Ashton and S. Hurter (eds.) *Studies…M.J. Price* (London, 1997), 55–7, 'Overstrikes at Neapolis and coinage at Poseidonia-Paestum'. H. Horsnaes, *JRA* 17 (2004), 305–11, 'Romanization at Paestum in the 3rd century BC: a note on the chronology of the PAISTANO coins and the interpretation of the wall-paintings from the Spinazzo cemetery', argues in basically the same sense, but unfortunately continues to print Greek *pi* instead of Latin *p*; and I think it very rash to identify the subject of one of the paintings with a magistrate of the Latin colony.

[43] See A. Cocchiaro (ed.) *Nuovi documenti dalla necropoli meridionale di Mesagne* (Fasano, 1989) (*non vidi*); G.J. Burgers, in E. Lo Cascio and A. Storchi Marino (eds.) *Modalità insediative e strutture agrarie nell'Italia meridionale in età romana* (Bari 2001), 249–66, 'L'archeologia e l'Italia meridionale post-annibalica: una prospettiva regionale e diacronica', at p. 263.

[44] D. Gasparri, in *Le ravitaillement en blé de Rome* (Collection de l'École Française de Rome 196, 1994), 149–58, 'Nuove acquisizioni sulla divisione agraria di Paestum'.

[45] Although there is no explicit reference, this calculation presumably supersedes that reported by E. Greco, *DdA*, ser. 3, 6, 2, 1988, 79–86, 'Archeologia della colonia latina di Paestum', at p. 86: 4 *actus*!

[46] E. Greco, ibid.

[47] Information from A. Serritella and M. Viscione; I am baffled by the conflicting claims of M. Torelli, *Tota Italia* (n. 2), 51–2, that the rural sanctuaries of Poseidonia came to an end in the Lucanian period, except for Capodifiume, which continued in the colonial period also; and that it was the colony which put an end to the religiousness of the territory.

[48] See L. Jannelli, in *Paestum* (n. 22), 96.

[49] E. Greco (n. 45), at p. 85.

[50] E. Greco and D. Theodorescu, in *Poseidonia e i Lucani* (n. 10), 184–200, 'La città e il territorio nel IV secolo a.C.' (the north-eastern corner was restored some time after the third century BC); contra M. Torelli, *Tota Italia* (n. 2), 46–7, who links the walls round the eastern half of the city with the colony.

[51] So E. Curti, E. Dench, J.R. Patterson, *JRS* 86, 1996, 170–89, 'The archaeology of central and southern Roman Italy', at 186.

[52] A. Burnett and M.H. Crawford (n. 42); *contra* R. Cantilena et al. (n. 7), 99, *if* the publication of the coins from the fill is accurate, the late coins are not from the surface

or even from near the surface. The account in T. Potter, *Roman Italy* (London, 1987), 72–3, is almost wholly fictional.

[53] E. Greco and D. Theodorescu, *CRAI* 1994, 227–37, 'L'agora de Poseidonia', at 232; I. d'Ambrosio, in *Poseidonia e i Lucani* (n. 10), 27–8.

[54] *Poseidonia-Paestum* III (n. 28), 27–36; L. Richardson, in *Cosa. III. The Buildings of the Roman Forum* (Rome, 1993), 253–64, argues that the Comitium was not round at the moment of building, but is refuted by E. Greco, *Poseidonia-Paestum* IV (n. 15), 3, n. 1.

[55] *Poseidonia-Paestum* III (n. 28), 63–7.

[56] See *Poseidonia-Paestum* III (n. 28), 20–1, for the presence of *tabernae* at Paestum and Alba, but their absence at Cosa.

[57] *Poseidonia-Paestum* IV, 3–7.

[58] M. Torelli, *Tota Italia* (n. 2), 54–6 and 61–71, engages in reckless attribution of the various temples to deities of the colony, in order to attribute to Paestum a copy of part of the sacred topography of Rome.

[59] For the area in general, see I. d'Ambrosio, in *Poseidonia-Paestum* IV, 36–53.

[60] M. Torelli, *Tota Italia* (n. 2), 61–2.

[61] See P. Vitti, in *Poseidonia-Paestum* IV, 83–105, refuting the attribution to 100 BC by M. Torelli.

[62] Poseidonia-Paestum IV, 7; Fig. 1 is misleading, but Fig. 20 shows the road just north of what will in a later age be the apse of the Baths; E. Greco (n. 30), 73–4; the 'deviazione' of a wall is not properly explained.

[63] M. Mello and G. Voza, *Iscrizioni latine di Paestum* (Naples, 1968–9), no. 142.

[64] See M. Torelli, *Tota Italia* (n. 2),128–9.

[65] M. Torelli, *Tota Italia* (n. 2), 67–8.

[66] E. Greco, *PdP* 40 (1985), 223–32, 'Un santuario di età repubblicana presso il foro di Paestum'; *Poseidonia-Paestum* III (n. 28), 41–9, 60–2; M. Torelli, *Tota Italia* (n. 2), 65, n. 141.

[67] F. Krauss and R. Herbig, *Der korinthisch-dorische Tempel am Forum* (1939); F. Krauss, *Der Athenatempel* (1955); for the date see *Poseidonia-Paestum* III (n. 28), 27–36: a second-century BC fragment in the fill of the podium.

[68] D. Theodorescu, letter of 7/2/1988; *contra*, M. Torelli, *Tota Italia* (n. 2), 65 n. 143. The associated altar and base are of the first half of the first century AD (*Poseidonia-Paestum* III (n. 28), 15–24).

[69] The Rostra in front of the temple and Comitium are of the first half of the first century AD (*Poseidonia-Paestum* III (n. 28), 35–6).

[70] M. Torelli, *Tota Italia* (n. 2), 68–9 with p. 47, fig. 26, no. 3.

[71] I. d'Ambrosio, *Poseidonia-Paestum* IV (n. 15), 39.

[72] J. de la Genière and G. Greco (n. 32); G. Greco and B. Ferrara (n. 33).

[73] See M.H. Crawford, *Roman Republican Coinage* (Cambridge, 1974), 28–9, n. 4.

[74] See Pedley and Torelli (n. 34), chap. 7.

[75] The phenomena discussed here are ignored by M. Torelli, *Tota Italia* (n. 2), 77–8.

[76] M.H. Crawford, *Coinage and Money in the Roman Republic* (London, 1985), 71–2; I do not share the doubts of P. Visonà over the continuation of the coinage of Heraclea, *JRA* 10, 1997, 334–5, reviewing F. van Keuren, *The Coinage of Heraclea Lucaniae* (Città di Castello, 1994).

[77] M.H. Crawford, *Roman Republican Coin Hoards* (London, 1969), no. 103;

R. Cantilena et al. (n. 7), 70 (not recognized as a hoard).

⁷⁸ See C. Ampolo, *Scienze dell'Antichità* 3–4, 1989–90, 271–9, 'Fra economia, religione e politica: tesorie offerte nei santuari greci'; P.G. Guzzo, in S. Adamo Muscettola and G. Greco (eds.) *I culti della Campania antica* (Rome, 1998), 27–36, 'Doni preziosi agli dei', collects some examples of precious metal offerings; compare Livy 6.4.3 (dedication by Camillus, 388 BC); 10.23.13 (dedication to Ceres, 296 BC); 26.47.7 (dedication at Nova Carthago, 210 BC).

4

COLONIAM DEDUCERE: HOW ROMAN WAS ROMAN COLONIZATION DURING THE MIDDLE REPUBLIC?

Edward Bispham

1. Introduction

Towards the end of the reign of Augustus an altar was dedicated to his *numen* in the colony of Narbo Martius (modern Narbonne). An inscription (*CIL* XII 4333) preserves the text of the *lex* or formal pronouncement made by a local magistrate, by virtue of which the altar was dedicated. One of the most interesting aspects of this text is the way in which matters pertaining to the use of the altar, but not dealt with by the dedicatory formulae inscribed, are to be regulated: 'other laws for this altar and its inscriptions shall be the same as for the altar of Diana on the Aventine', that is, in Rome. What makes the choice of *those* Roman sacral regulations as the model (rather than any others, Roman or Narbonnese) more interesting, is that the text of a *lex* dedicating an altar to Iuppiter Optimus Maximus (the principal god of the Roman pantheon) in the colony of Salona on the Dalmatian coast, in AD 127, has an almost identical provision: 'other laws for this altar shall be the same as the law pronounced for the altar of Diana on the Aventine Hill' (*CIL* III 1933). A third such document, its heavily abbreviated text implying a very familiar practice, comes from the colony of Ariminum in Italy, from the first century AD (*CIL* XI 361).[1]

As Beard, North and Price point out, the historical role of this sanctuary in regulating Roman agreements with allies must play a part in the choice of its regulations rather than any others (1998, 1, 330). It is also hard to resist the impression that, while the initiative for adopting the Aventine *lex* is local, this identical choice on the part of all three colonies, irrespective of the deity to whom the altar is dedicated, reflects a shared understanding that there were accepted modes of behaviour and means of expressing identity, which were common to Roman colonies in the imperial era.

This epigraphic evidence, then, reveals Roman colonies behaving in a uniform way, using the same set of Roman ritual rules to express the same conception of their relationship to Rome. Conversely, Rome is often seen to have had a uniform view of her relationship with her colonies. Modern interpretations of literary evidence for colonization, Greek and Roman, have tended to construct it as a 'statist' (i.e. state-organized) activity, designed to meet public aims (strategic or economic; and for Roman colonization, settlement of veterans, Sherwin-White 1973, 76–80, 82, 84, 93) or problems (land hunger). The colony is further seen as having strong ties with the mother-city: affective, juridical or both. On some accounts, Greek colonization was one stimulus to the crystallization of a higher form of communal organization in Old Greece, namely the *polis*.[2] Happily, archaeological discoveries have brought to light colonial 'type sites' (most famously Megara Hyblaia in Sicily, and Cosa in Italy), which seem to bear out the statist interpretation drawn from the literary sources.

The model works fairly well for classical Greece, or late republican and imperial Rome; but arguably not so well for earlier periods; nevertheless at all periods colonists sent to Roman (as opposed to Latin) colonies retained their Roman citizenship. Osborne (1998) has even argued that 'colonization' should be abandoned as a term used to describe Greek overseas settlement in the archaic period, which, on his view, is ill-characterized by the statist model. My concern is with Roman colonization in the fourth and third centuries BC, including new foundations of the Latin name (*nomen Latinum*): was a statist agenda manifest, and, if so, how important was it? To address these issues, I shall in this chapter look at specific ways in which both the prevailing historiographical model of colonization, and the category 'Roman colony' can be deconstructed. This in turn will lead us to question both the dominant model, and some of its statist implications.

Especially through archaeological discoveries, the category of colony has been almost reified in historical discourse: we know what a Roman colony is without having to see one, or hear it described. Each has an urban 'kit', modelled on core elements of the political and religious topography of Rome: a citadel, or *arx*, with a temple dedicated to the Capitoline triad, dominating a central political space (*forum*) containing a *comitium* (assembly place) and a *curia* (senate house). These spaces host modes of communal behaviour implicit in those core structures.[3] The foundation ritual, too, is familiar. Firstly, the *deductio*, or marching out, of the colonists from Rome to the site of the colony; there a *deductor* (founder), in ritual dress (the *cinctus Gabinus*), ploughs the *sulcus primigenius* (the original furrow), tracing the line of the future walls and instantiating a ritual barrier, the *pomoerium*.[4] As a standard text-book has it, 'When the Romans founded new towns…as part of their colonizing activity in the fourth century BC and later, they inaugurated them with a set of rituals…including the ceremonies of plowing the ritual furrow…of the *pomoerium*…and placing the first fruits of the earth in a ceremonial pit called the *mundus*, "world" '.[5] All these rituals coalesce to produce a community which, after a famous phrase of Aulus Gellius, is often called a 'little Rome'.

This model is all very well for the Augustan period, and, with qualifications, for the late Republic (by which time Latin colonial status had become titular, and involved no formal act of *foundation*). Augustan Roman colonies did not look much like Rome, but they did look like each other (cf. Laurence 1999, 199). They also, however, looked unlike each other in various ways. To privilege the Roman-looking aspects, or the 'Capitoline kit', may be to lose part of the picture of colonial identity, and here our argument touches on far-reaching reassessments of Romanization recently undertaken.[6]

As for the foundation ritual, the standard accounts are synthetic and synchronic, and may thus be misleading.[7] For a start, the 'set' of ritual acts is one constructed from a variety of late accounts, primarily of Romulus' foundation of Rome (such as Plutarch's account in the *Life of Romulus*), itself a 'charter' myth, purporting to explain customs which later Romans actually used in city foundations. Consequently, the 'set' of rituals at the foundation is not clearly defined: accounts of foundations do not always include, besides the ploughing of the original furrow, the burial of first fruits from the mother-community in a sacred pit.[8] Finally, Peter Wiseman has reminded us how many stories about the foundation of Rome the pre-Augustan period knew, stories which gradually lost ground to the 'canonical' myths of Romulus and Remus, and Evander;[9] we should not expect one set of procedures to be common to all these variants. The synthetic accounts thus represent late-republican or Augustan 'takes' on the formative moments and ideals of the Roman community, the latter from a time when Rome was being effectively refounded, with the protagonist toying with the idea of calling himself Romulus.[10]

'Little Romes', founded after ritual ploughing, and kitted out with a standard topography and infrastructure which recall the *urbs* (city), have, then, to be treated for what they are, namely late-republican and Augustan discourses, which evolved in the context of re-shaping an identity for a far-flung and recently divided empire. These discourses created new symbolic associations between Rome and her *coloniae*. These were especially important in the Augustan period;[11] but they are present earlier as well. The *lex*, or charter, of the Caesarian civilian colony at Urso in Spain states that 'whoever as IIvir or prefect shall be in charge of the jurisdiction in the *colonia Genetiva*, whenever the decurions shall have decided that he is to lead out the colonists…under arms for the purpose of defending the territories of the colony,…that IIvir or whomever a IIvir shall have placed in charge of men under arms is to have the same right and the same power of punishment as a military tribune of the Roman people has in an army of the Roman people …'[12] It would be a mistake to think that we can read off the colonial activity of earlier periods against this late ideological yardstick. What colonies and their foundations were like, and what the category 'colony' meant, in the third century BC or earlier, are not necessarily to be deduced from the 'Romulean' ideology (for the term see Torelli 1988, Fentress 2000b) of the age of Augustus.[13] This is, nevertheless, what has been done, aided and abetted, as we shall see, by archaeological discoveries and their interpretation.

In what follows I shall attempt to ask, under two particular headings, what can be said about the process of colonization in the middle Republic; and consequently to suggest what sorts of things should not be said. My focus will be on material culture; topography and nomenclature; and on colonial cults. It will be predominantly urban,[14] and in this sense is still constrained by the urban matrix in which the images of a 'little Rome' are generated in modern discussions. Nor will it seek to deny the Roman state an important role in colonization. That Roman strategic control of Italy was achieved by the mechanism of Latin colonies is manifest in their role in the Italian and Hannibalic wars. Filippo Coarelli has demonstrated how one transformation of the Italian landscape – road building – is closely bound up both with cementing the conquest and with colonization, especially the Latin variety (Coarelli 1988):[15] here statist agendas are clearly visible.[16]

The common metaphor of the *plantation* of Latin and Roman colonies across Italy is an agricultural one, conjuring up a transformed landscape. I shall not discuss, however, the broader impact of colonization on the Italian countryside, an area worthy of detailed investigation: not least in terms of the ecological impact of Roman resettlement, in terms of what was grown, where, and by whom; how it was stored and redistributed, and the processes of appropriation involved in all these activities.[17] Such a study would follow the work of Horden and Purcell, who focus particularly on the impact of colonization as an example of a transformation of the 'social relations of production' ('producers' relations with each other, their tools and the land', 2000, 270), affecting the nuanced game of risk and survival (2000, 278–87).[18] They set colonization alongside other forms of exogonous exploitation such as 'slavery, share-cropping dependent tenancy…serfdom, allotment, confiscation' (277; see also 274–8 on the 'powerful').

Allotment and exploitation of land are connected to the replication of particular social relations in Roman and Latin colonies. We know that, from the late third century BC, the size of *Latin* colonial allotments was differentiated along pseudo-military lines, with lots of diminishing sizes going to classes of *equites* (cavalry) and *pedites* (infantry).[19] The stratified nature of

Roman society, as well as the ideology of the citizen small-proprietor, were thereby perpetuated.[20] All this needs to be viewed within the larger context of changes in the Roman state, whose institutions and structures were, we suppose, being replicated. If these divisions were 'di regola' (routine) in the early second century, as Gabba has claimed (1958, 98), does that mean that we can retroject that regularity into the evidential black hole of the early third century and before?

Scholars have been inclined to think so. Indeed, Coarelli (1992) argues for a strong vein of continuity in Roman colonization from the archaic period onwards. More cautiously, Gabba thinks the fourth century a plausible starting date for such colonial structures, arguing for demographic and social motives, alongside military ones, for colonial foundation (1988); Bandelli (1988, 106) seems to argue for a politics of colonization beginning with the distribution of the *ager Gallicus* in the third century.[21] In that case, we might be able to relate the creation of state-constituted wealth classes (like those of the Roman census), within which all property holders are nominally equal, to the 'liberation' of the plebeians from the arbitrary domination of the patrician elites, which was finally ended in the early part of the third century.[22] How, though, would individual third-century *coloni* (colonists) fit into the Horden and Purcell outlook? How were they part of a 'centrally managed landscape' (2000, 265), and did the demands of the powerful intersect with the equality of land-holding which seems to have formed the armature of their settlement? An appeal to a structural similarity between allotment and latifundism at a 'macro' level does not answer all of these questions.

These are issues for another occasion, however. The present chapter builds on (and in some particulars corrects) work on Ostia in a recent article (Bispham 2000),[23] but it draws its main inspiration from a short but provocative piece by Michael Crawford, in the memorial volume for Ettore Lepore.[24] Crawford poses important questions about the nature of the common models used to understand Roman colonization, and the historiographical tradition in which they are embedded. The approach underpinning Crawford's article, and the questions it raises, can be set beside the work of other scholars, such as Mario Torelli and Lisa Fentress. The extent of my debt to these writers will be clear, although I cannot subscribe to all their conclusions. Equally, what follows also engages with older (now orthodox) scholarship, in a fashion which is deconstructive, but I hope not wantonly destructive. I shall disagree with some of the views advanced by scholars like Salmon and Brown; much remains with which to agree.

The classic synthesis on Roman colonization is still E.T. Salmon's *Roman Colonization* (1969).[25] This study took as normative what we may call the Gellian 'model' of colonization, which assumes that Roman (and by extension, Latin) colonies were indeed *quasi parvae effigies* and *simulacra*, 'small representations and images of a sort' of Rome.[26] At the same time, it revealed Salmon's awareness of the crucial importance of archaeological evidence, especially when he drew on the ongoing excavations at Cosa.[27] There, assumptions similar to Salmon's about what a Roman or Latin colony should look like were being made by Frank Brown and others, and these informed their interpretation of the site.[28] Thus (leaving aside for the moment religious buildings) they identified the following elements of an urban 'kit', all also found in Rome: a *forum* – linked visually by a clear line of sight to the *arx* (citadel)[29] – fitted with post holes for Roman-style group-voting channels; a *comitium* and *curia* complex facing the *arx* across the *forum*, complete with a Graecostasis; a *carcer* (prison) and Tullianum; *atria publica* (public halls); and a *forum piscarium* (fish market).[30] The conclusions were encouraging, and could be extended to illuminate what was then known of other Latin colonies: Brown wrote of a 'master plan' (1980, 42, 44, 58), and saw second-century colonial *fora* as 'planned by the colonial office in Rome' (1980, 43).[31]

Brilliant and ground-breaking as the excavation of Cosa was in many ways,[32] the picture of a Latin colony which emerged was not so much an analysis as a self-fulfilling prophecy. Problems are at once apparent with Brown's method. Let us take the example of the *atria publica*: 'the Atria around the Forum of Cosa may give a glimpse of what [the Roman Atria] were like, and, conversely, the Roman Atria may suggest the varied functions which the Cosan Atria served', he wrote (1980, 36). The assumption that Cosa should be like Rome is just that, an assumption; to go further, and read back from the hypothetical derivation to illuminate the archaeologically unknown at Rome is a circular argument.[33] For the *forum*, recent excavations have shed new light, which seems to undermine Brown's intrepretation of these structures, suggesting that they may in fact have been private houses of high-status colonists (Fentress 2000b, 15–17; cf. Taylor 2002, 61).[34] *Wholesale* application of a Cosan blueprint to Italy should likewise be treated with caution. The numbers of voting passages at Cosa (5 in the mid-second century (Brown 1980, 41 n. 11) are not matched at Alba Fucens, where there are three (later twelve) such channels at the same period (Torelli 1988b, 136).[35] Inter-colonial diversity is an important theme, to which I shall return.

2. Historiographies of colonization
'But the bond of colonies [to Rome] is different [from that of *municipia*]; for they do not enter the [Roman] citizenship from without, nor are they

supported by their own roots, but they are as it were propagated from the citizenship, and all of their laws and customs are those of the Roman people, not of their own choosing. This status, however, although it is more submissive and less free, is nonetheless thought to be preferable and more worthy on account of the greatness and majesty of the Roman people, of whom those very colonies seem to be, in a manner of speaking, small representations and images of a sort; and at the same time because the laws of the *municipia* are imperfectly known and fallen into disuse, they are no longer able to use them on account of their obscurity.'[36]

Aulus Gellius' brief characterization of the difference between colonies and *municipia* has regularly been taken out of context, and been made to serve as a building block for a very dirigiste, statist view of colonization. I have elsewhere (Bispham 2000, 157 f.) tried to offer a more contextual reading of this far-from-innocent imperial perspective; without it, our views of colonization might be very different. As it is, Gellius' legacy, the idea of the colony as a 'little Rome', was given a new lease of life as a result of archaeological discoveries during the twentieth century. The interface between the two strands of evidence on Roman colonization, and their mutual appropriation, call for closer inspection.

Two decades after Salmon's work on colonies appeared, and almost a decade after Brown's synthesis of Cosa's republican history (1980), R.T. Scott could write that the archaeological discoveries made at Cosa proved Gellius right when he talked of colonies as *simulacra* of Rome, and that this formulation could confidently be extended to Latin colonies in general. The view that a Latin colony should be a very Roman place is alive and well.[37]

Yet with Gellius and his modern disciples, we see the tail wagging the dog, surely? One small *Antonine* literary passage has so conditioned our understanding of *republican* Roman colonization that scholars now expect to find Gellius lurking under every bed, or on every *arx*. Small wonder that the excavators 'found' what they did! We shall return below to the religious topography and cults of Cosa, and other colonies, and ask whether a dispassionate assessment can really support the prevalent model for understanding Latin, and by extension, Roman colonization.

The Gellian model has already been challenged, above all by Mario Torelli, who has stressed how much of our information about early Roman colonization is filtered through late-republican and Augustan ideological matrices:[38] 'modern historiography, in blindly following the lines traced by the antiquarians of the late Republic, has envisioned the ideological components of colonization as confined within the limits of the ritual canonized by the legend of the *conditor urbis* [city-founder]' (1999, 15).[39] We shall return below to the antiquarians and their influence. For the moment, we must refrain from treating the manifestations of this late 'Romulean' ideology, over-emphasized in syntheses like those of Salmon, as normative. This is true both of mid-republican ritual (such as foundation rites) in particular, and more generally of the proposition that Roman colonies were little Romes.[40] Torelli stresses that instead we need to reconstruct an 'ideological picture' which is valid for the fourth and third centuries, if we are to get a better approximation of what colonization in the middle Republic was about.[41]

Yet, despite ingeniously revisiting the material evidence unearthed at Cosa, Alba Fucens and Paestum, Torelli does not seem to me to have broken free from the approach which he has himself criticized. He is able on the one hand to suspect the literary sources as too 'Romulean', but on the other to accept 'Romulean' interpretations of Brown's finds, since they are, after all, archaeological and not textual evidence. Yet material culture speaks through the excavator – and an excavator is no less fallible than a Verrius Flaccus.

Torelli's detailed knowledge of the archaeological, epigraphic and textual evidence for mid-republican Rome, and especially its cults, seems to promise the construction of an ideational world which is much closer to that which enmeshed earlier colonies than the one criticized. Yet understanding of colonial cults follows, for Torelli, from the possession of one or more keys, and these keys are all derived from the ritual topography and iconography of mid-republican Rome itself. The resulting picture of colonial cult is much more finely nuanced than what it replaces; yet one cannot help but feel that structurally both exegeses are fundamentally similar. Torelli twists the colonial data sets over the Roman reference points; once a precise correspondence emerges, it becomes a fixed point, from which others are inexorably nailed down *on the basis of the Roman arrangement*, sometimes regardless of plausibility.

In this process, once the interstices of Roman and colonial are located, everything else follows 'logically'. The results are interesting (e.g. the 'flat' Aventine of Paestum, 1999, 52–6), and Torelli deploys them cleverly in a wider historical context (note the plausible plebeian tinge which he discerns at Paestum on the basis of cult and votive offerings: Torelli 1988b, 143 f., 1999, 73–6, 78 f.). The problem is that the underlying approach is to seek a replication of Rome, which will underpin a further series of cultic reproductions, in which mythical, ritual and topographical associations come to operate *as they do at Rome*. Thus Torelli says of the intervention in the existing religious set-up consequent upon the Latin colonization of Paestum that it 'helps to clarify a design consistent with Roman politico-religious ideology, which wished the colonies to be fashioned as *effigies simulacraque parva urbis* [representations and small images of the city]' (1999, 62). Gellius would have approved.[42]

Salmon's titles for his chapters II–IV are revealing. Here we find the normative categories into which scholars divide the various Roman colonial foundations in Italy: 'Priscae Latinae Coloniae' (Ancient Latin Colonies), 'Coloniae Latinae' (Latin Colonies), 'Coloniae Maritimae' (Maritime Colonies);[43] other terms are also found in the scholarly vocabulary, such as *coloniae civium Romanorum* (colonies of Roman citizens).[44] These terms are based unambiguously on the testimony of the sources, and use the comforting force of the distinctions of Roman juridical language in order to maintain themselves as discrete categories. Yet these categories may be themselves the inventions of the late Republic or the Augustan period: the earliest *contemporary* reference to any kind of *colonia* is from early-second-century Aquileia.[45] What is unclear is how Romans viewed the phenomenon of colonization and its development in the fourth and third centuries. What did the contemporaries of the great wave of mid-republican colonization think these foundations were? Was there any single normative ideology of colonization? Was there such a thing as a colony, as we would understand it?

This last problem has recently been raised by Michael Crawford.[46] He rightly points out ways in which the normative model may be suspect for the earlier phases of Roman colonization. His example is a passage of Asconius; the commentator seems (admittedly there is a textual problem at this point[47]) to say that Placentia, founded in 219, was the 53rd Roman colony to be founded: 'eamque coloniam LIII <*lacuna*> deductam esse invenimus, deducta est autem Latina' ('and we find that *colonia* to have been founded as the ?fifty-third, but it was founded as a Latin *colonia*').[48] The context of this remark is Cicero's description (correct for his day) of Placentia as a *municipium*. Asconius (wrongly) thought it was always a colony, and it is salutary to note that his diligent researches overlooked the community's change of status consequent upon enfranchisement under the *lex Iulia* in 90 BC. Asconius seems to have consulted an antiquarian source, which told him: 'duo porro genera earum coloniarum quae a populo Romano deductae sunt fuerunt, ut Quiritium aliae, aliae Latinorum essent' ('there were furthermore two classes of these colonies which were led out by the Roman people, such that some were of the Quirites, and others of the Latins').

Asconius' source seems to be the only one to have reached us which uses the term *Quirites* of the inhabitants of what we call *Roman* colonies (ancient sources and scholars prefer *cives Romani*, Roman citizens), and the use of the term surprises in view of the *military* function often ascribed to these colonies. What is odder is that Placentia should, or indeed could, be considered the 53rd colony (or 54th, if the true reading were 'LIII[I]'): there were not enough predecessors to make up so large a number by the time Placentia was founded.[49]

In fact there is no shortage of apparent 'eccentricity' in discussions of, or references to, colonies in our sources. By far the most 'heterodox' is the only surviving ancient 'history' of Roman colonization, that of Velleius Paterculus.[50] His chronology disagrees with that found in the Livian tradition; and Roman and Latin colonies are indiscriminately mixed up, or rather, the distinction which we saw was fundamental to Asconius and his source, between Quirites and Latini, is absent. Velleius' list of colonies begins after the Gallic sack, and ends with the foundation of Eporedia in 100 BC. As Crawford remarks, such a time frame makes Claudius Quadrigarius a prime suspect as the original source of Velleius' material – he seems to have begun his historical narrative after the Gallic sack.[51] We might imagine a situation in which an account of colonization, written shortly after the Social War, could have deliberately obscured the juridical division Asconius' source insists on, perhaps a reflection of the equalization of status between Roman and former Latin colonies recently effected by the *lex Iulia*.

There are other skeletons in the colonial closet, which suggest more strongly that we may have to rethink our cosy position. Indeed, it is likely that what we take as normative categories were not in fact timeless truths, but the product of debate and dispute thrown up by changing political circumstances in the first century BC.[52] For Crawford, 'La verità è che non abbiamo la minima idea di ciò che significasse il termine *colonia populi Romani* per i Romani della fine della Repubblica' ('the truth is that we do not have the faintest idea of what the term 'colony of the Roman people' meant for the Romans of the end of the Republic').[53] What *colonia populi Romani* could be made to refer to is illustrated nicely by an example not discussed by Crawford. In 209 BC the complaints of the Latins and allies about the apparently unsustainable Roman demands on their manpower to fight Hannibal mutated into flat refusal to supply troops. The complaints and the incident's conclusion are well known.[54] Livy focuses on the punishment of the recalcitrant Latin colonies. He introduces them in a striking way: 'triginta tum coloniae populi Romani erant' ('at that time there were thirty colonies of the Roman people', 27.9.7), and goes on to list the defaulters: Ardea, Nepet, Sutrium, Alba, Carseoli, Sora, Suessa, Circeii, Setia, Cales, Narnia, Interamna.[55] These are what ancient sources and modern scholars term Latin colonies – this is uncontroversial. Yet Livy's characterization of these colonies as *Roman* cannot be dismissed as an oversight. He goes on to say that the consuls 'admonerent non Campanos neque Tarentinos esse eos, sed Romanos, inde oriundos, inde in colonias atque in agrum bello captum stirpis augendae causa missos. quae liberi parentibus deberent, ea illos Romanis debere, si ulla pietas, si memoria antiquae patriae esset' ('warned them that they were not Capuans or Tarentines, but Romans, with their origins in Rome, and sent from Rome into colonies and into the land captured in war for the sake of increasing the [Roman] race; they owed to the Romans what children owed to their parents, if they retained any sense of duty, and memory of their old fatherland', 27.9.11).

Now, the story illustrates a shocking breach of ties of *pietas* towards Rome, and the perils consequently facing her.[56] Livy's rhetoric well conjures up the sense of shock: 'non enim detrectationem eam munerum militiae, sed apertam defectionem a populo Romano esse' ('for this was not an evasion of the duties of military service, but an open revolt from the Roman people', 9.9); cf. the 'tantus pavor' ('such great fright', 9.14) of the Senate. To call the Latins Romans, and contrast them with Capuans (also Romans until their defection in 216 BC) and Tarentines, polarizes the issue, and throws the Latins' crime into sharp relief. Yet the appellation Roman still remains, and the words 'coloniae populi Romani' (9.7) are more in the manner of a factual aside than of heated oratory. It is difficult to see this use of the term 'Roman colonies' as an Augustan mistake. It must be at least possible that Livy has taken the formulation from a second-century source: the Gracchan period would be suitable, notable for the *defectio* (revolt) of the Latin colony of Fregellae, concern with the Roman birthrate, and the proposal of C. Gracchus to make the Latin colonies Roman.[57] If so, it would be valuable evidence for how labile our cherished colonial categories and terminology are.[58] We have no right, as Salmon did (1969, 52 n.62), to ignore what Livy *says* in favour of a different terminology, unless we can offer a justification: despite Salmon, Livy nowhere in this passage uses the term *Latini* after 9.2.[59]

Not only can the clearly bounded category of 'Roman' or 'Latin colony' be called into question. The idea of any sort of canonical *number* of colonies must also come under threat if we take Asconius' source remotely seriously. A higher number of colonies than that derived from the standard accounts might be explained by supposing that some sites abandoned by the late Republic had briefly been colonies, or what in an earlier period counted for a colony (such as a garrison). Alternatively there may have been a range of possible solutions to those problems (military and other), which the foundation of what we call colonies seems to have been designed to address.[60] Later, as canonical accounts of the history of colonization began to be formed, the history, and even the collective knowledge, of such places may have been marginalized (see below, section 7). At any rate, we can be reasonably sure that there were disputes among antiquarian and historical writers, in the Gracchan period, and in the first century BC after the *leges Iulia* and *Pompeia*, about what the term *colonia* meant, about different types of colony, how they differed, what their rights and responsibilities were, and how many of each kind had been founded.[61]

Such uncertainty, or rather the existence in the Middle Republic of a diverse and unregimented colonial phenomenon, might explain the anomalous *pro coloniis* of the *lex agraria* of 111 BC, preserved on the Tabula Bembina:

> [quibus colonieis seive moi]nicipieis, seive quae pro moinicipieis colo[nieisve, ceivium Rom.] nominisve Latini, poplice deve senati sententia ager fruendus datus [est, quo agro eae coloniae eave moinicipia seive qua]e pro colonia moinicipiove prove moinicipieis fruentur, quei in trientabule[is est, quod eius agri ---].[62]

We might draw an analogy with the difference between consuls and proconsuls: no one doubted what a consul was; equally, someone who was *not* a consul (but normally had been one) could be considered equivalent to one (*pro consule*) for a specific period and purpose. It is not my aim here to investigate the phenomenon of the *pro colonia*, merely to point out that its existence suggests that the juridical boundaries which we are accustomed to draw between colonies and other types of settlement, and between Roman and Latin colonies, do overlap in large measure with those found in the late second century BC evidence, but at the same time they do not adequately describe the colonial situation of that period.[63]

Disputes about the meaning of *colonia* can be inferred from other passages, where the variant explanations should be read as part of an ongoing and politicized debate, not simply as the echoes of a sterile squabble about etymologies. Two examples will suffice. Servius (*ad Aen.* 1.12) tells us:

> sane veteres colonias ita definiunt: colonia est coetus eorum hominum qui universi deducti sunt in locum certum aedificiis munitum, quem certo iure obtinerent. alii: colonia est quae graece apoikia vocatur; dicta autem est a colendo; est autem pars civium aut sociorum missa, ubi rem publicam habeant ex consensu suae civitatis, aut publico eius populi unde profecta est consilio. hae autem coloniae sunt quae ex consensu publico, non ex secessione sunt conditae.[64]

The differing explanations which Servius preserves are all strongly statist, but the last clause may hint at a rival suggestion that not all colonization happened as organized mass movement of citizens as a result of regular political decisions. This possibility is alien to our normative picture of Roman colonization, but familiar from the world of archaic Greece, or of the Hellenistic Mamertini at Messana.[65] Is this a trace of another contested meaning? Theorizing is at play in all our explanations, seen for example in the comparison with Greek practice; on a more fundamental level the definitions are all ideologically charged and idealizing to some extent, whether they concern the 'ready-made' physical centre (see below), the emphasis on agriculture (see Horden and Purcell 2000, 80–7, 197–200, 270–8 on the ideological hegemony of the cultivator), or the statist tinge.

Siculus Flaccus has a very different emphasis, this time military; note also that here a sub-category of colony is the subject of antiquarian debate, its meaning less clear to Romans of the late Republic and early empire than it is to us:

> coloniae autem inde dictae sunt, quod [populi] Romani in ea municipia miserint colonos, vel ad ipsos priores municipiorum populos coercendos, vel ad hostium incursus repellendos. colonias autem omnes maritimas appellaverunt, vel quod mari in his deduceretur, vel, quod pluribus placet, maritimas appellari existimant ideo, quod Italia ab Alpibus in mare porrigatur a<c> tribus lateribus exteras gentes intueatur.[66]

Salmon (1969, 15) cites this passage as evidence that 'the chief consideration [in founding colonies] was the defence of Roman soil and the establishment of future bases for military operations', a view familiar from Cicero's formulation in a speech to the people in 63 BC.[67] This interpretation is not wrong, but what matters is that Flaccus shows how little agreement there was about the purpose and nature of *coloniae*; this implies a 'fuzzy set' of colonial entities, rather than a neat textbook case study.

The labile nature of scholarly categories, and the contingent nature of ancient conceptions of colonization, should be clear by now; so too the importance of understanding the historiographical processes by which our monolithic idea of colonization has been generated. It is time to turn now to Rome's relation to her colonies as a symbolic norm, the possible existence of a colonial religious template derived from Rome, and to the relations of colonies to indigenous populations.

3. Material culture and colonization

While the individual buildings and urban plans of various colonies have been seen by scholars as marking little Romes, other areas of material culture have received less analysis in this respect. In this section I shall look at one element from mid-republican colonies, namely Black Gloss fine pottery (see Morel 1981).

First, some theoretical premises. I shall take it as axiomatic that, in the well-worn post-processual phrase, 'material culture should be seen as meaningfully constituted'. Such a position is not uncontroversial, but neither is it without use. Yet in the application of this approach *classical* archaeology lagged behind other branches of the discipline until about fifteen years ago. In a stimulating recent discussion of the methodologies appropriate to using material and literary evidence together to approach the history of archaic Greece, Ian Morris argues that 'archaic Greeks, like humans everywhere, used material culture to say things about themselves' (Morris 1998, 4, cf. 68 f.), and that as a result, not only is the entire range of material culture useful to historians, but also it demands two related modes of interpretation. One of these is that individual elements of material culture be interpreted contextually across time, beside other categories of available material. The other is that our interpretation of material culture is an interpretation of objects already implicated in a 'symbolic field', already manipulated by individuals 'in pursuit of goals' (1998, 4, cf. 79). The materials in the archaeological record are the building blocks of a 'symbolic language', and have meaning only in the context of the whole dynamic non-verbal linguistic system; this is a compromised and directed entity since it is used by competing discourses in communication.

As a result we cannot 'see the physical remains…as a transparent window onto the realities of the past', but we are rather looking at a contextual web in which everything is in some sense constructed, in which 'we cannot reduce cultural practices to underlying economic and social realities which have analytical priority' (Morris 1998, 5 f., cf. 74). Archaeological and literary evidence can operate in symbiosis, since literature provides broad parameters to limit possible interpretation, and the broad brush of shared elite culture expressed in the literary evidence can be nuanced in the regional variations of the material culture (Morris 1998, 6 f.). For Morris, *contexts of behaviour* (such as burial, settlement and sanctuary) are also important as the settings which give meaning to artefacts (1998, 8–10; even within these, objects have a context-dependent meaning).

Space does not permit anything approaching an examination of 'total material culture' here. At the very least, in order to provide a proper context for the claims I am about to advance, I should have to consider, for example, the totality of republican ceramic evidence from more than one Latin colony, coarsewares beside finewares, imports and local production. What I do want to do is to draw on at least some of Morris' ideas in a preliminary way, by trying to suggest possible implications of one type of material culture, aware that my study of the pottery is very incomplete and the conclusions therefore very tentative. I hope to suggest what ranges of meanings might be predicated of a small class of objects: ways of cracking part of the symbolic code, given their context. Of course such artefacts are intrinsically polysemic, but they are also embedded in a series of social relations, and processes of social reproduction, which are at the heart of the community making and using them.

Let us begin by discussing briefly the locally made Black Gloss (hereafter BG) finewares of Ariminum. Experts have been struck by their 'Romanness'. By this they refer to a stylistic similarity with BG production from Rome and its immediate environs, which distinguishes the output of Ariminum (and also those of the Latin colony of Cales and the Roman colony of Minturnae) from those of other centres such as Cosa, Alba Fucens and Paestum.[68] From Ariminum come some four dozen BG *pocula deorum* (cups dedicated to a god); they were found in contexts of redeposition, but one bowl base was impressed with the prow / Roma side of a mid-third-century *uncia* before firing. Given this, and the date of this class of object elsewhere in Italy, the Ariminate examples are probably not to be dated later than *c.* 240 BC.[69]

The BG production of Cales also had strong stylistic affinities with Roman output. The Calene origin of this pottery is advertised by the makers on a number of vessels; in a market where Calene wares were both popular and imitated, this is easily understood.[70] Given the similarity of Calene and Ariminate BG to Roman production, and thus to each other, we may ask at a more general level whether ties to Rome were important to colonial populations, and if so, how they manifested themselves. Ariminum and Cales probably 'felt' very 'Roman' in the third century, at least in some contexts, for example cultic ones.[71] This can be read in the material culture, where claims about Romanness were being made through fine pottery, both the *pocula* used in religious dedications, and a wider range of BG vessels used in domestic contexts, perhaps suggesting a Roman identity projected onto the domestic sphere and social interaction within it.

One piece of Calene BG contains a remarkable graffito, which complicates the question of Roman influences, and leads me to make a retraction. In Bispham 2000 I discussed ways in which Ostia might, and might not, during the Republic be considered a small image of Rome.[72] I there went so far towards debunking the idea of early Roman or Latin colonies as 'little Romes', that I asserted that all the evidence for the adoption of Roman toponyms in colonies was imperial in date, and that the practice itself could not be retrojected to the Republic. I must now correct myself: a relief-*patera* (dish) of the first half of the third century BC bears the inscription 'K. SERPONIO CALEB. FECE. VEQO ESQUELINO C. S.' (= 'K(aeso) Serponio(s) Caleb(us) fece(t) veqo Esquelino c(um) s(uis)?').[73] Despite Mingazzini's claims, it seems perverse to argue that the vase was made anywhere other than Cales;[74] the potter asserts that he worked in a part of Cales called the Veqos Esquelinos, that is, a *vicus* named after the Esquiline in Rome. Here, then, is a clear republican antecedent of the divisions of Italian cities, well-attested in imperial inscriptions, into areas homonymous with places in the city of Rome.[75] It must, I think, be admitted, that were our evidence for the middle Republic better, we would probably have similar examples from elsewhere; although from which places, as we shall see, is a moot point.

What are the wider implications? That one can, on the basis of such evidence argue, with Morel, 'Que les colonies de Rome, y-compris (et peut-être surtout) les colonies latines, se veuillent de petites Romes, c'est ce qu' indique éloquemment leur toponomastique' ('that Rome's colonies, including (and perhaps above all) the Latin colonies, wished to be little Romes, is eloquently indicated by their toponymy'), is far from clear.[76] In interpreting the significance of this piece of toponymy in the colonial setup we are faced with a choice between 'top-down' and 'bottom-up' models. *Either*, when the colonial commissioners carried out the *deductio*, they not only accomplished a basic division of the future urban area, but also gave evocative Roman names to the resulting regions; *or*, the names were given locally, to recall the mother-city, by ex-Roman colonists, perhaps by the colonial elite. In other words: did these names appear as a direct consequence of the decision of the Roman assembly to found the colony, as part of the deliberately prescriptive measures taken by the *triumviri* (the three-man founding commission)? Or were they an informal reminiscence of Rome, which hardened into customary usage (as commonly found in emigrant communities)?[77] Certainly the adoption of the rare, aristocratic, *praenomen* (forename) Kaeso (a reminiscence perhaps of the *triumvir* K. Duillius, or of the *gentes* (clans) Quinctia or Fabia, both of which used it) by the potter Serponius (or his parents) was a voluntary act, not an imposition.[78]

'Top-down' evocations of the colonizing city can certainly be found. At Ariminum, the chief magistrates of the colony (as at the other Latin colonial foundation of that year, Beneventum) were called *cosoles*, that is, consuls.[79] We could not, it seems, wish for a more unequivocal recall of Rome and her institutions, nor one made in a more fundamental context within the new state.[80] Surely these colonial toponyms are simply another manifestation of the same wish to replicate the Roman? Perhaps. One thing is notable: to our knowledge, the experiment of Latin colonial consuls was not repeated, in all probability not considered worth replicating.[81] By the second(?) century Ariminum's chief magistrates were *duoviri* (*ILLRP* 545) – no great emotional investment seems to have been made by Ariminum in keeping the prestigious consular title.[82] Why, then, was it granted?

The context of the foundations of Ariminum and Beneventum needs to be considered more closely. Ariminum, one of Rome's furthest outposts at the time of foundation (Torelli 1988b, 140; Tramonti 1995, 239 f.; Cicala 1995, 360), might want to feel close to the colonizing city, and to compensate for her exposed geo-political position with familiar titulature, a miniature Roman magisterial structure (and timocratic social structure to boot). The anti-marginalization argument also works, although a little less clearly, for Beneventum, founded to seal the definitive subjection of the Samnites after the Pyrrhic War, in a resentful area.[83]

One explanation for the magistracy may be sought in the changing circumstances of Rome's control in Italy, and her relations with her allies. In 268 it may not yet have been as hard to recruit colonists as it later became;[84] but a sea change was already underway within the various juridical statuses employed in Italy.[85] The practice of incorporating conquered peoples as *cives sine suffragio* (citizens without the vote) was not, so far as we know, extended beyond this year; and, in the course of the third century, the Romans began to promote some *cives sine suffragio* to full citizenship, starting with the Sabines in 264.[86] The privileged status of Latin colonists might have seemed threatened. It does seem that in 268 a new definition of colonial Latinity was reached, one which should be considered in the light of Latin loyalty in the struggle against Pyrrhus, and a possible conflict with Carthage. Cicero (*Caec.* 102) mentions Ariminum as one of the *XII coloniae*; it is often held that these were Ariminum and the eleven Latin colonial foundations (including Beneventum) which followed (after which no more were established).

What the status of the Twelve Colonies was, and how it differed from that of the others, is unclear, and cannot be pursued here in any case.[87] It may, however, have sought to buttress the position of Latin colonies *vis-à-vis* Rome, in terms of both concrete legal privilege and ideological baggage. The creation of consuls as the magistrates of Ariminum and Beneventum may have been a short-lived attempt to pack such baggage into these two colonies, but it should be stressed that not only does this seem like a move contingent on the shifting dynamic of status and privilege within Roman Italy, but also it lapsed after perhaps a couple of generations.[88] If nothing else, the case underlines how colonization is a moving target.

Another explanation, not incompatible with the first, might be offered in terms of Roman projection of power within Italy, indeed, with the creation of a new conception of Italy itself. There are signs that the conquest of Italy was perceived as coming to an end in precisely these years, with the subjection of Picenum, and the colonial foundations of Ariminum and Beneventum being seen as in some sense providing closure to the narrative of the Roman conquest.[89] The extent of Roman Italy was now to remain fixed, juridically, until the Social War. Conceptual boundaries and legal ones rarely match: the conceptual frontiers of the large block of *ager Romanus* (Roman territory) now established in central Italy were protected against Rome's most worrying or most recently pacified enemies (Gauls and Samnites) by two colonies which marked the boundaries of a new Roman state within a new Italy, and were themselves in some respects very Roman. The sequel, however, showed that neither Roman ambitions nor Italy as a concept would stay still: Rome's interests and reach continued to extend; the need to 'close off' a conquest, which was obviously no longer complete, faded, and with it perhaps the overtly Roman titulature.

Finally, in the case of Ariminum, it seems that its practical importance to Rome may have influenced its treatment, and underlined the bond between colony and mother-city. Ariminum seems to have been a forward command centre for Roman campaigns in Cisalpine Gaul. For all that it was an independent city, some evidence suggests that the sphere of action in northern Italy assigned to consuls in the third and second centuries, often called 'Italia' and sometimes 'Gallia', could also be called 'Ariminum'.[90]

To return to our toponyms. Roman place names, in so far as they may have existed in colonies under the Republic outside the Calene *vicus Esquilinus*, were not ephemeral phenomena like the grand magisterial titles at Ariminum and Beneventum; I suggest that they were the products of very different processes. Strikingly, Cales and Ariminum between them produce (under the Empire) most of the Roman or Romanizing urban (or presumably urban) toponyms known from Italy (although Beneventum also figures, and at Augustan Puteoli, for which our epigraphic evidence is quite rich, we can observe the same phenomenon).[91] Cales and Ariminum, founded sixty-six years apart, were also, at the times of their respective foundations, at the limit of Roman hegemony within Italy. Although Roman political influence in the late fourth century quickly fell over the rest of northern Campania and the Caudini, the artistic output and styles of Cales and Capua remain distinct through the third century, despite the granting of *civitas sine suffragio* to the Campani. This division, which can be mapped not onto regional divisions (e.g. that between Latium and Campania), but roughly onto parts of the map of changed juridical status which came in the wake of conquest, has led Morel to talk of a Romano-Latin artistic *koine* (community) comprising Rome, South Etruria (especially Caere), Latium Vetus and the area of Roman and Latin colonization.[92]

While to talk of such *koinai* is also to obscure local differences, for example between colonies themselves, as Morel points out,[93] the distinction that this *koine* embodies is nevertheless useful. It enables us to understand the 'frontier' status of these two Latin colonies, which at their foundation stood on the edge of Roman aspirations, looking into an uncertain and hostile yonder. The divide between Romans or Latins and the Celts of the *ager Gallicus* is easily envisaged (although evidence from 'Gallic' sites like Monte Bibele should make us wary of monolithic ethnic or cultural characterizations in the north[94]); the hostility first generated by the Roman annexations would be ended only by the more-or-less complete extirpation of some Celtic tribes in the early second century.[95] Campania was to prove a battle ground in the First Samnite War, and in the Second Samnite War, only a generation after the foundation of Cales, a Samnite force penetrated as close to Rome as Ardea (Salmon 1967, 235). In such uncertain circumstances, one can understand the need for strong affective ties which expressed the desirable link between Rome and these colonies. It is no accident, then, that Cales was the seat of a Roman quaestor,[96] or that Ariminum at one time gave its name to a *provincia Ariminensis* (Ariminate area of operations).

Not that this explains all. The 'frontier of Latinity' moved ever deeper into Italy, away from the Tyrrhenian epicentre; further work of this kind is needed on the ceramic assemblages (and other aspects of material culture such as votive terracottas[97] and coinage) of colonies like Luceria, Saticula, Venusia and Beneventum,[98] which in their turn faced some of the problems which had faced Cales in 334 BC. The results might surprise. The pottery of Brundisium, the most distant Latin colony from Rome, and at a crucial interface not just with Messapic peoples but also potential transmarine enemies, seems less 'Roman' than that of most colonies; this underlines our ignorance of many Roman and Latin colonies, and their artisan output, in the third century.[99] So the 'frontier factor' does not explain all.

Morel also suggests that the origin of the colonists may be another factor.[100] A strongly Roman contingent might be thought to be more vocal in recalling Rome than a more heterogeneous group of colonists, including other Latins and indigenous inhabitants.[101] Yet here, again, there are complications: how Roman *were* the populations of the two colonies in question? Morel suggests that some of the last Etruscans living in Campania may have formed part of the original colonial settlement at Cales.[102] The republican epigraphic record from Ariminum boasts a number of names, which scholars have argued, with varying degrees of caution, should be attributed to *non-Roman* immigrants, chiefly *incolae* from older Latin colonies; some of these inscriptions might be as old as the third century.[103] The Romanness of the population of Ariminum is striking on one level, but is elusive when viewed from other angles.

What then of our *veqos Esquelinos* at Cales? In one sense, given the strongly 'Roman familial' characteristics of Calene and Ariminate BG, and the undoubted Roman origin (direct or indirect) of some of the Calene colonists attested in the third century (e.g. the pottery producing Canoleii, Morel 1983, 23 f.), it should not surprise us that Cales, and perhaps Ariminum too, in their exposed positions on the edge of a very un-Roman, un-Latin, world should have Romanizing toponyms of this sort as early as the third century, and in the case of Cales, perhaps earlier.[104] None of this need mean the imposition of names by the founding commissioners, who may have been in no hurry to complete every last detail of the colonial set up. The motivation for adopting such names could easily have come from below, just as the propensity for the production of very Roman finewares and the use of Roman *praenomina* were certainly not part of a Roman-imposed blueprint.

In fact, given what we know of Cales, it seems quite comprehensible that such names should have emerged from the imagination of the colonists, and quickly become part of customary usage. It should also be borne in mind that many of the colonial toponyms from Italy (like *vicus Esquilinus*) are *not* the Roman names of districts of Rome, but the re-application of place-names from Rome to colonial geography to produce new toponyms: Roman topography acted as a matrix, from which *new names*, and inevitably new associations, were generated. Our colonial toponyms are *Romanizing*, not Roman, and are the product of an *autoromanizzione* (self-romanization), explained by the particular circumstances in which these colonies were founded, rather than a heavy-handed dirigiste approach on the part of the *triumviri*. The claim, made by Sanesi (1978, 77), that the existence of the *vicus Esquilinus* shows 'un ben preciso programmo politico di Roma nell' organizzazione e nell' amministrazione delle colonie fin dall' inizio della conquista' ('a very precise Roman political programme, employed in the organization and administration of the colonies since the beginning of the conquest'), seems to me unsustainable.[105]

It seems, then, that one thing that is being said in the symbolic language of material culture, or at least one subtype in one particular context, is similar to what the words on our Calene *patera* imply. A set of associations are used to evoke the colonizing city, Rome. This evocation is not straightforward: the *patera* need not mention a real Roman place; but a place that could only be Roman, and has been instantiated in a colonial context. The exaggerated stylistic affinities of the BG production of some colonies with Rome are not simply ways of 'pretending' to be Roman; they evoke Roman models, within the changing kaleidoscope of the conquest of Roman Italy, when what it meant to be Roman, Latin or ally was not itself static. These evocations of Rome may be in large part produced under the pressure of settlement in what were frontier areas. They should, furthermore, be read as a 'construction' as much as a simple 'affirmation' of an identity, prescriptive as well as descriptive; indeed, the first-order level of inference implied by the term 'descriptive' is in fact unlikely to be available to us from material culture. We should also note that the associations generated and manipulated by these pots and their inscriptions seem to be informal and spontaneous, not part of a directed 'Romanizing', master-plan. Finally, it is important that we can see these sorts of things in *colonial* contexts. Torelli argues in a study of Daunia (1999, 103), that Romanization affects local ideology and customs, but not local artisan production in this period.

4. Colonial cults
One context that generates meaning for our BG pottery, especially for the

Ariminate *pocola*, is the religious sphere. Let us turn, though, from objects given a 'Roman' meaning as appropriate offerings to the gods, to look more broadly at the worship of gods in colonies.

Colonization, and the corresponding creation, or reorganization, of urban centres, brought important changes to local religious structures.[106] Temple building, together with defensive circuits, is an early and a major form of public construction in many colonies.[107] Over the course of time temple-building seems to remain a preferred expenditure of resources in Latin colonies in particular, although not to the complete exclusion of other manifestations of the new Hellenistic style of architecture, which filtered through from the East and from Rome during the second century BC.[108]

Colonial cults have received much attention themselves, above all the Capitoline Triad. I shall argue that *for the middle Republic*, Latin colonies, better known archaeologically than citizen colonies, should be entirely cut out of this Capitoline discourse.[109] As for Roman colonies, the presence of Capitolia has often played a crucial role in discussion, as a barometer of Gellian 'simulacrity'. Vitruvius (*de arch.* 1.7.1) advised that a city's tutelary deities, and Iuppiter, Iuno and Minerva, should be housed on the *arx*. This prescription is often read back into the Republic. Thus, Zanker writes: 'The formula [*sc.* the subordination of Roman political life to the gods] can be found already…in the small civilian colonies of the fourth century BC. The combination of the Capitolium and a central gathering place in the middle of the city embodied the Roman self-image more perfectly than was the case even in Rome itself.'[110] But is this true?

The importance of the Capitolium within the Roman colonial urban image is clearly seen at Luna, where the *forum* was dominated by a temple to the Capitoline Triad from the foundation in 177 BC; later examples include the conversion of the existing temple of Iuppiter at Pompeii into a Capitolium by the Sullan colonists.[111] For earlier periods, as we shall see, this situation is hard to verify. I have elsewhere attempted to show that, at Ostia, the Capitoline triad was a relatively late arrival, and that the core religious elements in the colony's make-up had been, and remained, the cults of the Castores, of Hercules, and above all Vulcan; and that these elements were taken over from, and ensured symbolic continuity with, the archaic settlement, which, I argue, preceded that colony.[112] I would like to consider now further ways in which the Capitoline model might be deconstructed. This requires a survey of colonial cults: my examples come from both Roman and Latin colonies.

I outlined above the criticisms levelled against the study of colonial cult in the middle Republic by Mario Torelli, and offered my own critique of some of his methods. It is only fair here to stress how much I *do* owe to Torelli's work in this area. He has shown that when we study the evidence for cult in the mid-republican colonies, far from witnessing a uniform imposition of an unambiguously Roman series of cult practices and places at the expense of the indigenous element, we can see a striking degree of survival of local cults. Of course, the impact of conquest and colonization changed them, adapting them to serve the interests of the colonists. Yet Torelli is right to stress not only the pliability ('duttilità') of local cults within the framework of Roman hegemony and colonization (a framework predicated on a certain willingness to be flexible), but also the diversity of religious topography, practice and ideology apparent in the mid-republican period.[113] This is not to say that the religious make-up of Roman colonies has no Roman elements at this period, but simply that the colony often sees the persistence of the local in an adapted form.[114] Alongside this, there is an emphasis on particular cults which could be called Roman, and which, while they may have analogues in Rome, are not necessarily those which, to us, signify the ascendancy of a model predicated on the dominant state cults of the Roman *res publica*, especially that of Iuppiter Optimus Maximus.

Torelli is also right to stress that beside the Roman element we must acknowledge the Latin. He points to the type of the large sanctuary, where a plurality of gods seems to be worshipped in connection with a single function, as particularly Latin. The type-site would be the sanctuary of the Thirteen Altars at Lavinium, which Torelli sees in some sense reproduced in the sanctuary of the *lucus* (grove) at the Roman colony of Pisaurum (see next section). Whether or not one wishes to cavil at e.g. the detail of Torelli's interpretation of the Lavinium sanctuary (1984), it is clear that we should be open to the identification of Latin as well as Roman elements in the cultic matrix of the colonies. Again, at Paestum, it might be the case that one particular group of temples can indeed, as Torelli suggests (1999, 52–6), be mapped onto an 'Aventine archetype'; this symbolic *arx* would carry within it a nexus of meanings and ideologies appropriate both to the plebeian character of the colony, and to third-century plebeian Rome. Yet the identifications which underpin this theory, while ingenious, are not all convincing (e.g. the 'pan-Latin *Liberalia*', 1999, 56).[115]

Yet the idea that we might look for an *Aventine* triad (Liber, Iuppiter and Minerva) as the core religious structure of a Latin colony is novel, and represents at least a partial breaking of the mould. Indeed, for Torelli, the Capitoline triad should not be sought in Latin colonial contexts until after the revolt of Fregellae. While I shall take issue with this position, it is refreshingly original, and allows us to see things Capitoline as historically contingent rather than in any sense 'givens' in the colonial context. Again, after the tantalizing suggestion of a Paestan 'Palatine perspective', Torelli goes on: 'However, rather than a deliberate attempt to imitate the capital city's topography of sacred buildings, it could equally well be interpreted (at least in the case of the presumed *aedis Matris Magnae*) as a reference to the *origo Troiana* [Trojan origin] of the Latins and of Rome' (1999, 65). As we shall see, allowing due weight to Latin elements in Latin colonies is extremely important, as are the implications of dynamics of interaction between Roman and Latin elements.

4.1 *Cosa* (*Fig.* 1)

Let us now turn from models to evidence, beginning at Cosa: a site coloured, as we have seen, with the excavator's expectations almost before a pick had been stuck in the ground. Trying to forget the familiar (for a summary of the current orthodoxy see Taylor 2002, 66–8), we shall re-examine the evidence for religious developments there, to see whether it will support the weight of the hegemonic 'Gellian' interpretation long since placed on it. The earliest religious activity attested seems to be represented by the deposition, in a natural fissure in the rock of the '*arx*', of sacrificial debris. This assemblage, called 'Deposit A' by the excavators, contained carbonised vegetable matter (Brown, Richardson and Richardson 1960, 9–16; Brown 1980, 16 f.), and pottery dating to the third century BC, including Genucilia plates, and BG from the *petites estampilles* (small stamps) workshop,[116] including some carrying dedications to Hercules (Taylor 1957, 75–91; see further below for this class of pottery).[117] Traces of a square structure (25 x 25 Roman feet), the median line of which ran through the pit, were interpreted by Brown as a raised platform or enclosure, the colony's first religious space.[118]

Brown put a very Roman construction on this physical evidence, and imagined around it a foundation ritual synthesised from literary sources.[119] The fissure in the rock was for him the *mundus* into which the first fruits of the new community were deposited.[120] Beside this, another very Roman founding ritual on the *arx*, the setting up of an augural *templum* (sacred precinct): from the *arx* an augur would certainly have had a clear line of sight over the city and its *territorium*.[121] The Roman model assumed to be fully operative here emerges even from the first chapter title in Brown, Richardson and Richardson 1960: 'Cosa Quadrata', invoking the supposed earliest phase of Rome's urban history, as Roma Quadrata (Plut. *Rom.* 9, Festus 310, 312L). Some of these ritual acts may have happened: an inauguration of the colony and its *ager* (territory) from the *arx* seems plausible. At the same time, it is methodologically dubious to assume that the late-republican and Augustan evidence can be simply retrojected into an era for which we do not know this 'Romulean' foundation ideology to be applicable. Roma Quadrata, far from being a pattern we can expect to see replicated in city foundations,

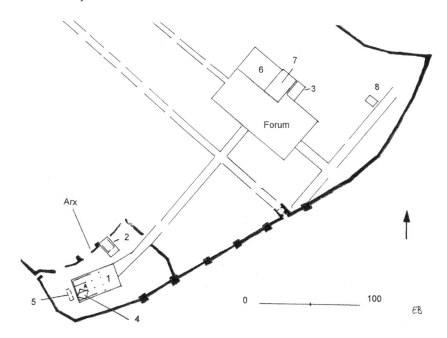

Fig. 1. Cosa, main republican structures. A: fissure containing deposit A. 1: 'Capitolium'. 2: temple D. 3: temple B. 4: site of possible *auguraculum* under 'Capitolium'. 5: supposed site of third century temple. 6: *basilica*. 7: *comitium/curia*. 8: eastern height – possible temple.

is a mystery (see now Mastrocinque 1998). Moreover, some elements, like the pottery dedicated to Hercules, are unexplained on Brown's model (he assumed that Iuppiter Latiaris, as god of the Latins, was invoked from the first ritual onwards: 1980, 16). Indeed, as we shall see in examining the temples built on the *arx* over the next century, there is no shortage of dubious assumption and uncertain logic underpinning the 'story' of religious development at Cosa.

Two religious buildings of the republican period were brought to light on the *arx* during the early American Academy excavations: the 'Capitolium', and Temple D, oriented at right angles to it, to the north. The terracotta decorations recovered at the time were, however, divided into *three* separate series, based on size, decorative characteristics and to a certain extent, findspot (Strazzulla 1985, 98). The earliest 'series', thought to be almost entirely represented by revetment plaques[122] and antefixes, was attributed by the excavators to an, as yet unlocated, third temple, earlier than the two then known (Brown, Richardson and Richardson 1960, 151–79; Strazzulla 1985, 98).[123] Such a structure was originally thought to be located immediately to the east of the 'Capitolium' (Brown, Richardson and Richardson 1960,

19–23, Strazzulla 1985, 98). Subsequently a 'footprint' (where the bedrock had been cut to receive foundations) of a small temple with an elongated single *cella* (chamber) was identified, behind the 'Capitolium', to make room for which it was supposed to have been demolished (Brown 1980, 51; Scott 1985b, 95; Strazzulla 1985, 98; Scott 1992, 92).[124] Rabun Taylor, while not denying the existence of an early series of terracottas (he identifies two *sima* subtypes as belonging to this category), has cast doubt, in my view rightly, on this supposed location for the building which carried them, and instead proposed that the first temple on the *arx* was the square structure on its summit, identified by the excavators as the *auguraculum* (augural platform) (Taylor 2002, 66 f., 69–71, 73, 77–80).[125]

The date of this first temple is uncertain: the excavators, while recognizing the lack of direct evidence, consistently opted for a third-century date, not earlier than the end of the First Punic War (Brown 1980, 25 f. and fig. 25; Scott 1985b, 95; Scott 1988, 75 f.; Scott 1992, 92 f., 94, 96; Torelli 1999, 39; for an earlier date see, however, Strazzulla 1985, 98; cf. Fentress 2000b, 13, and Taylor 2002, 66, 69, arguing that we lack firm evidence for third-century religious activity).[126] The early terracottas (on Brown's and the Richardsons' view) are not that dissimilar from those found in nearby Etruscan sanctuaries, and Tarquinian parallels, and indeed manufacture, are often invoked (Brown, Richardson and Richardson 1960, 156 f.; Brown 1980, 26; Strazzulla 1985, 99). The antefixes, however, have been compared to Campanian rather than to Etrusco-Italic production (Strazzulla 1985, 99; Scott 1992, 93; Torelli 1999, 39, agnostic about attribution to a particular temple). Yet it is clear that they have nothing in common with Campanian types, and it seems that the belief that they do is based only on the excavators' claim that Hercules appears only once more in Etruscan antefixes (at nearby Talamone, see below), but that he and Minerva do appear in Campanian examples.[127]

The first temple is conventionally (Strazzulla 1985, 98) attributed to Iuppiter.[128] The reason is that some of the antefixes from the earliest decorative cycle are thought to have been reused on the temple identified by the excavators as a Capitolium.[129] This reuse of material is taken to imply continuity of cult between the two temples. Since, as we shall see, Iuppiter was worshipped in the 'Capitolium', Brown suggested Iuppiter Latiaris, appropriate to a Latin colony, as the god worshipped in the first temple (1980, 55; cf. Torelli 1999, 39 f.; Fentress 2000b, 13).[130]

It should be stressed that there is little evidence for (or against) this 'hypothesis' (Scott 1992, 93, cf. 1988, 76). The only relevant data are the antefixes just mentioned, depicting, alternately, Minerva and Hercules (Scott 1992, 93; Taylor 2002, 66), some of which were sealed in the construction layer of the 'Capitolium'.[131] Now antefixes do not represent the deities worshipped at a sanctuary; such identifications are difficult to arrive at even from well-preserved pedimental groups, and inscriptions, cult images and a good sample of all fictile decoration are needed to make a firm attribution. The presence of Minerva and Hercules does not rule out the attribution of the first temple to Iuppiter; it does however provide two variables, which must condition the identification and significance of the deity to whom the temple was dedicated. That is to say, that the deity ought to stand in some mythical relationship to Minerva and Hercules.[132] To this problem we shall return.

Can the claim of continuity of cult be sustained, though? In its favour two arguments have been adduced: (i) the contiguous locations of the first temple and the later 'Capitolium', and (ii) the apparent reuse of the early antefixes in the 'Capitolium' (Brown, Ricardson and Richardson 1960, 20). (i) is not weakened by Taylor's relocation of the cult building, but, if anything, strengthened. (ii) is, however, problematic, as it forms part of a reconstruction that does not rest on clear stratigraphic evidence.[133]

What then of our terracotta antefixes? Some fragments seem to come from replacements for damaged antefixes – the moulds in which these had been made were very worn, suggesting that they continued to be used for replacements for some time, after the first temple had been demolished.[134] Yet, as Taylor points out (2002, 66, 78, cf. Brown, Richardson and Richardson 1960, 154 f.), many antefixes were found buried in the construction layers of the 'Capitolium'; there is an obvious logical difficulty in interpreting the same material as constituting both construction fill and current decoration in the same building. Now, superfluous, or superannuated, temple decorations and dedications often end up deliberately buried, in many cases ritually broken, within the sacred precinct in which they had functioned; this happens in the case of rebuilding as much as in that of decommissioning.[135] On the other hand, burial is not the same as reuse. Of course, it might be argued that some antefixes were 'ritually buried', others reused; but the case for reuse seems so problematic that it should not be used to support the argument for continuity.[136]

So we have slender grounds for suggesting continuity of worship; Iuppiter, certainly worshipped in the 'Capitolium', cannot be excluded as a recipient of cult in the earliest temple. Even granted continuity of cult, however, we would be wrong to expect continuity of ideology; rather, we must allow for evolution. We cannot simply read back, for example, a Roman Capitoline ideology from the supposed 'Capitolium' to the first temple. There are many non-Capitoline manifestations of Iuppiter: we have noted Brown's preference for a Latin Iuppiter. It is surely poor method not to give due weight to the *caesura* inherent even in a mutation of the *epiklēsis* (surname) of a deity, but to assume full compatibility and to stress continuity rather than change in such situations (as does, e.g., Brown [1980, 26]: 'The god and his image were incorporated into the new temple and with him all of the decorative elements of his new house').[137]

A second temple, with a square *cella* (Temple D), appeared on the *arx* some years later, on its north-east side, facing out to sea. Recent discussion favours raising the date of construction to *c.* 205 BC, on the basis of a sextantal *as* found under the floor of the *cella*, but above the *podium* fill, giving a *terminus ante quem non* for the later stages in the temple's construction (Scott 1988, 76; 1992, 95).[138] Its decoration is described as more modern than that of the first temple, owing more to Roman or Latin than to Etruscan repertoires.[139] To this decoration can be ascribed the pedimental figure of a cuirassed warrior, which, along with other terracotta fragments from the south slope of the *arx*, *may* have once formed part of a closed pedimental group, perhaps representing the sacrifice of Iphigenia (Scott 1992, 94; Taylor 2002, 73). The dedicatee of this temple seems to have been a goddess, as suggested by remains of what was almost certainly a draped female cult statue. Which divinity has been much debated; tentative suggestions identify Mater Matuta.[140] It was thought at one time that this temple formed a pair with the 'identical' extra-mural one overlooking the port and lagoon, which was ascribed to Portunus; it may rather be to Neptune (Fentress 2000b, 21).[141]

Finally came the very large temple, often referred to, on account of its triple *cella*, as a Capitolium.[142] With this most 'Romanizing' structure the wish-fulfilment of the excavators seems strangely guilty, and there may be a hint of illicit affinity with Rome in the way in which it is also referred to repeatedly as the 'Capitolium style building' *vel sim.* (e.g. Scott 1992, 96).[143] Generally, however, the interpretation of this building is as a 'no-holds-barred', deliberate attempt to recreate at Cosa the substance and setting of the Roman Capitolium.[144] For Scott the temple 'seems intended to evoke the *area Capitolina* [Capitoline precinct] in Rome, as we know other temples and areas of the capital were recalled in other Italian settings' (1992, 96), and he writes of the 'multiple Roman accents visible on the Arx in the second century' and how the building can be seen to 'stress Roman inspiration in large detail and small' (1992, 97).

The detail of the Romanizers' case is as follows. The temple's proportions are similar to Vitruvian recommendation for a 'Tuscan temple' (4.7.1–5), which are in turn supposedly based on the proportions of the Roman Capitolium (Brown 1980, 52); the heavy, archaic profile of the podium (base) moulding apparently recalls that of the Roman Capitoline temple (Brown, Richardson and Richardson 1960, 69–73; Brown 1980, 53 f.);[145] roof tiles and revetment plaques from the first temple were reused in lining the temple's cistern (Brown 1980, 54); the stone gable of the cistern is thought to be based on those of the Roman Capitoline cisterns, or *favissae* (Brown, Richardson and Richardson 1960, 108; Brown 1980, 54; but see the criticism at Fentress 2000b, 21 f.); the temple forecourt apparently copied the *area Capitolina* at Rome (yet the Cosan altar's position was determined by the existing location of the *arx*'s sacred pit), and was related augurally to the layout and centuriation of Cosan territory (Brown 1980, 54; Scott 1985b, 95; Scott 1992, 92; doubts: Taylor 2002, 78, 80).

The case does not stand up: its weaknesses and circularities are clear. To which god(s) then was this temple sacred? The terracotta decoration provides our only real evidence. The remains of a pedimental group, which may show a sacrificial scene (Strazzulla 1985, 98), or a procession or assembly of the gods, could be reconciled with a number of scenarios.[146] Two beam-end sculptures, however, offer more hope: one shows Hercules, the other Ganymede being snatched by an eagle (Strazzulla 1985, 98).[147] The depiction of a moment in the Ganymede myth does seem strongly to suggest Iuppiter as one of the three deities housed in this temple. Yet one swallow does not a summer make: what evidence is there for the worship of Iuno and Minerva?

As we have seen, the presence of Minerva on the third-century antefixes is not proof that she was worshipped in the first temple, and it need not imply her worship in the three-*cella* temple either. For Iuno there is little evidence, it seems, and we should take the time to consider other possible candidates for the two lateral *cellae*. After all, a Capitolium in a Latin colony in Italy is simply anomalous at this period. There were less unusual ways of celebrating Cosa's ties to Rome; to say with Scott that the decoration of the temple was 'redolent of the heightened associations of Roman victory and triumph and their expression in Hellenistic terms' (1992, 97) is to go further than the evidence allows. We must be prepared for some lateral thinking, to unseat the hegemonic Capitoline model.[148]

There are a number of three-*cella* temples from Italian towns in this period. Some have been thought to be, and have been called, Capitolia, but for none of them is this claim supported by a shred of evidence. An example is the temple on the *arx* of the Latin colony of Signia, which a third-century BC bronze *lamina* (sheet), once attached to a dedication, shows to have been sacred to Iuno Moneta (Coarelli 1982, 177 f.). Other three-*cella* temples which were not Capitolia, and which seem variously to have housed between one and four gods, are known from Veii, from the Latin cities of Cora and Lanuvium, and from the Latin colony of Ardea, whose Casalinaccio temple offers perhaps the closest parallel to the mouldings from the podium of the Cosan 'Capitolium'.[149]

Brown, to his credit, was aware that identifying the deities of the Cosan *arx* was not straightforward. His Capitolium was terribly Roman, but it was also, so to speak, a broad church, which could in some sense incorporate Iuppiter Latiaris, as well as the Etruscan Tinia of *Cusi (the defunct Etruscan centre beneath modern Orbetello), and 'Argive Hercules, to whom one of the wellheads in the pronaos was dedicated', the local god of the Portus Herculis (1980, 55 f.).[150] We noted above the presence of pottery dedicated to Hercules in the early Deposit A on the *arx*: if this deposit is in any way connected with the foundation of the colony, the devotion to Hercules must imply some significant role for him in the new venture. Scott too seems aware that his Capitoline model may be perverting the outcome of the analysis, and adopts a broader perspective when he suggests that the reference of the terracottas may be local, and that Hercules may be seen as a Latin deity, while Minerva (as part of the Capitoline Triad) is surely Roman.[151] Assessment of non-Roman and local ingredients in Cosa's religious make-up may indeed provide a broader interpretative matrix for our three-*cella* temple.

The Ganymede beam end can be paralleled elsewhere, but not in a Capitoline context. Ganymede appears in the Lo Scasato II pedimental group from Falerii, in which a group very 'similar' (Torelli 1999, 137) to the Capitoline triad is prominent: Minerva, Iuppiter and Iuno. The group comes, however, from a temple which has been attributed to Minerva (Torelli 1999, 134–9, with bibliography).[152]

The pairing of Hercules and Minerva in the antefixes, and the possible Hercules beam-end sculpture among the terracottas of the 'Capitolium', are also suggestive.[153] An acroterial group of Minerva leading Hercules into Olympus decorated the archaic temple of Fortuna in Rome, a sanctuary replaced in the middle Republic by twin temples to Fortuna and Mater Matuta. The latter has been suggested as the goddess worshipped in temple D, and has the kind of Latin connections which are clearly of potential importance at Cosa.[154] We should note also the terracotta antefix of Minerva from the Latin colony of Beneventum (mentioned above; Giampaola 1991, 127 f. and figs. 6 and 7, Giampaola 2000, 36), dated late-third to mid-second century. The treatment of the hair and the aegis recall that on the Cosan Minerva antefixes (but the fact that the Beneventan Minerva wears a torc, unlike her Cosan counterpart, but recalling the Minerva in the antefixes from Talamone – for which see below – should encourage us not to press such similarities too far).

As significant as possible Latin aspects of the deities of the *arx* are parallels closer to Cosa. The temple at the nearby Etruscan centre of Talamonaccio, ancient Talamone (see Torelli 1999, 145 f.) seems to have undergone a restoration, perhaps in the early second century, with a new cycle of terracotta decorations. For Strazzulla (1985, 99) these repairs, and accompanying new pedimental sculptures, share with Temple D at Cosa motifs inspired by Roman production, in the newest style (see also Brown, Richardson and Richardson 1960, 156 f., suggesting a Tarquinian workshop; Scott 1992, 95; von Vaccano 1992, 64 f., 73 f., declining to draw political conclusions from stylistic affinities; Taylor 2002, 68).

This second phase of architectonic decoration at Talamone includes antefixes with nimbate heads of Minerva and Hercules, which while not replicas of the Cosan antefixes discussed above (Hercules, importantly, is beardless, and Minerva sports a torc), display clear affinities with them.[155] Their date is unclear, with third- and second-century chronologies proposed (see now Taylor 2002, 62, 64). A third-century date might demonstrate the influence of Cosa's religious architecture on the Etruscan centre. Others, perhaps rightly favouring a later date, have argued for a more political dimension to the creation of these 'Romanizing' pieces, seeing in them a reflection of a renewed Roman interest in this part of coastal Etruria in the first quarter of the second century, which saw the reinforcement of Cosa, and the settlement of Saturnia (see von Freytag-Löringhoff, 1992, 69 f., for doxography).

For neither date, however, should we consider as satisfactory an interpretation which simply looks to Rome as the source for everything, and denies any local input. The decorative idiom may ultimately be Roman, and probably derives from the terracotta cycles of Roman Italy, and Roman and Latin colonies, but the *subject matter* is well suited to local traditions and concerns. Massa Pairault has seen Hercules and Minerva as both linked to the Argonautic myth, and as used to convey local identities and elite aspirations in Etruria in this period. The relevant part of the Argonautic myth sees Hercules, companion of the Argonaut Telamon, defeat Laomedon and besiege Priam in Troy. Thus, she argues, local legend reconciled Etruscans to Roman ideology, through the link of Telamon to the Trojan myth.[156] On a less cosy reading, we might stress the *conflict* between Hercules (and Telamon) and the Trojans: in my view von Freytag-Löringhoff is rightly cautious about explaining these terracottas in Romano-centric terms.[157]

In either case, I suggest that, whatever their other associations for the colonists at Cosa, Hercules and Minerva, as worshipped there, also reflect an engagement with, and an appropriation of, these two deities as important parts of a *pre-existing religious environment*.[158] As such they have an important role to play in mediating Cosa's relations with Etruscan communities: local religious continuity accounts in part for their presence here, and they manifest once more the workings of Torelli's *duttilità*.

We should therefore be wary of accepting Torelli's contrast between the religious situation at Cosa, and that at Alba Fucens (on which see below).

Torelli sees, probably correctly, Hercules at Alba as having an integrative role in an environment where the indigenous inhabitants played a much bigger part. In contrast he imagines a de-Etruscanized zone confiscated from Vulci, including the *ager Cosanus* (territory of Cosa) (1999, 41). Yet the situations at Alba and Cosa are not comparable; and I am not sure that the 'ethnic cleansing' view of the Roman appropriation of the *ager Cosanus* adequately describes the situation, or that Etruscans were absent from the world view of the colonists, or isolated within the wider region.

What, then, have we discovered about Cosa's three-*cella* temple? If it was a Capitolium, it would be unique at this period in a Latin colony; and in that case, special pleading would be required, not least for the absent Iuno. Equally significant must be the fact that three-*cella* temples in Etruria were very far from being uncommon.[159] We cannot show that Hercules and Minerva occupied the lateral *cellae* of this temple. The evidence for *their* association with the *arx*, and their relevance to the wider region, and thus Cosan identity, is good, however; and cult activity relating to Hercules seems to go back to the earlier years of the colony. Any reconstruction of religious activity on the *arx* has to involve these two deities, as well as Iuppiter, and the goddess worshipped in temple D, whether Mater Matuta or not. A Capitolium by default will not do.

Let us briefly consider Cosa's other main temple (Temple B), which dominated the *forum*.[160] The chronology of this temple is uncertain: a date around or after the first quarter of the second century is proposed for its completion; in any case, it clearly forms part of the monumentalization of the *forum* which took place during that period.[161] The deity in question is probably female, given the discovery of fragments of female draped terracotta statuettes dedicated to her. A reused inscription found nearby was taken to show that she was Concordia (Brown 1980, 38 f.; cf. Strazzulla 1985, 98), but early on Ceres was offered as a possible alternative (Scott 1985c, 97). The theme of the temple's decorative frieze, which may show the recognition of Paris (Scott 1992, 95), is not easy to fit into either interpretation.[162]

More suggestive was a fragment of the snout of a terracotta sow, probably of the second century BC, which Brown (1980, 39) linked to the Latin myth of the *scrofa Laurentina*, suggesting an assertion of Latin identity by the colony. Torelli then offered an intriguing reading of the relationship between this myth and the cult of Concordia, arguing that it asserted *concordia* (harmony) between Rome and the loyal Latin colonies in 209 BC in the face of the refusal by others to meet Roman demands for troops (see above).[163] Re-examination of these terracotta fragments, however, by E. Richardson (cited in Fentress 2000b, 20 f.), seems to show that the sow was *held* by a life-size votive bust of the goddess, who Richardson suggests was Ceres,

Persephone or Libera. Thus Latin connections cannot be pressed in the current state of the evidence.

In summary, then, what reflections are suggested by the cumulative evidence for the public cults of this Latin colony? Important deities seem to be Hercules (from early on), followed by Iuppiter and Minerva. The only monumental cult centre in the *forum* housed a deity associated more with a plebeian outlook – Ceres or Libera (compare the contemporary foundation of Paestum, as analysed by Torelli 1999, 71–9). The evidence for designating the three-*cella* temple a Capitolium is weak, and some other explanation, taking into account Latin- and Etruscan-compatible elements in Cosa's pantheon, is called for. It is important also to note that the three-*cella* temple was built at Cosa only in the generation following the sending to the colony of a *supplementum* (reinforcement) in 197 BC. Its presence must also be understood in the context of the other monumental building carried out in the colony, especially around the *forum* at this time (Scott 1988, 76 f.; Torelli 1983, 244–7). The changed situation in the early second century must be taken into account (see below), as well as possible continuity. It does not seem satisfactory to argue (as does Fentress 2000b, 13) that the Cosan boom of the early second century was simply a realization of what had been planned in the third century but not realized because of manpower shortages.[164] It is unlikely that it was only in the first quarter of the second century that Cosa was finally able to realize plans made a hundred years earlier (although the improved demographic situation after 197 was hardly a negligible factor). There already existed material manifestations of the colony's religious and cultural identity: the first temple on the *arx*, later demolished (and perhaps partly recycled) to permit the building of what, I argue, was something essentially new.

Earlier in this chapter we questioned the extent to which Cosa can be seen as a little Rome, and the methodologies and expectations underpinning that interpretation. Let us now return briefly to these claims. Even if a monolithic 'colonial mentality' was being expressed at Cosa, as Scott claims,[165] it is simply wish-fulfilment to see it as expressed by the building of a 'Capitolium'. Even *were* the three-*cella* temple a Capitolium, it would still be the case that for some hundred years prior to its building, through two Punic Wars, in which her loyalty to Rome had been tested and proven, Cosa had managed to express an identity without it. Any sense of Romanness at Cosa, or of a special relationship with Rome, was for the first period of the colony's life demonstrably not expressed through any 'Capitoline ideology', but via other religious matrices, within which the part played by Hercules was early and probably significant. There might, as assumed by Scott and others, be 'multiple evocations of Rome'[166] on the *arx* (even this term, as Taylor 2002,

60 points out, is a loaded one) and in the *forum* of Cosa; and, for the second century, they might well have been 'sponsored' by Rome. Such later development was bound up with the profits of imperial conquest, and with new architectural models reaching Rome and Italy, along with the appearance of new construction techniques such as *opus incertum*.[167] Yet we struggle to see a clear attempt made to evoke the Roman *area Capitolina* at Cosa, either in terms of micro-topography, with its overlying mesh of myth and meaning, or at a general level. Indeed, the simple picture of earlier accounts must now be adjusted to take account of new discoveries: like temple B in the *forum*, the new temple on the eastern height was found to have replaced earlier housing; and traces of possible housing on the same alignment as the colony's street plan, have been found on the *arx*; it is impossible to disprove stratigraphically their co-existence with temple D (Fentress 2000b, 14; Taylor 2002, 70).

A strong evocation of Rome is to be found on the Cosan *arx*, but, ironically, it comes from a period when the colony's autonomous existence had been cancelled out by the acceptance of municipal status after the Social War. The evidence comes again from terracottas, this time from, probably, an Augustan restoration associated with the Capitolium (Scott 1985b, 95; Taylor 2002, 60, 75 – assigning the campana plaques to this phase, 81). This restoration is represented by a very Roman terracotta cycle, perhaps from a portico built around the three-*cella* temple; Strazzulla notes the presence of similar themes and treatment to those of the terracottas of Augustus' prestigous sanctuary of Apollo Palatinus (1985, 100).[168] Perhaps Apollo should be added to our list of Cosan deities – a not insignificant addition, as we shall see. In any case, the closest evocation of Rome to be found at Cosa comes within the context of a *post-colonial* imitation of the art and architecture of the new régime at Rome in the late first century BC.

4.2 *Alba Fucens* (*Fig.* 2)

The Latin colony of Alba Fucens[169] was founded in 303 BC, to buttress Roman expansion into Aequian territory. Both the circuit of the walls and some monumental building seem to date from the middle of the third century.[170] Interestingly, sondages conducted across the line of the wall-circuit have revealed architectural terracottas and pottery which seem to predate this phase of monumentalization. Some of this material could come from the first years of the colony,[171] but much of it seems in fact to predate the foundation (although none of it is to be dated earlier than *c.* 350 BC).[172] There is thus a good chance, as Mertens argues, that the colony was implanted in a pre-existing Aequian *oppidum* (fortified settlement), perhaps one of the thirty-one reported by Livy as destroyed by the Roman campaign.[173] No occupation horizons from such an Aequian *oppidum* have been found, but if

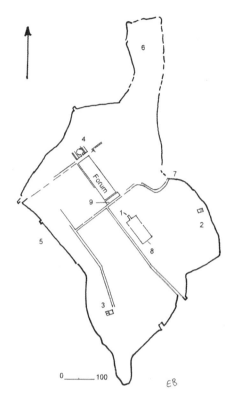

1. *sacellum* of Hercules
2. Pettorino temple
3. S. Pietro temple
4. *comitium*
5. colonial walls
6. Alba Vecchia
7. *Porta di Massa*
8. *forum pecuarium*
9. *basilica*

Fig. 2. Alba Fucens.

the architectural terracottas did derive from this putative pre-colonial settlement, we would once again be faced with the question of how the Romans
reacted to the presence of local cults in conquered cities.[174]

At Alba destruction seems to have been the first reaction, as Livy believed.
The possible pre-colonial material noted above was found reused as fill,
mainly in ramparts behind the walls.[175] Yet destruction need not preclude
some sort of cult continuity; the colony's early religious development does
not seem to follow a 'Capitoline' model. Instead, the earliest sanctuary
seems to be that of Hercules.[176] This occupies a central position in the saddle
in which most of the colony lies.[177] Later the sanctuary was monumental-
ized as a *sacellum* (shrine) dominating the long axis of the *forum pecuarium*
(sheep market). The form of the sanctuary now visible is essentially of early-
first-century date (Torelli 1988b, 137); neither plan nor elevation of the
earlier phases is known, but a circular basin associated with late-fourth- and
early-third-century pottery seems very likely to have been part of the cult
apparatus. In the area later occupied by the *forum pecuarium* itself, limited
sondages produced BG pottery associated with coins belonging to the
second quarter of the third century (*c.* 269 BC according to Mertens), as well

as two BG cups, described as 'Campanian', with the H marked on the base (thus dedicated to Hercules, like the Cosan examples discussed above), found under the later *porticus*.[178]

There are clear signs of the chronological priority of the Hercules sanctuary with respect to other important public buildings at Alba. It is with this sanctuary, not the later *forum* and *basilica* complex, that the *comitium*,[179] built at the northern end of the saddle, is aligned. This is highly suggestive, as is the fact that the Italic temple on the hill of Pettorino was also oriented on the Hercules sanctuary.[180] While Mertens suggests (1988, 104) that the central sanctuary may not have belonged to any one deity in particular, its subsequent development, and the dedication of early votives to Hercules alone, do make it likely that he dominated cult here.[181] This cult was, physically and conceptually, the focus of civic life in the early colony.[182]

Hercules' function(s) here cannot be explained simply; we should bear in mind his enormous popularity in the upland Apennine regions of Italy, a phenomenon quite independent of the Roman conquest, and one which has often been related, through the story of Herakles' lost calf, to the practice of transhumant pastoralism among the Italic peoples.[183] Hercules probably evoked a number of responses for the Roman and Latin settlers placed here in the mountainous frontier looking out over the heartlands of the Aequi and Marsi, peoples with a life-style different (perhaps imagined as more different than it was) from that of the urbanized Tyrrhenian plains which they had left behind. The god may equally have served as a way in which local populations, or such as remained after the Roman conquest, could be in some way conciliated, and even integrated into the colony and the new organization of society, territory and economy. Following earlier observations by Coarelli, who rightly emphasized an imperial dedication from Alba to Hercules Salarius (Coarelli 1984, 87, citing *CIL* IX 3961),[184] Torelli wrote (1999, 39; cf. 1993, 111–15, 1988b, 137):

> The case of the religious and cultural roots of the cult of Hercules Salarius in Alba Fucens is very useful in showing that even in the rather inconspicuous appearance of the local cultic system remarkable care was taken in exploiting Roman and Latin tradition to favour the economic integration between the new foundation and the surrounding areas, an integration which should better be described in terms of strengthening the socio-economic domination of the urbanized Latin colonists over their non-urbanized Marsian areas.

We should, nevertheless, give due weight to the importance of Hercules in indigenous society, which made such manipulation of cult possible in the first place.

Other cults at Alba Fucens, although given monumental sanctuaries later than Hercules', are of interest too. Apollo has been identified as the deity of the hill-top S. Pietro temple, as the Roman Apollo Medicus. This identification may be supported by the discovery nearby of anatomical ex-votos in the Romano-Latin tradition (see on the phenomenon, and its association with healing, De Cazanove 2000). Unusually, this temple has a double-*cella*, and this may well imply the presence of Diana, Apollo's sister. The double-*cella* may be a sign of localized religious difference at Alba, since the Pettorino temple also has one.[185] Vulcan was also worshipped somewhere in the colony, perhaps implying (so Liberatore 2001, 190, 192) imitation of Rome, although a great antiquity for the cult at Alba is not attested.

4.3. *Ariminum*

We have already considered ways in which some Ariminate material culture, at least in a religious context, laid claim to a particular form of Romanness in the third century, and how issues of perceived identity and isolation may have shaped attitudes to Rome, and their expression. Ariminum's earliest religious practices may also embrace an indigenous substrate.[186] Let us begin by looking again at the 'Romanizing' third-century BG wares from the colony, other than the *pocula deorum* already considered.

Morel has drawn attention to the predominance of related types of BG pottery associated with, or evoking, Hercules and his cult, in a number of third-century BC colonial contexts.[187] Firstly, we have the so-called *Heraklesschalen* (Herakles-vessels): cups or *paterae* figuring Hercules in the central zone. They were made principally in Rome; and are found in small numbers at certain Roman and Latin colonies (possibly with limited production at Paestum), and more commonly across the *ager Romanus*, in northern Etruria, and even, in one or two cases, outside Italy; they seem to be cult objects, with a commercial distribution not restricted to colonies.[188] Secondly we have Calene-style *paterae* featuring the apotheosis of Hercules on the *umbilicus* (centre), made at several centres in central Italy.[189] Thirdly, vases with a stamp figuring Hercules' club and sometimes other Herculean attributes (found at Rome; Minturnae; Alba Fucens, Paestum, Cales, Interamna Lirenas, and Fregellae; the allied communities of Teanum and Aquinum, and one example in Spain).[190] One production centre for these vases, termed the *gruppo erculeo* (Hercules group), has recently been identified at Cales.[191] Finally, there is a group of vases related to the *atelier des petites estampilles*, with the letters 'H', or 'HR' *vel sim.* in ligature, stamped, cut, or painted, usually in the *tondo* (inside base) of the vase; these are found in Rome from the late fourth century until near the middle of the third; in Latium and S. Etruria; at Ostia, Minturnae; Paestum, Cales, Fregellae, Alba Fucens, Cosa and Ariminum during the third.[192] The last two types are, according to Morel, characteristic of a 'popular' piety.[193]

At Ariminum the cult of Hercules is attested, at various social levels, through the BG pottery. He is not the only deity who figures there: the *pocola* also name Ceres and Apollo for example (see Franchi de Bellis 1995). Other evidence for the worship of Hercules, even if later, may be added here: it seems that he may have had a sanctuary in the *vicus Cermalus*, (note the Romanizing name: *CIL* XI 6787; Susini 1965, 147 f., 148 n. 1).[194] Diana is also important, not as a Roman element for (in some ways) a very Roman community, but rather as a manifestation of the devotion of what was, after all, a Latin colony, to the federal Latin cult at Nemi. A bronze tablet found there in late 1886 or early 1887 (*ILLRP* 77), which should belong to the third century (so Degrassi *ad loc.*, Cicala 1995) reads: 'C. Manlio(s) Ac[---] f. / cosol / pro / poplo Arimenesi'.[195]

Here we see the public face of the Ariminate *community*, which addresses itself through its chief magistrate (see above on the Ariminate consuls) to Diana Nemorensis,[196] the deity of the old Latin federation whose prestige was said to have driven king Servius Tullius to found the cult of Diana *in Aventino* as a rival (see Introduction above, on Ariminum and Aventine Diana). Now, the old Latin League was no more after 338, but some of its religious observances seem to have survived it, and it is not surprising that Rome exploited them, or allowed them to be used, to perpetuate and strengthen a shared sense of purpose among the Latin colonies, whether founded before or after 338. Yet more than a sense of shared Latinity may be read from Ariminum's choice in making a dedication here at Nemi. Ariminate devotion to Diana seems indeed to be pre-eminent; in the imperial period there was a *vicus Dianensis* at Ariminum (*CIL* XI 379), and Ariminates also set up a dedication to Diana at Rome (*CIL* VI 133).[197] The deity had a special place in the local hierarchy, and from an early date (Cicala 1995, 358, 361 is probably right to situate her at the very foundation of the colony). This, however, was not simply a local phenomenon; deliberately or otherwise, it came to provide another channel by which Ariminum, as a geographically peripheral community in the third century, could relate itself to the core. That core is not simply Roman, it is also Latin. By setting its worship of Diana within this particular matrix, the colony seems to be trying to associate itself with one of the oldest strata of Latin cult, and obtain thereby a vicarious antiquity for its religious identity, which compensated in some measure for isolation, real or perceived (on which see above).[198]

The presence of Apollo, Diana's brother, is not accidental either, nor the somnolent reflex of an innately Roman religious nervous system. The importance of his presence at Ariminum (and Adriatic Pisaurum), has been stressed by Susini among others.[199] Susini relates Apolline prominence to the expulsion of the Gauls from Greece *c.* 279–8 BC after the sack of Delphi (a theme recalled in the terracotta decoration of the temple at Civitalba in Umbria, Torelli 1999, 142–4). Apollo also became more important to Romans as their relations with Greeks grew from the First Punic War onwards, reflecting increasing awareness of Apollo's role as Archegetes for the Greeks of the West, and as protector of strangers. For Susini (1965, 148), there is more than a whiff of colonial 'policy': 'on ne saurait exclure enfin que, dans le cadre de la politique d'implantation coloniale du IIᵉ siècle av. J.-C., Apollon…ait été invoqué également dans les nouvelles colonies comme dieu de bon augure' ('finally it would be difficult to exclude the possibility that, in the setting of the politics of colonial foundation of the second century BC, Apollo…was invoked equally in the new colonies as a god of good omen'). Likewise for Ortalli (2000, 503) the Ariminate *pocola*, dedicated above all to Apollo and Hercules, are 'tra l'altro collegate a rituali migratori e di fondazione' ('among other things, tied to rituals of migration and foundation').[200] In any case, Apollo and Diana, and also Hercules, emerge in public (and perhaps in private) contexts as the pre-eminent deities of Ariminum for some time after the foundation.

4.4 *Tarracina (Fig.* 3)

Literature on the Roman colony of Tarracina still commonly names the great extra-urban sanctuary which dominates the height to the E. of the city as that of Iuppiter Anxur, the poliadic deity of the community. Some years ago, however, Coarelli mounted a convincing challenge to this identification, proposing instead to see the sanctuary as dedicated to Venus Obsequens (Coarelli 1987, 113–40). The first significant phase of the visible remains (the 'small temple' and the upper terrace of the main complex) seems to belong to the third quarter of the second century, with the lower terrace of the main

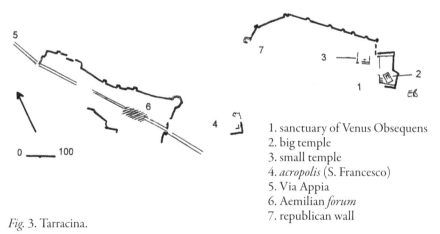

1. sanctuary of Venus Obsequens
2. big temple
3. small temple
4. *acropolis* (S. Francesco)
5. Via Appia
6. Aemilian *forum*
7. republican wall

Fig. 3. Tarracina.

complex dating to the first decades of the first, perhaps after 83 BC (Coarelli 1987, 115–17, 121, 125). Earlier activity seems to be implied, however, not only by the evidence for oracular activity on the lower terrace of the main complex, but also by two terracing walls in polygonal masonry (Coarelli 1987, 120 f.), which excavated material from the nineteenth century seems to suggest could be contemporary with the foundation of the colony in 329 BC.

Other cults may have shared this complex, perhaps Iuppiter Anxur (for the literary evidence on him, and on Feronia, see Coarelli 1987, 123, 126 f.), for whom Coarelli suggests a primary temple within the colony, on the site of the convent of S. Francesco, rather than either the 'small temple' (to Feronia? Coarelli 1987, 123–6) or the small temple *in antis* on the upper terrace (1987, 122 f.). Feronia, another prominent deity perhaps worshipped here and elsewhere in Tarracina, well illustrates the adaptive nature of local cults in relation to forces and phenomena external to the community. As Torelli (1993, 99–101) notes, Feronia was a Sabine goddess with (here) a maritime emporic function, exercised in a community which lay at the end of a transhumance route leading from the Monte Lepini to the sea.[201]

Coarelli (1987, 121) makes an interesting case for the presence of an (admittedly extra-urban) *auguraculum* on an upper terrace at Monte S. Angelo, which he thinks might go back to the fourth century BC, but suggests that such a feature has a Latin rather than a Roman colonial pedigree. As elsewhere, the classic colonial marker, the Capitolium, is attested only late on: whichever of the two large temples in the centre of Tarracina was the Capitolium, whether it should rather be associated with the possible 'Sullan' forum or the 'Aemilian' one (see for various arguments Coppola 1984, 328, 348, 364–6, 371 f.), the earliest certain date for its construction cannot be pushed back before the first century BC.

The fourth-century colony seems to have revered Iuppiter above all, but as the young Anxur, not as Capitolinus or Optimus Maximus; and Feronia may have been more important, probably because of her oracular aspect, than the Capitoline cult, even in the first century BC. A substantial shift in cult pratice, and in religious and communal ideologies (perhaps related to the Sullan victory in the Civil War), can be detected with the institution of the cult of Venus Obsequens on Monte S. Angelo; this arguably represents a bigger change in the religious sphere than anything associated with the first colonization (Coarelli 1987, 127–38; but note 131 f., for links, via Venus Erucina, to Iuppiter Capitolinus).

4.5 *Minturnae* (*Fig.* 4)
Finally Minturnae, a Roman colony, founded in 295 BC. Dea Marica was worshipped nearby at the mouth of the Garigliano river from at least the

sixth century BC.[202] This sanctuary clearly remained an important point of reference within the colonial world view, another example of Torelli's flexibility of local religion:[203] in 207 BC the Minturnians reported to the Roman Senate that the *lucus* of Marica had been struck by lightning (Livy 27.37.2–3). By then the colony had acquired other religious buildings: a temple of Iuppiter was struck at the same time.[204] This temple has been convincingly identified with the 'Tuscan' temple next to the Augustan temple A (Torelli 1988b, 150; Guidobaldi and Pesando 1989, 39, 51 f.). It is a moot point whether it should be described as a temple with three *cellae*, or a single *cella* with *alae* (Bispham 2000, 158, with bibliography on the post-191 'Capitolium'), although Guidobaldi calls it a Capitolium (1988, 129; cf. Guidobaldi and Pesando 1989, 51).

At all events, a Iuppiter temple existed by the late third century. How long, though, had it been in existence? Guidobaldi and Pesando (1989, 39) assume its existence since the foundation of the colony; yet there is no stratigraphic evidence to support this claim. As I hope to have shown (Bispham 2000, 174 f.), the temple of Iuppiter at the citizen colony of Ostia has no good claim to be older than the late third century, and indeed Ostia may never have had a Capitolium. Perhaps Minturnae's religious topography developed on a similar chronology. It should be stressed that the temple of Iuppiter here lies *outside* the original *castrum* (fortification) of the colony, and therefore is probably not contemporary with the foundation.

As at Cosa, though perhaps starting slightly earlier, the first half of the second century saw substantial monumentalization of public space at

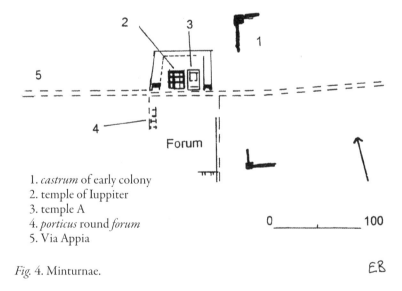

1. *castrum* of early colony
2. temple of Iuppiter
3. temple A
4. *porticus* round *forum*
5. Via Appia

0 _____ 100

Fig. 4. Minturnae.

EB

Minturnae. The *forum* porticus seems to date between 190 and 150 BC. It extended and improved the colony's public space, providing a foral area, something not included in the original colonial plan (1988, 129; Guidobaldi and Pesando 1989, 39–60; Coarelli 1987, 30 and n.22, 1992, 28; Guidobaldi and Pesando 1989, 39, for parallels with the decoration of the sanctuary of Aesculapius at Fregellae). This monumentalization can be linked to the phenomenon exemplified by the wave of colonial modernization described by Livy for 174 BC (Guidobaldi 1988, 129; Guidobaldi and Pesando 1989, 38–45; Torelli 1988b, 151; see further below).

5. Gods of colonization?

Certain deities recur in the colonies. Hercules is prominent everywhere, and probably across multiple social strata and groupings, as shown by the dedication across central Italy, especially in the colonies, of votive vases. There are early dedications on the Cosan *arx*; in the iconographic nexus surrounding the later *arx* temples at Cosa, Hercules again figures prominently. His sanctuary is central in more ways than one at Alba Fucens. At Paestum, Torelli's identification of the amphiprostyle temple as Hercules' (1999, 62–4) seems convincing, as do the proposed links to Mater Matuta (and note that possibly Mater Matuta shared the *arx* at Cosa). At Brundisium, the area probably occupied by the main *arx* of the colony (formerly the area of the Messapic settlement), and therefore by a temple or temples, is little known, but produced a monumental statue of Hercules.[205] At the Roman colony of Ostia Hercules is a precolonial, perhaps emporic, deity, whose sanctuary, whilst outside the mid-republican *castrum*, remains one of the colony's three most important cult sites throughout its history.[206]

Apollo and Diana also figure, certainly or with high probability, at Alba Fucens, Ariminum, and elsewhere.[207] Both appear, for instance, among the deities whom the *cippi* (inscribed stones) of the *lucus* at the Roman colony of Pisaurum (founded in 184 BC) commemorate (*ILLRP* 13, 21). The frame of reference of all of these deities is not necessarily Romanocentric, but probably encompasses Latin, local, and in the case of Hercules and Apollo, Mediterranean elements. It seems that during the Middle Republic, these deities were in some sense 'gods of colonization', as some scholars have suggested. Yet caution is required before we try to give overarching explanations for their widely diffused presence in colonies.[208]

If we are to use the phrase 'gods of colonization', we must use it in a more nuanced way than simply to denote gods, who, together with their myths and rituals, were used to mediate and propagate new ideologies of power, and make clear the new order of Roman conquest and local subjection. This may be a role assumed in the Roman colonial context from the second century onwards by Iuppiter Optimus Maximus, but Hercules will not be made to lie down in such a Procrustean bed. Studies of the impact and diffusion of the cult of Greek Herakles in north-west Sicily and the hinterland of Metapontion in south Italy have suggested that it fulfilled a complex integrative function.[209] Herakles' mythical achievements can be seen as paradeigmatic of the colonists' experience, in terms of bringing 'civilized' values and of promoting cultural and economic interaction. Appeal to the past via the hero's myths and cult also legitimated changes in indigenous society, for which interaction with Greeks was a vital catalyst: the cult may even have validated the participation of local communities as autonomous agents interacting with Greek colonial settlements (see Giangiulio 1993, 46–8).

We have argued that local situations, where myth and cult act as vehicles for changing identities, must be taken into account, and that the Romans did, as others have shown, shape those situations for their own ends. Deities prominent in indigenous cult and subsequently in a colony must not be torn from the local context which gave meaning to their worship. Within their local context, they formed part of a religious landscape and an ideational realm. Although Hercules is found in a prominent role at Ostia and in other colonies, we must remember that at Ostia he co-existed with the Castores and Vulcan, for whom such 'colonial' roles have not been claimed. At Cosa he shared the *arx* with Iuppiter, Minerva and perhaps Mater Matuta. Ceres may have dominated the Cosan *forum*, and she is not held to be particularly colonial; she is probably, like many of the gods and goddesses on whom we have focused here, to be found worshipped, in some context and at some level, everywhere.

There are two instances where we can glimpse the breadth of the religious devotion of particular *groups* within colonial societies, demonstrating again the importance of contextual study, and of being able to look at a collection of evidence which forms a unity, not a series of bits and pieces. I have in mind two groups of inscriptions: the *cippi* from the *lucus* at Pisaurum from the early second century, and the early-first-century inscriptions of the *collegia* (associations) of Minturnae (reused in the podium of Temple A). The former group needs to be understood as prominently associated with *matronae* (free married women); the latter is an expression of the religious activity of collectives of freedmen and slaves. At Pisaurum we find dedications to (besides Apollo and Diana) Fides, Iuno (additionally as both Lucina and Regina), Mater Matuta (twice), Salus, Diva Marica, Divi No[v]esedes, Feronia,[210] 'Lebro' (*ILLRP* 14–20, 22–60).[211] At Minturnae *collegia* (associations) of slaves and freedmen set up dedications to Ceres (*ILLRP* 729), Spes (*ILLRP* 730, 740), ?Venus (*ILLRP* 737), and Mercury Felix (*ILLRP* 742).[212]

The local context will always impede and deconstruct the identification of 'colonial' roles for these deities, whether we think these arose spontaneously, or were the result of conscious 'state' policy. Diana seems to have strong Latin overtones. Hercules seems almost too ubiquitous and malleable to be useful (cf. D.H. 1.40.6: besides the Ara Maxima in Rome 'in many other places in Italy, precincts [τεμένη] are set up to the god, and altars are dedicated to him, both in cities and along highways; and one could scarcely find any place in Italy in which the god happens not to be honoured'). Apollo clearly means one thing in Alba Fucens, where he probably has a healing role, and another in the *ager Gallicus*, where the repulse of the Gauls from Delphi is a principal intertext.[213] I shall be content here to underline the recurrence of certain deities in Roman and Latin colonial contexts. They appear either alongside, or as, local survivals; they are worshipped within their own cultic matrices, dependent on the particular and the local as much as the general and the Roman. Their *repeated* presence is, however, not fortuitous. I shall restrict myself to two sets of general remarks here: firstly on some colonial aspects of the cult of Hercules; and then on the notable mid-republican absentee – Iuppiter.

What might Hercules mean? There were some statist overtones to his cult: Morel notes the Roman state taking over the cult at the Ara Maxima from the Potitii in the fourth century (D.H. 1.40.5).[214] Yet the god is multi-faceted, and public or private interests are reflected in a variety of functions and *epiklēseis*. Hercules might for example figure in colonies as protector of trade and commerce, as recipient of *decumae* (tithes), or as the apotropaic Hercules Tutor.[215]

But might there nevertheless be Roman mentalities constructed through the colonial cults of Hercules? It may be that a passage of Dionysios of Halikarnassos can help us here. After describing the slaying of Kakos by Herakles, Dionysios goes on to tell the 'truer' story of Herakles' presence and exploits in Italy ('which has been adopted by many who have narrated his deeds in the form of history', 41.1); rounding up stray calves was clearly insufficient reason for them (cf. 41.2, 42.4, 43, on Dionysios' heterodox genealogies).[216]

The reason for Herakles being honoured as he is, says Dionysios, is that he destroyed, at the head of a great army, every tyranny in all the land within the Ocean, 'that was grievous and painful to its subjects, or any *polis* (city) which outraged and mistreated its neighbours, or any rule (ἡγεμονία) of men who practised a savage way of life and unlawful murders of strangers; he established instead law-abiding kingdoms and temperate governments (πολιτεύματα) and humane and sociable customs for life' (1.41.1). In the process Herakles mingled Greeks and barbarians, inland and coastal dwellers, 'those who hitherto had been having mistrustful and unsociable dealings with each other'. Finally, he built *poleis* in barren places, drained land and built roads through mountains, and opened up land and sea for the use of all. This required some heavy fighting in places, and Dionysios singles out the Ligurians or Ligues (41.1–3), a 'numerous and warlike race' (41.3, cf. 40.3, from the first, 'legendary', version of the story, where the Ligurians are called 'lawless men'), who tried to bar Herakles' way into Italy.[217] Some cities (those either weak or Greek) surrendered to Herakles as he made his way through Italy, but others had to be taken by siege (42.2); among these was that of Kakos, who was 'an entirely barbarian chief who ruled over wild men', holding 'fortified places', and being 'painful' to his neighbours. Kakos had attacked and stolen from Herakles' army (42.3), but in revenge his 'citadels' (φρούρια) were stormed and he himself killed. His former citadels were demolished, and the surrounding lands given to Evander and Faunos (42.1). Finally, Herakles settled the prisoners, taken earlier, in newly won regions. 'It was because of these deeds that the name and glory of Herakles became very great in Italy, and not because of his journey through the country, in which nothing noble was involved' (42.4).

Now, it does not seem that Dionysios' narrative is simply an Augustan myth; indeed, by differing from the version found in the *Aeneid*, it sets itself apart from the dominant Augustan version (note his citation of earlier writers). Some elements of the account are required by the mythic setting; others, however, seem to come from old strata of the myth, not least the characterization of Kakos as a robber chieftain.[218] The core of Dionysios' material seems, then, to derive from (a) republican account(s) of Herakles' exploits, which addressed the deity's popularity across the whole of Italy.

Yet those who, like Scott, argue that 'beyond providing the Latins with an appropriate heroic pedigree, Hercules' civilizing activities in Italy became emblematic of those of the Roman colonies from the later fourth century onwards' (Scott 1992, 93), make an attractive case. Within the narrative of suppression of tyranny, misrule and lawlessness, and the building of roads and cities, opening up Italy to all, it is possible to see the outlines of a justification of the Roman conquest as aiming at the same ends, and commemorated across Italy by the universal veneration of Hercules. The settling of Arkadians, Aborigines and prisoners in territories conquered by others, and above all the building of new *poleis* and roads, recall colonization.[219] The settling of prisoners might be thought to be a means to justify mass movements of population instigated by the Romans in the third and second centuries. Strabo (5. 4.13 = 251C) mentions Picentine deportations to Campania, Livy (40.38, 41) the deportation of Ligurians (note their presence in the Hercules myth above) to Samnium (where – as in the rest of central Italy – the worship of Hercules was very popular).[220]

It is tempting, then, to see, behind Dionysios' rationalizing account, a later-second-century BC historical source, using Herakles' Italian wanderings as a charter myth for Roman conquest and colonization as it had been known up to that point.[221] The archaeological evidence for the antiquity and ubiquity of Hercules' cult in colonial contexts seems to find in Dionysios an echo which may allow us to restore at least *some* of its original ideological content. Hercules had more varied local meaning than perhaps any other deity;[222] but he was also susceptible, at least by the second century, to being made to carry a number of messages about what the Romans were doing in Italy, and what their colonies stood for; and carrying them in a way which, moreover, looked familiar in a local context. That large parts of central Italy had enthusiastically embraced the cult of Hercules since the archaic period meant that for a Roman Hercules carrying such messages, there was a 'Sabellic' Hercules who might act as an interlocutor, as at Alba Fucens.

6. What about Iuppiter?[223]

'The colonies of Rome contained their versions of the Capitoline Temple of Jupiter, evoking the hill at the heart of the mother city and the ruling god who guaranteed Roman military success' (Horden and Purcell 2000, 457). That it was partly through cult, and the reproduction of cult (Horden and Purcell 2000, 457–9), that colonizers and colonists conceptualized their world and the multiplicity of their relations, seems clear enough for later periods than ours. We have just reviewed ample evidence, however, that mid-republican Roman and Latin colonies began life as communities oriented by cardinal points of cult place and practice which, while they may find points of correspondence, if not more, in Rome, may also equally be transformed survivals of local religious practice. Furthermore, it remains to be demonstrated that they used the cult of Capitoline Iuppiter as a cultic cardinal point, as a method of understanding their cosmos. The cult of Iuppiter was of supreme importance at Tarracina, but this was the local Iuppiter Anxur. At Tarracina, Ostia and Minturnae, at Ariminum, Cosa, and Alba Fucens, it seems that Iuppiter Greatest and Best came late, if at all, under the Republic. Despite the imperfections of our evidence, it seems clear that where he was present, it was as a junior partner. Local deities, especially perhaps Hercules, overshadow the Capitoline triad so completely as to leave it almost totally blotted out.

Here, of course, it is vital to distinguish between Roman and Latin colonies. Granted, however, that Iuppiter Optimus Maximus would be odd in a Latin colony, nevertheless his other *epiklēseis* are hardly prominent before the end of the third century. Only, perhaps, at Cosa, was Iuppiter – in an unknown manifestation, perhaps Latiaris – important from an early date, and there traces of the worship of Hercules seem to have chronological priority. Replication stands beside re-invention. The world viewed and understood through the geography and topography of cult was not that of the late Republic; and it was different for Romans and Latins, for almost as long as their difference from each other meant anything.

By the late Republic the Capitoline Triad had established itself as the normative model of Roman colonial cult (Latin colonies in Italy had by then ceased to exist). Ch. 70 of the *lex* (charter) of the Caesarian colony of Urso in Spain specifies, for example, *ludi scaenici* (games with theatrical entertainment) in honour of Iuppiter, Iuno and Minerva. More than a century earlier at Luna, a Roman colony founded in 177 BC (Liv. 41.13.4; Harris 1989, 114–18 on the historical context), a three-*cella* temple, unmistakably a Capitolium, seems to have been built in the first years of the colony's life (Rossignani 1985, 55–7) (*Fig.* 5).[224] The rise of the Capitolia profoundly altered the cultic balance of Roman communities, their physical appearance, and their sense of identity. When did it happen, and why?

The growth of the Capitoline cult as a mould for expressing Roman identity and power was a gradual product of three interlocking processes. Firstly there is the increasing dominance of Rome's position in and beyond Italy in the third century. Within a generation of the battle of Sentinum (295 BC), which effectively ended the possibility of challenges from within the Italian peninsula, Rome was embroiled in an ambitious and far-reaching war with Carthage. Victory here, partly dependent on skilful manipulation of her Italian resources, gave Rome a new confidence, which reached stratospheric levels after the end of the second Punic War (Gruen 1992, 131–82). From this point we witness, proportional to the growth in Roman power

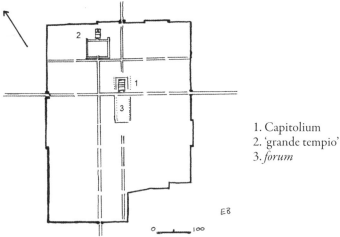

1. Capitolium
2. 'grande tempio'
3. *forum*

Fig. 5. Luna.

and influence, the gradual worsening of relations with her Italian allies, and a corresponding increase both in the value of Roman citizenship and the importance of Roman identity.[225] This confident season, at the turn of the third and second centuries, was the point at which Romans, beginning with Fabius Pictor and Cincius Alimentus, first felt the need to formulate *in extenso* (and historiographically, Curti 2001, 21; Beck and Walter 2001, 17–19, 22–6, 48) who they were, and how they had got to where they were, adapting the Hellenistic medium of prose history. Such assessments of Rome's character, achievements and mission were for internal as much as external consumption.

Secondly, the growth of Roman power, and the new formulations of its ideologies, were based on, and visible in, new wealth: the profits of conquest and empire, which mainly ended up in elite Roman hands. Much of this wealth was spent on private luxury, some on public munificence, employing the new media of Hellenistic art and architecture, together with new techniques such as concrete construction, to begin embellishing Rome, through competition rather than centralized direction, as a city worthy of imperial aspirations. Such innovations were, however, slower to reach parts of Italy away from the Tyrrhenian littoral (and slower in some of those areas than others).[226] Colonies no less than allied cities were relatively, perhaps increasingly, isolated from the main currents of cultural change. Perhaps because of the relatively small territories of citizen colonies,[227] some local elites may have lacked the resources to undertake energetic monumentalization on the scale, or in the style, required by the new *Zeitgeist*.[228]

Thirdly, and less directly, the elites of the older Roman colonies will have heard about the new Roman colonies founded in the north of Italy in the early second century BC, and felt some need perhaps to emulate, or try to keep up with, the urbanistic standards of these new foundations, which in size, prosperity and opportunities had effectively replaced the Latin colony as a vehicle of Roman military and social policy. After 184 BC Graviscae was the only old-style *colonia maritima* founded;[229] the older ones may have felt culturally marginalized.

How did these new outlooks and pressures change Rome's conceptions of herself and her colonies, and the faces of the colonies themselves? Let us take urban change first. Where local economic constraints meant that cities and their elites could not follow the Roman model unaided, the *urbs*, or her leading men, stepped in to complete prestige projects of communal value, such as temples.[230] Much intervention happened through manubial benefactions – related to the creation of ties of *clientela* (patron-client relationships) – by individual generals,[231] and through the activities of Roman censors. These developments mainly affected the *ager Romanus*, above all citizen colonies, but urban change was not confined to juridical limits. The Roman-inspired monumentalization of both Minturnae and Cosa[232] should be viewed as different manifestations of the power of the same Roman urbanistic dynamo.[233]

The most striking example of censorial intervention in Italy is that of Q. Fulvius Flaccus and A. Postumius Albinus in 174.[234] It is important to note that the works listed are paid for from colonial funds (*ipsorum pecunia*), not Roman. Unusual are (a) the fact that Roman censors held the *locatio* (bidding for contract), and (b) the unprecedented scale of the work. It is worth setting out in full Livy's account (41.27.5–13); the text is corrupt at crucial points, and I have not gone beyond what is printed in Briscoe's 1986 Teubner edition.[235]

> (5) the censors for the first time ever awarded contracts for paving the roads in the city in basalt, and for building up the roads outside the city with gravel, and defining their edges, and for building bridges in many places; (6) and for providing a stage for the aediles and the praetors; <and> starting-gates in the circus, and eggs for ?numbering the signs (of the laps) for the chariots…and the turning posts…and iron cages b<y which wild beasts> could be introduced…festivals on the Alban mount for the consuls. (7) And they saw to the paving of the Capitoline slope in basalt, and a porticus from the temple of Saturn up to the Capitolium as far as the *senaculum* [place of assembly for the Senate] and beyond that the *curia* [Senate house], (8) and outside the *porta Trigemina* they paved the *emporium* [business area] with stone and fenced it off with bollards, and saw to the rebuilding of the *porticus Aemilia*, and made an approach with steps from the Tiber into the *emporium*. (9) And within the same gate they paved a porticus onto the Aventine with basalt, and made…public? … from the temple of Venus. (10) The same censors awarded contracts for building walls at Calatia and Auximum; and when public spaces had been sold there, they spent the money which had been realized in surrounding the *forum* with shops on each side. (11) And one of them, Fulvius Flaccus – for Postumius ?said that he would award contracts for nothing unless on the order of the Roman Senate and people…– ? let a contract with the money of those colonists (?) for a temple of Iuppiter at Pisaurum and at Fundi and at Po<t>entia, also for bringing in water, and at Pisaurum for paving the road with basalt, (12) and at Sinuessa…? for bird-keeping …, and in these both for bringing round sewers and a wall…and for closing off the *forum* with porticoes and shops and building three arches. (13) These works were contracted out by one censor to the great gratitude of the colonists.[236]

This activity led to a quarrel between the censors, with Postumius objecting to the scale of Flaccus' proposals: the role of the Fulvii in the foundation of Pisaurum and Potentia perhaps explains in part Postumius' opposition to intervention which would disproportionately benefit his colleague (Guidobaldi and Pesando 1989, 43). Note how the embellishment of Rome is matched by building work in the *ager Romanus*; it was within precisely this sort of state-stimulated urbanistic activity that Brown (1980, 44) contextualized the building activity in the Cosan *forum*, with its new architectural styles.[237] Nevertheless, there was apparently no matching, state-stimulated, intervention in Latin colonies in 174 (Guidobaldi 1988, 129; Guidobaldi and Pesando 1989, 41), and this is probably (as Brown suggests, 1980, 44) related to their independent status. Those Latin states with access to new cultural models had to fend for themselves, while Roman (or Fulvius Flaccus') interest focused, as Livy's comment (*haec ab uno censore opera locata cum magna gratia colonorum*) shows, on Roman colonies and colonists.[238]

Calatia (not a colony) and Auximum, which perhaps was one at this point, were given walls, even full circuits; the colonies of Pisaurum and Potentia, as well as the *municipium* (chartered town) of Fundi had temples of Iuppiter built, and enhancements to their water supply; in addition, at Pisaurum a road (the *decumanus maximus*, the main street?) was paved with basalt. At the colony of Sinuessa there was substantial building work which affected the walls and sewers, and saw the recreation of the *forum* as an enclosed Hellenistic-style space surrounded by shops and porticoes, and served by three arches or Iani.[239] Through this building work Q.Fulvius Flaccus was facilitating the closure of what had become an urbanistic gap between new and old colonies, by modernizing and monumentalizing. The developments at Minturnae form part of the same phenomenon, and may have been sponsored by local elites.[240]

What is significant for us is that part of the official package in 174 was the creation of new temples of Iuppiter in two colonies; besides these we first hear of the Minturnian and Ostian Iuppiter temples in the late third and early second centuries respectively. These temples of Iuppiter do not in themselves signify the genesis of a Capitoline ideology in Roman colonies from the late third century onwards; but they do look like a more significant clustering of attestations when set beside changes in the ideological value of the Capitoline cult at Rome in exactly these years.

I have argued that Rome's successes during the third century went hand in hand with an adjustment of identity which finds clear expression in the first Roman histories. One concern of the new historical paradigm for Rome was to present a past which gave assurances of future greatness, as well as one from which egregious weakness and failure, at least on the part of the commonwealth, had been edited out. Above all, Rome must never have known absolute defeat or capture; and, unparalleled as such a state was in the mutable world of the Mediterranean, it must depend on the especial favour of the gods: see, for example, the straight-faced claim in an official letter to Teos, early in the second century, that the support of the supreme deity had been responsible for Roman success (Sherk 1969 no. 34 [= Sherk 1984 no. 8] l. 15).

It was, of course Iuppiter Optimus Maximus who guaranteed the fundamental and immutable victory of Rome across the years, and who guided its destiny. As a corollary, while the bulk of the city might lie in ruins, Iuppiter's shrine must remain untouched: hence, as scholars have argued, the story in which the Gauls did not sack the Capitol. This seems to have replaced another version, only scrappily represented in the surviving sources, which knew of a capture of the sacred hill (Skutsch 1968, 138–42; Sordi 1984; Williams 2001a, 150–70). Small wonder that the earliest Roman history, that of Fabius Pictor, shows a particular interest in the Capitolium: it contained the story (F 12P) of the naming of the Capitolium from the *caput Oli* (the head of Olus), a story which marked the status of the Capitoline hill and temple as, in Williams' words (2001a, 170), the 'symbol of the eternity of the city *par excellence*'.[241]

Such stories may have been invented by Pictor, but they are more likely to have evolved across the second half of the third century, reflecting changing Roman self-perceptions, shaped by victory and survival against the odds, the Celts, and Carthage.[242] It is beside this reshaping of Capitoline history in Rome that we must locate the appearance of colonial Iuppiter temples and Capitolia. Colonies now began to be seen increasingly as replicating and underpinning a particular type of Roman power, that of the eternal imperial city, whose *imperium* was guaranteed by Iuppiter himself; as a consequence, beginning in northern Italy, Roman colonies became more similar to each other.[243] In the late third century Iuppiter becomes a noticeable part of the colonial pantheon for the first time, and by the time of the foundation of Luna in 177, it was becoming unthinkable that a Roman colony should not have a temple to the Capitoline triad.[244]

7. Conclusions

Conventional 'Capitoline' accounts of colonization have proven less than satisfactory. Much remains to be done to bring out the character and complexity of both Roman and Latin colonization in the middle Republic; a good start will be the questioning of articles of faith in our current models. Let us briefly take a single example.

Standard accounts see all Roman maritime colonies founded before the second decade of the second century BC as small garrison settlements of 300 souls. The clutch of colonies (Puteoli, Buxentum, Liternum etc.) founded in the 190s are explicitly said by Livy (34.45.1) to have had 300 colonists each, and there is no special reason to doubt this. The only other explicit attestation is for Tarracina in the fourth century, again from Livy (8.21.11). Here the size of the plots (2 *iugera*) is suspiciously small, corresponding to the traditional *heredium* (hereditary estate); yet the number of colonists may be correct: Coppola (1984, 326) points out how limited was the land available in the immediate vicinity of the settlement, squeezed as it was between the Monti Lepini and the sea. There is, however, absolutely no reason to assume that 300 colonists was a *standard* number for Roman maritime foundations in this period; in fact the only other figure attested for the number of colonists for this period is, as we shall see, 500. Assumptions about numbers of colonists, or attempts to work out how well or ill 300 men could have defended a colonial wall circuit, are baseless.[245]

Under 378 BC Diodoros (15.27.4) tells us: 'While these things were going on [the liberation of the Theban Kadmeia from the Spartans] the Romans sent out five hundred colonists with immunity from taxes to Sardinia.' This notice, and one in Theophrastos about Corsica, presumably also referring to the fourth century (*HP* 5.8.2, 'they say that the Romans, wishing to establish a city, once sailed to the island with twenty-five ships'), have been needlessly doubted by Salmon (1969, 14 n.7), and, with some honourable exceptions (e.g. Torelli 1982; 1993, 100 f.), have found little place in mainstream scholarly discussion of colonization. Yet the episode is entirely comprehensible: Cornell 1995, 212, 321 f., notes the synchronism with closer Roman relations with Caere, which certainly would have had trading interests on the islands, perhaps for Corsican fir, whose merits provide the context of Theophrastos' precious contemporary comment. Roman settlement in these islands in turn also allows us to make more sense of the prohibition in the second Romano-Carthaginian treaty recorded by Polybios (3.24.11), and normally dated to 348 BC, on Romans founding *poleis* outside Italy.

These two colonies either failed, or evolved very differently from their Italian cousins; in any event, they illustrate beautifully the breadth and diversity which we have to allow to the category of *colonia* before the second century BC. By that date, ideas of what was a colony were by no means fixed, but were already hardening, with clearer boundaries.[246] This, perhaps, is why the histories which began to be written in this period by Romans (as opposed to earlier Greek accounts) do not mention these settlements overseas. Politics hi-jacked history. The optimate opposition to C. Gracchus attacked his ill-judged attempt to found Iunonia (the names of his other colonies – Neptunia Tarentum, Minervia Scolacium, Vell. Pat. 1.15.4 – are intriguing) on the site of Carthage, using *mos maiorum* to bolster their attack. Never, it was said, had the *maiores* wished to found colonies outside Italy; this tradition is still clearly visible in Velleius' account of the events, for example (1.15.1, 2.7.6–8). Very probably it was this pseudo-history of colonization which misled Salmon and others into denying the fourth-century overseas colonies.[247]

Modern analysis has thus been conditioned by the second century BC propaganda which lies behind later literary accounts.

This chapter began with a sceptical look at the images often unreflectively and synchronically applied to Roman colonies, both as urban units, and in terms of their foundation rituals. Evocations of Roman religious topography we have discussed; political topography too often features in the standard accounts. Here the *comitium* (popular assembly-place) plays a major role: the fine circular *comitia* (or structures identified as *comitia*) at Alba Fucens, Cosa, Paestum and Aquileia have often been used, along with group voting, to show how Latin colonies (not Roman ones, note) consciously modelled their political process and civic community on those of the founding city.[248] These *comitia*, despite their differences, are very like each other; but are they like the Roman *comitium*? New research on the latter, above all by Carafa, has reduced the certainty which once existed about its form, leaving substantial doubts over the date, duration, and even the existence, of a circular phase, on which the Latin colonial *comitia* are supposed to be modelled.[249] Certainly the Latin *comitia* might be *symbolic* evocations of the Roman *comitium*, but in the present state of research it looks unlikely that they were intended to be close copies of it. Detailed evocations of the micro-topography of the Roman *comitium* are scarcely easier to see than those of the Roman *arx*.[250]

The synthetic picture of the foundation ritual often painted is, for the mid-republican period, equally unhelpful. Consider one counter-example, of a sort of ritual behaviour for which our literary sources do not encourage us to look. It may encourage us to think of diversity and difference, rather than pervasive little Romes. Recent excavations under a section of the first wall of the colony at Ariminum produced what seems to be a votive deposit connected with the building of the wall. It comprises three coins (one local, one cast pre-colonial Roman, and one stamped colonial), and the skeleton of a dog. The colonial coin seems to have been issued at the time of the foundation of the colony, and it is hard not to follow Ortalli, and interpret this as a sacrificial deposition, perhaps a foundation deposit.[251] Associated with the building of the wall, the deposit is thus associated with an early moment in the life of the colony, if not the foundation itself. Neither here, nor at Alba Fucens, where trenches near the Porta di Massa and elsewhere have produced complete open (thus probably votive) BG vases and large numbers of animal bones, associated with a rebuilding of the walls,[252] is there any trace of the *sulcus primigenius* sought by Brown at Cosa, and usually assumed elsewhere. Ritual ploughing was certainly happening in the first century BC (sometimes for colonies set up in existing settlements, as at Casilinum), but was it used for early colonies?[253] Varro (*LL* 5.143) says that towns founded by ploughing the original furrow along the line of the future walls are *urbes* (cities), and that 'therefore all our colonies are called *urbes* in ancient writings'; yet, writing in the first half of the second century BC, the Elder Cato, according to Servius (*ad Aen.* 5.755 = F 18P), says that ploughing the original furrow was the practice of founders of a *ciuitas* (community) – as quoted he says nothing about colonies.

It would be, of course, unreasonable to expect to find the traces of an ephemeral intervention like a plough furrow in complex urban stratification. We must take account of what we find from the time of foundation itself, before we read back later ideological matrices and their content, and extrapolate from the comfortable synthesis of late-republican and Augustan antiquarianism (and its modern followers). At Cosa, we have an early sacrificial deposit in a pit from the colony's high place, pehaps dating to the period of the foundation. It might be a *mundus*, but it is not at once obvious that it was; in any case, the presence in it of vessels dedicated to Hercules suggests that he was invoked at that early religious ritual. Whatever the relation of any foundation ritual to Iuppiter, Hercules is the deity with observable priority here. At Ariminum, the strength of the walls, and the symbolic barrier they embodied, seem to have been protected by the sacrifice of a dog, and the deposition of three different coins, at a time (again) not distant from the foundation. Whatever foundation means for us, it must be something which embraces this diversity of ritual beginnings, at least for Latin colonies; we need to accept that what was done to make the new community auspicious in the eyes of the gods *may have been nothing like what later writers represent*. There was a change, no doubt, and I have suggested above that it is related to the adoption of a more Romanocentric, 'Capitoline', colonial ideology, implicated in new manifestations of Roman power.

Leaving aside broad yet important similarities between Rome and her colonies (Roman or Latin), such as the augurally-rooted distinction between *urbs* and *ager* (Torelli 1999, 52–6), or the use of Roman units of measurement and their subdivisions (at Cosa the *actus*, Scott 1988, 75; Cambi and Celuzza 1985, 104; cf. Greco 1988, 86 for the *territorium* of Paestum), we might well ask 'what, if anything, was *characteristic* of Roman colonies in the third century?' For all Fentress' penetration in her deconstruction of Brown's assumptions in his interpretation of Cosa (2000b, 24, 'That Cosa was, in some sense, Rome seems to us unproven'), the underlying assumption is still that there is such a thing as a 'standard' colony. She writes (2000, 11) 'in many ways it is an odd colony'. Better to ask: which colonies were normal?

In a stimulating paper, Robin Osborne (1998) argued that archaic Greek colonization should be seen as the result of opportunistic activity by highly mobile groups and individuals, and that such colonies were neither sent out by, nor had (largely) exclusive relations with, 'mother cities': in fact that they were not colonies at all. The settlement abroad of Greeks in the eighth and seventh centuries should be distinguished from the state-organized emigrations of the classical Greek, and Roman,[254] periods. Of the latter it can generally be said that they envisaged equality of lots at a pre-selected site, under a named founder sent by the colonizing state, and often reflected commercial or 'military and agrarian concerns' (1998, 252, 254, 268).[255] The foundation stories of archaic Greek colonies, for Osborne, represent later attempts to account for success, to invent a prestigious and clear-cut past out of a fuzzy and often unflattering history (1998, 262–8). They are a later attempt, made for contingent political or cultural motives, to invent a 'big bang' (1998, 265; or a series of such bangs: Clarke 1999, 264–76 on foundation and refoundation in Strabo).

Such an argument, although not the last word (see Wilson 2000 for further reflections) has a lot to be said for it. Rather than enforce, however, the distinction between archaic Greek and Roman underpinning Osborne's analysis, we might want to steal his clothes, and deconstruct the idea of dirigiste state-organized colonization for the early and middle Republic. I have argued above that much of the canonical ritual and ideology (above all the Capitoline) in which colonization narratives are embedded is probably not that of the middle Republic, let alone earlier; and that the discourse of replication has no place at that period. What about stories of founders? It would be very comforting if, because Festus was an antiquarian, we could rely on the names he gives for the *triumviri* who led out the Latin colony to Saticula (313 BC, Festus 458L; note also Velleius' information on Setia, 382 BC, 1.14.2). Yet we cannot: Asconius' confusion over the identity of the *triumviri* at Placentia, in a later period, when they ought to have been known, surely shows as much (Crawford 1995, 188). The possibility remains open that the aura of state foundations, like canonical lists and definitions and sizes of colonies, is a retrojection, kitted out with plausible (perhaps correct) founders' names, to hide a fuzzier past.

In this paper elements of material culture, and evidence for colonial cults, have both been examined. They have been found to offer little or no comfort to 'Gellian' or 'Capitoline' models of colonization in this period. While we should reject a relativism which removes the brutal nature of Roman aggression and conquest, it is nonetheless true that Roman and Latin colonies adapted and transformed local cults, allowing greater integration with local populations.[256] The nature of the colony, its cults, its senses of identity and its relations to Rome were different, strikingly so, in the late Republic and early Empire from those which we can observe for the middle Republic.

When I first heard a report of the paper which became Osborne 1998, from David Ridgway, it was couched in the form of 'Osborne telling us not to think of archaic Greek colonization as being like Roman colonization'. The remark is *ben trovato* if not genuine. As far as the early and middle Republic are concerned, if we imagine the creation of Roman and Latin colonies as being less like 'Roman colonization' we will be doing rather well.

Acknowledgements

My thanks are due to the editors (and to Anton Powell) for their inexhaustible patience and helpful suggestions on content and style; to those who commented on the original paper, especially Michael Crawford, Irad Malkin, Lawrence Keppie and John North; to those who have helped since, by discussing ideas with me and answering questions: Lisa Bligh, Matthew Leigh, Stephen Mitchell, Llewelyn Morgan, Robin Osborne, Mara Pellegrini, Jordi Principal, Andrew Wilson; to Susan Kane for making temple terracottas interesting; and to Nicholas Purcell, who read the entire piece and made a number of provocative and penetrating suggestions. None of them, however, are responsible for my mistakes. All translations are my own unless stated otherwise.

Notes

[1] Translation from Beard, North and Price 1998, 2, 241 f.; discussion at Beard, North and Price 1998, 1, 329 f.

[2] See for example, Malkin 1987; 1994; but note Tréziny 1997.

[3] On the 'kit' and common city-plans of Augustan colonies, and their meaning, see Vitruvius, *De Arch.* 1.7.1. See generally Torelli 1988b, 132–47; Mouritsen 1998, 76, 118 (including Latin colonies); Laurence 1999, 150; Zanker 2000, 27 f., 33, 35 f., 40 f. For Zanker (2000, 26) colonial 'borrowings' from Rome may be limited to specific structures, which are the outward markers of political or institutional activity. As with political topography, political institutions are also modelled on those of Rome: Sherwin-White 1973, 117 f. (suggesting that Roman and Latin colonies borrowed from each other rather than directly from Rome), 413. On Capitolia: Barton 1982, 259–65; Stambaugh 1988, 247.

[4] *cinctus Gabinus*: Livy 8.9.9, 10.7.3; Servius, *ad Aen.* 5.755 = Cato F18P; Festus 251L., s.v. 'procincta classis' is about fighting not ploughing, and does not mention the head being covered with the toga; ploughing and first fruits: Varro, *LL* 5.143, Ov. *Fast* 4. 820–6, Plut. *Rom.* 11; burying objects of good omen in the ground: Festus 310, 312 L. A synthesis of these elements is the basis of accounts of foundation ritual in standard introductions to urbanism, e.g. Stambaugh 1988, 9 n. 2, Torelli 1988b, 141.

[5] Stambaugh 1988, 244.

[6] e.g. Woolf 1998; papers in Webster and Cooper 1996, Mattingly 1997, Fentress 2000a (esp. Zanker 2000), and Keay and Terrenato 2001 (note Terrenato 2001b on alternative constructions of the impact of Roman colonial settlement at Pisae and Luna, esp. 56); on the common characteristics of material culture across the Augustan empire: MacMullen 2000.

[7] Cf. Morris 1994, 10 f., on problems with synchronic accounts of ritual.

[8] In a footnote to the passage quoted just above, Stambaugh reveals the flimsiness of the construct, and the ways in which archaeological and textual evidence are invoked in

mutual support: 'No ancient text specifically states that these rituals were conducted at the founding of colonies, but it seems a safe inference, based on the allusions in ancient sources to the ritual at the foundation of Rome and the archaeological data from Cosa and elsewhere' (1988, 244 n. 2); as we shall see, the interpretation of the archaeological data is conditioned by the same literary sources which are supposed to provide independent confirmation.

⁹ Wiseman 1995; cf. Erskine 2001, chap. 1, esp. 26–36, on the Trojan myth as unremarkable and not central to Roman identity before Augustus, who transformed it (*contra* Torelli 1999, 165–81).

¹⁰ Cf. Rüpke 2001, 101. That late-republican and early imperial focalizations of the Capitoline Triad did not always overlap is suggested by a comparison of two versions of a speech attributed to Scipio Africanus before he ascended the Capitol in 187 BC, one in Valerius Antias (= Gellius *NA* 4.18.3) and the other in Livy (38.51.7–11): the latter has Scipio invoke the Capitoline Triad, the former only Iuppiter Optimus Maximus.

¹¹ For the Augustan period see Zanker 2000, 37 f., 39–41, on theatres and amphitheatres, and new forms of monumentalization of public space under the Principate.

¹² *lex coloniae Iuliae Ursonensis* (translation from Crawford 1996, I, no. 25), ch. 103. Sherwin-White perceptively wrote of this text: 'The citizen colony as the perfect image and picture of Rome makes its first appearance in our sources at the close of the domination of Julius Caesar' (1973, 80). In my view, however, this is not solely a function of the paucity of our sources for earlier periods, but tells us something about colonization and its contexts at this period; and what we see here is not simply *imitatio Romae* ('imitation of Rome'), but an attempt to ensure that in a non-veteran colony far from Rome, magistrates were obeyed without question in emergencies.

¹³ For Torelli, 1988b, 131 f., the 'Romulean' imaginary of the city is a fourth-century rationalizing construction, whose basis can be traced back through augural practice to much earlier times. Note, however, Zanker, 2000, 37, arguing for substantial continuity in 'the notion of the urban center as a political symbol' between the Middle Republic and Augustus.

¹⁴ For a deconstruction of the 'urban variable' as a separate category of enquiry (at least from an ecological point of view), see Horden and Purcell 2000, ch. 4, with 553–61.

¹⁵ Cf. the statist position of Coarelli 1992, 21–8. See also Potter 1979, 104; Laurence 1999, 5, 14, 19–26, 79–81, 94, 127, 188, 192, with further perspectives and contextual nuances (but note 25); ibid. 27, 33, 38, importantly setting colonization in a wider context of town-foundation; 36, 78 on the gap between the foundation of the colonies and the building of roads (but note Williams 2001a, 15: the reverse is true of the Via Aemilia in the second century); and 1999, 120, roads rather than waterways linked the first Cisalpine colonies; Zanker 2000, 29.

¹⁶ Zanker, 2000, 28 f., has a very statist interpretation of the rationale behind the basic armature of colonial urbanism. Laurence, 1999, 26, notes how Rome's main ports were colonies.

¹⁷ One might look in such terms at the impact of the supposed 'ethnic cleansing' of the *ager Cosanus* in the third century BC, for which see Fentress 2000b, 12 f.

¹⁸ See also 189, 212, 219 f., 229, 248, 254, 256, 260 f., 265, 294, 318, 323, 328 f., 334, 582 f., 592–4, 600 on interventions in various environments associated with resettlement and colonization; 426, 430, 434 f., 436, 457, 627, 631 on religion and colonization; and 344, 347, 348, 349, 352 f., 376, 379, 383, 385, 386, 388, 395–400, 469, 607, 609, 616,

617, 618, 619, 620 f. on connectivity and colonization. To list individual page references to colonization here is, however, to ignore the wider context of *mobility* of all types, frequencies and intensities, within which the authors locate our phenomenon.

[19] *pedites* and *equites*: Copia-Thurii (Livy 35.9.7–8, lots of 20 and 40 *iugera*); Vibo Valentia (Livy 35.40.5–6, 15 and 30 *iugera*); Placentia (Asconius p. 3C, 200 hundred *equites* out of 6,000). Three property classes: Aquileia: Livy 40.34.2; Bononia: Livy 37.57.7 f.; 40.34.3–4; see Bandelli 1988, 107–9. For a later differential between *pedites*, centurions and *evocati* (veterans called back into service): Caes. *BG* 1.17. 4. For Salmon, 1969, 15 n.9, these divisions (and the use of *adscribere* – Livy 31.49.6 (Venusia, 200 BC), and *scribere* – Livy 37.47. 2 (Cremona and Placentia, 190 BC) for enrolling colonial supplements) underline the military nature of the colonies; the other passages cited by Salmon refer instead to the raising of Latin military forces. As for the 'military structuring' of these colonies, if accepted, how far back in time can it be read? The new theory of differential house-plot size propounded by Fentress (2000b, 15, 18; for a different, functionalist, interpretation of these data, see Torelli 1988b, 141), on the basis of the recent excavations in the *forum* at Cosa, is referred to the second rather than the third century. It is not even a given that these status divisions 'simply mapped in an orderly fashion Rome's own foundations in rank and order' (Fentress 2000b, 20). I do not propose to discuss here the supposed archaic *heredium* of 2 *iugera* (accepted, for example, for historical colonization by Torelli 1988b, 128 f., 148), on which see Drummond 1989, 121, with bibliography there cited.

[20] On this see Bernardi 1946; Gabba 1958, 98; 1988, 20 f.

[21] See also Oebel 1993, on the distributions of the *ager Gallicus*.

[22] Gabba 1988, also seeing Latin colonies as vehicles for integrating non-Roman elements (*incolae*) into Roman-style social structures.

[23] On Ostia see now Torelli 1999, 29–31.

[24] Crawford 1995.

[25] Cf. Salmon 1954. See also Torelli 1988b, 127–32, and from a different perspective, Gargola 1995.

[26] On this passage of Aulus Gellius (*NA* 16.13.8–9) see Bispham 2000, 157 f.; on its Hadrianic context, namely of increasing municipalization in the Roman Empire, and the aspirations of provincial cities to the title of *colonia*, given by a reluctant Hadrian, see Sherwin-White 1973, 253, 257, 262 f., 267, 272, 274, 378; and ibid. 362 f., 376, 413 f. (Hadrian talking about republican or triumviral *municipia* only).

[27] Note especially the appendix to Salmon's introduction: 'Cosa: a typical Latin colony' (1969, 29–39). On Latin colonies see also Bernardi 1973. For the continuing importance of Cosa as a type-site for Roman colonization, see Gargola 1995, 83.

[28] Fentress 2000b, 11, points out that Brown *set out* to study Etruscan town planning, and the wider impact of Rome on urbanism.

[29] Zanker 2000, 35, rightly argues that while this might evoke Roman topography, the general situation at Cosa is too common in Italy to be ascribed to a 'Roman' urban plan; Lippolis and Baldini Lippolis, 1997, 311, argue that the two possible *arces* at Brundisium recall the situation at Alba Fucens, and perhaps Rome too – but Rome had only one *arx*!

[30] Brown 1980, 11 and fig. 10, 36, 51 f.; 18, 24 f., 33, 41; 22–4, 27 (*curia* modelled on the Roman one 'as one must suppose'), 28 (cf. Varro, *LL* 5. 155); Scott 1985c, 96; Brown 1980, 31 f. (a 'rectilinear copy' of the Roman, 32), Scott 1985c, 96; Brown 1980, 33–6;

Scott 1985c, 96; Brown 1980, 36 ('Noting that Rome's fish market at the time adjoined one side of its Forum...'); Scott 1985c, 96; cf. Stambaugh 1988, 258. Torelli adopts a similar line of argument: the assemblage of public structures at Cosa at the start of the second century closely matches the typologies of public buildings found in Rome before the onset of Hellenization, underlining the degree to which Cosa depended on Rome for its spatial identity and building types (1983, 244–7). On Brown and the *comitia* of Cosa and Rome see Fentress 2000b, 22 f.

[31] Anachronistic language, but (at the period at which Cosa assumed its monumental republican form, i.e. the early decades of the second century) colonies very like each other were being founded as a part of the transformation of Gallia Cisalpina; the creation of a strikingly uniform and homogeneous 'provincial landscape' can in part be explained by the shared cultural values and habits of the Roman aristocrats who implemented these changes: Purcell 1990, Williams 2001b, 94–7; a colonial office of the mind, if you like.

[32] Cosa remains for Fentress 'a fundamental source for Roman colonization in the Republic' (2000b, 11); cf. Taylor 2002, 60, on the influence of Brown and Richardson's work.

[33] On Brown's method, circularity and begging of the question, see Fentress 2000b, 13, and for a fuller review, in the light of new evidence, of Brown's conclusions about the *atria publica*, 2000, 14–20. See also Terrenato 2001b, 65, citing Cosa as one of half-a-dozen 'over-played pieces of evidence' on the homogeneity of 'Roman' Italy – '[m]oreover, once the case-studies are fully contextualized, they can be thoroughly deconstructed and shown to be the exceptions rather than the rule'.

[34] Other queries might be made about Brown's conclusions, for instance on the *carcer*: '*Oddly enough*, Cosa's *carcer* seems to be the only one which has been identified outside Rome' (1980, 32), my italics.

[35] Note also the alternative interpretation: the post holes were for temporary stage buildings (Brown 1980, 41, Scott 1985c, 96); and now Mouritsen 2004.

[36] *NA* 16.13.8–9. *Sed coloniarum alia necessitudo est; non enim veniunt extrinsecus in civitatem nec suis radicibus nituntur, sed ex civitate quasi propagatae sunt et iura institutaque omnia populi Romani, non sui arbitrii, habent. quae tamen condicio, cum sit magis obnoxia et minus libera, potior tamen et praestabilior existimatur propter amplitu-dinem maiestatemque populi Romani, cuius istae coloniae quasi effigies parvae simulac-raque esse quaedam videntur, et simul quia obscura oblitterataque sunt municipiorum iura, quibus uti iam per innotitiam non queunt.* Zanker 2000, 41, takes Gellius to be speaking of the *maiestas populi Romani*, of which the built monumental environment can be seen as the reification; he takes *amplitudinem maiestatemque* as the antecedents of *cuius*, not of *populus Romanus*, as I have done (and as Sherwin-White 1973, 413 did). The direction of attention away from simple physical replication is in any case salutary.

[37] Scott 1988, 73; cf. 75, where the early layout of Cosa is described as 'characteristic of the Roman inspired organization of the colony'; and Brown 1980, 12, 17: 'the ancient ritual of plowing the boundary, *however that may have been accomplished on the rocky hillside*, enclosed the town...' (my italics); 75: Cosa came down 'to archaeologists as the most perfect example of a Roman town in the making during the third and second centuries BC', cf. Scott 1985, 95; 1992, 97. See Fentress 2000b, 11, on Brown's view.

[38] Torelli 1988a, 65–72.

[39] Torelli 1999, 15: 'the reconstruction of the religious phenomena in the earlier...col-onization has been modelled on the situation prevalent in the latter days of the Republic

and in imperial times'.

⁴⁰ Torelli 1988a, 65 f.; Bispham 2000, 157 f.; Torelli 1988b takes a slightly different view, it seems: he asserts that the rituals described in the traditional synthesis were used in foundation (127 f.); and that in the case of Roman colonies, the Romulean imaginary of the fourth century, shaped by and expressed through augural practice, determined the form of the early colonies as *effigies parvae simulacraque* (a tendency from the second century onwards transferred from the urban ensemble to individual buildings, 1988b, 145), but (interestingly) that Latin colonies, while sharing augural practice as a cultural trait with Rome, were not bound to follow the same archetype, hence their (for Torelli, Greek-inspired) physical difference from the Roman *castrum* form.

⁴¹ Torelli 1988a, 66.

⁴² Cf. 1999, 73. For Torelli's more nuanced view, see below.

⁴³ Salmon 1969.

⁴⁴ e.g. Salmon 1969, 70; Siculus Flaccus p. 135 L = 102.22–8 Campbell.

⁴⁵ *CIL* I² 621 = *ILLRP* 324. 'L. Manlius L. f. / Acidinus triu(m)vir / Aquileiae coloniae / deducundae' ('Lucius Manlius Acidinus, son of Lucius, *triumvir* for leading out the colony of Aquileia'). This statue base is to be dated not much later than the foundation of the colony, according to Mommsen (*ad CIL*). For the foundation (181 BC) see Livy 40.34.3.

⁴⁶ Crawford 1995.

⁴⁷ Between three and eight letters are missing according to Clark's apparatus: Crawford suggests 'a.u.c.' *vel sim.*

⁴⁸ *Pis.* p. 3C.

⁴⁹ Some forty *deductiones* are known or confidently surmised. As Crawford has shown, Salmon's attempt (1969, 67–9) to salvage Asconius' credibility, or rather, to damage it by assuming he had confused the original foundation with the refoundation of 190, will not work: 1995, 190.

⁵⁰ 1.14–15. For Velleius as interested in Greek colonization and Italian foundation dates, see Starr 1981, 164; see also Laurence 1999, 169–71.

⁵¹ 1995, 187.

⁵² Crawford 1995, 190.

⁵³ 1995, 190.

⁵⁴ Livy 27.9, esp. 2–3, 5, 7, 9, 11, 13–14. The complaints were first made *in conciliis* ('in assemblies') (2); refusal is made to the consuls when Latin *legationes* ('embassies') arrive in Rome (7); money to pay these troops is also an issue: 7, cf. 14: *quae daretur in stipendium* ('what should be given as pay'). See Nicolet 1985.

⁵⁵ For an interesting case for including Interamna Nahars as a Latin colony, thus breaching the canonical number of 30, see Bradley 2000b.

⁵⁶ Cf. Bispham 2000, 172 on Florus 2.21.12.

⁵⁷ Appian *BC* 1.23. Sherwin-White (1973, 116) is wrong to refer Pliny *NH* 3.30 to this period. In the Social War Venusia joined the enemy, and Aesernia was captured, but such a context is less attractive.

⁵⁸ So too the ideology expressing the closeness of the tie with the Latin colonies, and their role in keeping up population levels.

⁵⁹ Sherwin-White (1973, 36) pointed out that Livy also uses *coloniae Romanae* of Latin communities at 2.16.8, cf. 9.23.2. I would not use the passage under review as evidence in his wider argument about Latin colonies. Sherwin-White's explanation (1973, 99)

of the term *Roman* in our case (based on heavy Latin military contributions to Roman wars) is unconvincing; better to point to what he himself notes elsewhere (1973, 99 f.), namely that these colonies were Roman foundations and heavily populated by Romans (as the Senate itself argued); see further 1973, 102–4, 106.

[60] Crawford 1995, 190 f. with further discussion, noting Philip V's estimate of Rome as founding 70 colonies in his second latter to Larisa (*SIG*[3] 543 [= Austin 1981, no. 60] 29–34).

[61] Festus 276L (*priscae Latinae coloniae appellatae sunt, ut distinguerent a novis, quae postea a populo dabantur*, 'the old Latin colonies were so called, so that they might be distinguished from the new ones, which afterwards used to be granted by the people'); this might reflect another such argument, namely, which *were* the 'old Latin colonies'? Crawford (1995, 191) suggests the early second century as a possible context for the beginning of a process of 'normalization' in the discourse of colonization, at a period when the relative status of Roman and Latin colonies was being debated, with the concept of Latinity being stretched in other ways, as with the granting of Latin status to Carteia in Spain (171 BC, Livy 43.3.1–4).

[62] '[to whichever colonies or] *municipia*, [or] any equivalents of *municipia* or colonies [(there may be) of Roman citizens] or of the Latin name, land [has been] granted by the people or by a decree of the Senate to exploit, [which land those colonies or those *municipia* or any] equivalent of a colony or *municipium* or *municipia* (there may be) shall exploit, which [is] in the *trientabula*, [whatever of that land ---]'. Text and translation from Crawford 1996 I, 116 f., 145.

[63] I deal with this passage further in Bispham, forthcoming chap. 2.

[64] 'Indeed old writers define colonies thus: a colony is a group of those men who were all led out together into a certain place provided with buildings, which they occupied with a fixed right. Others (say): a colony is that which is what is called *apoikia* in Greek; moreover it was called from 'colere' (to till); moreover it is part of the citizenry or allies sent out, where they hold the state by decree of its citizenry, or by the public intention of that people from whom they set out. Moreover colonies are those which were founded through a decree of the people, not through secession.'

[65] Note that the 'Roman' garrison put into Rhegion in the Pyrrhic War, which went on to seize the city, was (according to Polybios, 1.7.6–12), imitating the Mamertini, and numbered 4,000 – a similar size to a Latin colony of these years. In 186 BC some Transalpine Gauls tried to occupy a site near what would later become Aquileia, *oppido condendo*, 'to found a town'. In response to a Roman embassy, it emerged that the emigrants were acting without the *auctoritas* ('authority') of the Gallic *gens* ('people'), who had no idea what they were doing in Italy. I think that we must wonder whether the Gauls really understood the Roman question; in any case, the hegemony of the statist model of colonization by Livy's time, and the deprecation of Gallic randomness, are implicit in the story.

[66] 'But colonies are so called for this reason, because the Romans sent settlers into those *municipia* ['towns'], either to keep under control those very former peoples of the *municipia*, or to repel the attacks of enemies. Indeed they called all the colonies 'maritime', either, in some authors, because the foundations were made by the sea, or, and this explanation satisfies more authorities, they think that they are called maritime, for the reason that Italy extends from the Alps into the sea, and faces external enemies on three sides'.

[67] *De Lege Agraria* 2.73, where he asserts that the Roman *maiores* ('ancestors') *colonias sic idoneis in locis contra suspicionem periculi collocarunt, ut esse non oppida Italiae, sed propugnacula imperii viderentur* ('thus placed colonies in suitable places to guard against suspected danger, such that they should seem to be not towns of Italy, but the ramparts of the empire'). Cicero has an axe to grind here, and his statement must be read in its context; cf. Bradley, this vol. Salmon (1969, 56 n. 68) cites the 'vetus...fama' ('old...story') of Horace *Sat.* 2.1.35–7, that Venusia was founded to protect Rome from attack.

[68] Morel 1988, 62; Ortalli 2000, 503: the ceramic evidence serves to 'comprovare i tenaci legami che la [sc. Ariminum] legavano alla madrepatria' ('prove the strong ties which bound [Ariminum] to the motherland [Rome]'); cf. Fontemaggi and Piolanti 2000, 510: all the *pocola* show 'stretti legami con Roma e l'area laziale' ('close ties with Rome and Latium'); Franchi de Bellis 1995, 369.

[69] Zuffa 1962; Susini 1965, 146–51; Coarelli and Morel 1973; Morel 1988, 60; Franchi de Bellis 1995, 369 (giving a date range of 300–260 BC for the *pocula*); Giovagnetti 1995; Ortalli 2000; and Biordi 1995, 430 and fig. 8 for the coin-impressed cup.

[70] Sanesi 1978, esp. 75 n. 9; and see Morel 1983, 24 and 1988, 54–7, on some implications of potters' signatures; also Hayes 1997, 15–17 on provenance stamps (genuine and other).

[71] Sadly the Ariminate BG under discussion seems either to come from contexts of random redeposition, probably as rubbish (Fontemaggi and Piolanti 2000, 510–11), or not to have been recovered together with useful stratigraphic data (Franchi de Bellis 1995, 368), which means we must substitute speculation for contextual interpretation.

[72] Bispham 2000, 158.

[73] *ILS* 8567: 'K. Serponius made this at Cales in the *vicus* Esquelinus with his (?slaves)' (this resolution of the two final letters is rejected by Morel 1983, 23 and n. 19, who sees our potter as possibly a freedman, on grounds unclear to me; he also reads 'fece(i)', 'I made...'). On the vase see Pagenstecher 1909, no. 121 and Taf. 13 (find spot uncertain), Rocco 1953, 5; Mingazzini 1958; Sanesi 1978, 74 n. 3; Morel 1988, 55, 60 f.; Sanesi, 1978, 76 for the date, surely correct.

[74] Mingazzini 1958.

[75] Sanesi (loc. cit.) sees the *vicus* as a suburb of Cales, perhaps on the basis of the locations of known kiln sites.

[76] Morel 1988, 60, with previous bibliography; Susini 1965, 150.

[77] For the archaic Greek west, shared toponyms are a 'common colonial strategy': Wilson 2000, 39, arguing that they do not prove a link between colony and 'mother-city'.

[78] Morel 1988, 61 and n. 128.

[79] *ILLRP* 77 (Ariminum) on which see Cicala 1995; *ILLRP* 169 (Beneventum, also mentioning *praetores* – a later addition?), 553 (Beneventum).

[80] Cf. Sherwin-White 1973, 99, who includes our colonial consuls among examples of how 'the *coloniae Latinae* appear to imitate Roman institutions with riotous abandon', cf. 117, 'Romanizing tendency', 229; the colony was 'the most definitely Roman of all the...constitutions known to Rome' (speaking of the Augustan period).

[81] Admittedly an argument from silence. We know too little of the magistracies of Aesernia (founded 263 BC; *ILLRP* 526: *II vir*; 527: 'pr(aetor)'?) and Firmum Picenum (264 BC; *ILLRP* 593–4) to exclude a repetition of the experiment there.

[82] *ILLRP* 169 (Beneventum), to judge from its spelling, is a second-century text. The title may have endured for two or three generations. Interestingly, this is the timescale on which ideological and institutional change operates, and it is at this level, what Braudel called 'social time' (1972, 20 f.), rather than that of *histoire événementielle*, that we should be looking to understand this change. A parallel might be the introduction of new tribal names at Sikyon by the tyrant Kleisthenes, which despite being (to Herodotus at least) offensive and anti-Dorian, endured for sixty years (= two generations?) after Kleisthenes' death in *c*. 570 (Hdt. 5.68): the change and its longevity must be explained in terms of evolving *mentalités* as much as snap decisions by individual reformers. For one critique (among many) of Braudel see Horden and Purcell 2000, 36–9; for an application of Braudelian approaches to archaeological analysis, see Barker 1995, 1–11; and Morris 1998, 69–79 (arguing for a methodology where archaeology and literature, social and individual timescales, illuminate each other).

[83] It is true that Beneventum was isolated politically from Roman territory, a Latin island in a sea of *socii* (allies); her two main communication routes to Campania ran through Samnite territory. The mass of Monte Taburno is also a psychological and physical barrier of the first order.

[84] See Guidobaldi 1988, 125 f., on the relative popularity of Roman and Latin colonies in the late fourth and early third centuries, and change in the perception of Roman colonies (or rather Roman citizenship through colonization) by the early second century. Viritane assignations should be factored into this equation.

[85] Torelli 1999, 44.

[86] See Sherwin-White 1973, 205–14, for the suggestion of a model different from that adopted here.

[87] See Mommsen 1887, 623–5; Bernardi 1946, followed by Bandelli 1988, 112 (guarantee of wider *commercium* [right to make legally binding business deals with Romans] and *ius suffragii* [right to vote]); Salmon 1969, 92–4; Sherwin-White 1973, 102–4 (against the creation of a new type of Latinity, with doxography), 109; De Martino 1972–5 II, 99–102, Galsterer 1995; Torelli 1988b, 144, Torelli 1999, 44. *Contra* Coarelli 1985–7, followed by Bandelli 1988, 112: if Luca is counted as a Latin colony, then the identification of the XII colonies gets complicated.

[88] Galsterer, 1976, 122 sees this change as one to modern institutional titulature from one which was perceived as anachronistic.

[89] On Italy see Williams 2001a, 128 f.; on the painting of Italia in the temple of Tellus, see Wiseman 1986, 91; and on Ariminum and Beneventum see Purcell 1990, 10; also Bispham forthcoming, chap. 1.

[90] Liv. 24.44.3, 28.38.13; note also Pomponius Mela 2.4, calling Ariminum a *terminus* (boundary-stone) between Gallic and Italian peoples. See Amat-Seguin 1986, 100; Oebel 1993, 129 f.; Brizzi 1995; Ortalli 1995; Tramonti 1995; Williams 2001a, 133.

[91] Bispham 2000, 158 n. 5. This epigraphic evidence is all imperial. The Puteolan material seems to reflect an Augustan reorganization of the colony, although individual place names may be Republican. It was unknown to Mommsen, who nevertheless suggested that the Ariminate toponyms should be associated with the foundation of the Colonia Augusta Ariminensis (*CIL* XI p. 76). This remains an attractive hypothesis, and it may be that overall the regional nomenclature known from Ariminum is Augustan, incorporating *some* or none of the earlier names (Sanesi 1978, 76 n. 15 raises the same possibility for Cales). Note the third-century BG *poculum* sherds from Ariminum,

mentioning 'PAGE FID' (Susini 1965, 150, no. 6); 'VEICI' (on which see Franchi de Bellis 1995, Tav. II, Fontemaggi and Piolanti 2000, 510, no. 180b); and 'PA' (all illustrated at Susini 1965, pl. 4); Susini (1965, 150 f.) thinks of a *pagus Fidenas*, recalling Fidenate colonists, linked to the *clientela* of the Livii, who played a major role in the conquest of Picenum; judgement is best suspended.

[92] Morel 1988, 62 f.

[93] Morel 1988, 62, applying the same criticism to the idea of the 'Etrusco-Latio-Campanian *koine*' often invoked by scholars, with or without Magna Graecia included: 'cela n'est exact qu'en gros, dans la mesure où l'Italie est une province de l'hellénisme' ('that is only exact in broad terms, to the extent to which Italy is a province of Hellenism').

[94] Torelli 1999, 3 f. for very brief overview, with bibliography.

[95] For the third-century situation, see Bandelli 1988, 105 f. In the second century Polybios normally uses Ariminum as his reference for the southernmost point of the Cisalpine plain (3.61.11, 86.2; but not in book 2: see Williams 2001a, 62–4).

[96] Sanesi 1978, 77.

[97] On Luceria see Torelli 1999, 92 f., 95, 172 (on Latin moulds for terracottas), and 124; and for the Lucerian votive deposit of the Belvedere: Comella 1981; Strazzulla 1981; 1987: 16 f.; D' Ercole 1990; and De Cazanove 2000, for the wider phenomenon.

[98] On the poverty of our knowledge of Samnite and Latin Beneventum, see Giampaola 1991, 123; one remarkable piece of artistic production is a terracotta head of Minerva, from an antefix, dating between the late-third and mid-second century BC; it was discovered in a context of redeposition, but probably comes from a major temple in the colony, possibly on the *arx* (Giampaola 1991, 127 f. and figs. 6 and 7, Giampaola 2000, 36).

[99] Morel 1988, 50; personal inspection of the ceramic material displayed in the Museo Archeologico in Brindisi in August 2001 noted a predominance of 'Apulian' red-figure and 'Gnathian' ware vases, both of which continue into the third century. Admittedly such displays may not be representative of the whole collection, and plain BG is less aesthetically pleasing. As for Beneventum, Morel 1991, 189–91, makes no mention of Beneventane BG production in his survey of fine wares from Samnium.

[100] Morel 1988, 62.

[101] Equally a Roman identity 'constructed' out of heterogeneity is possible: for such post-eventum constructions in the invented traditions of archaic Greek colonies, with one mother-city and a single oikist evoked from the ashes of past conflict and confusion, see Horden and Purcell 2000, 397; Osborne 1998, Wilson 2000. Cases like Zankle (colonized by pirates from Cumae, then again by men from Chalkis and other Euboians, with two oikists: Thuc. 6.4.5), and Himera (Chalkidian and Syrakusan colonists, three oikists, a dialect 'mixed between the Chalkidian and the Dorian', but Chalkidian institutions: Thuc. 6.5.1) were probably more common than our (often late) sanitized traditions allow.

[102] See Morel 1988, 57, with further bibliography.

[103] Bandelli 1988, 109 f.: Liburnius, Maecius, Manlius, Obulcius, Octavius, Ovius, Roscius, Vettius and Sabinus. On his reading, none of these *need* be names of Roman emigrant families; only Maecii and Manlii are probable. Bandelli's interpretation, while important as a corrective to Romanocentric assumptions, simply pushes the problems of

origins back another step: if we find Ovii at Fregellae and Venusia and Capua, how are we to say that they are indigenous to all or any of those regions, rather than products of earlier immigration? Furthermore, high *elite mobility* might be warping our picture of the overall ethnic composition of the colonial body. Nor do we know *when* many of these families arrived at Ariminum. Even the Ariminate BG *poculum* with 'Q. Oui' scratched on it, although once thought to be third century (Susini 1965, 146) has been downdated to the second century by Fontemaggi and Piolanti (2000, 510 f., fig. 180d); on the Ariminate Ovii see also the stimulating discussion of Donati 1995. For a pre-existing indigenous settlement from the fourth century (as at Alba Fucens and Brundisium) in what was later the northern part of Ariminum, see Ortalli 2000, 501. Presumably this was razed, and *some* inhabitants incorporated in the colony: see Bradley 2000a, 133 f. On the ethnic heterogeneity of colonial populations, and its basis in Mediterranean mobility, see Horden and Purcell, 2000, 395–400, esp. 396 f. Latin colonial names as later arrivals: Torelli 1983, 246, on the Roman 'destructuring' of conquered areas in S. Etruria in the second century BC, which manifests itself partly through the intrusion of Roman and Latin names and individuals into local society; not all of these intrusions are owed to colonization.

[104] Third-century organization into *vici* (whatever exactly these are) is attested by painted inscriptions on Ariminate BG pottery: see n. 91 above; and Fontemaggi and Piolanti 2000, 510 f., fig. 180b, interpreting 'veici' as a collective nominative signifying the dedicators, not a genitive.

[105] Sanesi 1978, 77, cf. 76.

[106] Torelli 1999, 52, discussing the abandonment of most Greek and Lucanian rural sanctuaries in the territory of Paestum after the foundation of the colony, extrapolates a general trend for Latin colonies. But see Crawford, this volume.

[107] Torelli 1999, 48.

[108] For an interpretation of the urbanism of Latin colonies as very traditional, Torelli 1983, 245.

[109] Zanker 2000, 35 is rightly cautious in the case of Latin colonies, denying that we can talk of a 'specifically 'Roman' urban plan', however much that urban plan might recall Rome (which I shall argue that it did not).

[110] So, recently, Zanker 2000, 27, 35. As I have argued regarding Ostia (Bispham 2000), the presence of a Capitolium from an early period is simply an assumption, and I think that there is no better evidence for one at any other mid-republican site (Zanker 2000, 33, has an interesting qualification: 'the central location of the principal sanctuary (*often* the Capitolium)' – my italics). Other 'givens' for Zanker, including the last two of his three 'important features' of Roman colonies (2000, 27), seem to me likewise to rest on inference and assumption: if we cannot prove an early Capitoline phase, we cannot argue that colonial Capitolia were central places along the principal axis of communication or that they dominated proto-*fora*; and whether 'political rights' could be exercised in the colony or not depends entirely on one's definition of those rights. Perhaps it is better to say that such rights could *also* be exercised at Rome, as far as they concerned the *res publica* (state).

[111] Luna: see below. Conversion of the Pompeian temple of Iuppiter: Barton 1982, 261 f., 1995, 75, Zanker 1998, 63–5. See Barton 1982, 262–6 for a list of known Italian Capitolia; that at Liternum (attested epigraphically) *might* date to the foundation of the colony in 194 BC (De Caro and Greco 1981, 91, Barton 1982, 265); and that at Faesulae

(*CIL* XI 1545) might be Sullan. Note also the conversion, in the Augustan period, of the temple of Iuppiter Flazios at Cumae to a Capitolium (no accompanying colonization: Barton 1982, 265).

[112] Bispham 2000, esp. 162–4, 174 f.

[113] Torelli 1999, 53, 56, 72 on Iuppiter and Minerva at Paestum; 63–5 on Herakles /Hercules; 93–7 on Athena Ilias and Trojan Venus. Diversity: Torelli 1988a, 68–72, esp. 71–2. Innovation is also present in colonial religion: Torelli 1999, 29, 31 f., and esp. 93–7 on the Roman adaptation of the local myth of Diomedes, above all in Daunia, with bibliography there cited. See also Torelli 1999, 128 f. for the lack of 'traditional' Latin-style terracottas at Paestum, suggesting a restriction of 'cultural choices' among the colonists, despite the considerable changes which they introduced.

[114] For a different reading of the Roman colony as *substitutive* and not *integrative*, see Coarelli 1992, 25 f., citing the cult of Marica at Minturnae.

[115] Cf. Torelli 1999, 65–71: the (over-ingenious) identification of an 'Aventine slope' complex around the *piscina publica* ('public pool') at Paestum, involving Venus Verticordia, Fortuna Virilis and Mens. The addition of a Forum Boarium / Forum Holitorium analogue (the temples of Aesculapius and Magna Mater: 1999, 57–65) seems to me to be a further step away from plausibility. On plebeian associations of Iuppiter Libertas and *pagi*, cf. Susini 1965.

[116] For bibliography and brief discussion of this ware see Bispham 2000, 167; add now Stanco 1994, 21–6, with Tavv. 1–7.

[117] It is difficult to reconcile Brown's 1980 description of Deposit A, and the material from it dedicated to Hercules, with the much earlier discussion of the pottery (Taylor 1957). The significant pieces in the latter's catalogue, which is almost exclusively concerned with vessel shapes, are A21C, with an 'H' painted on it (= *CIL* I² 3584a), A38, which reads 'pocolom' (the deity's name is lost); and perhaps A1.

[118] On Brown's interpretation, and his underlying concerns, see Fentress 2000b, 23 f.

[119] Brown 1980, 16 f. (and see section 1), Gargola 1995, 75. For Torelli 1988b, 128 'erano *rigorosamente* seguite *tutte* le relative pratiche augurali' ('*all* the pertinent augural practices were *scrupulously* followed', my italics), listing the usual set of rituals, and using the example of Cosa.

[120] Taylor 2002, 80 sees this assemblage as an ordinary votive deposit, not commenting on the date. Other supposed '*mundi*', equally problematic, both in Latium: Artena (see Lambrechts 1996, with reviews by Bispham, *CR* 1999, 306 f., and Morel 1999) and Norba (Torelli 1988b, 134).

[121] See also Scott 1988, 75 f., Stambaugh 1988, 255.

[122] Including *sima* and cresting decoration: Scott, 1992, 94 (but see ibid. for two heads of figures possibly from beam-end decorations from this series). Illustrations: Brown, Richardson and Richardson, 1960, Pls. XVI–XXII, esp. XVIII for the antefixes; note that some of the pieces attributed to the third century temple at 1960, 312–23, cannot belong to it.

[123] Even Taylor, who in a recent article casts doubt on the thesis that the variety of terracottas on the *arx* (some of which might be domestic) necessarily entails a third-century temple, admits that some of the terracottas sealed in construction contexts of the 'Capitolium' might be from a third-century building (2002, 70 f.).

[124] Scott 1992, 91 f., on the story and proposed locations of the temple, with Tav. II (not enormously convincing); Brown 1980, 25; Stambaugh 1988, 258.

[125] Taylor is disposed, on the basis of his restudy of the terracottas, to remove the first temple, i.e. the 'temple of Iuppiter', from the Cosan story completely. Yet all he has done is move it.

[126] Strazzulla 1977, 42 f., 1985, 98 f., is broadly critical of the excavators' datings of all the temple terracottas, arguing that some restoration work is as late as the first century BC; for a more searching critique of Richardson's dating of the terracotta series and the art-historical principles of seriation underlying it, see Taylor 2002, esp. 61–70, 72 f., 80.

[127] Brown, Richardson and Richardson 1960, 156 f. For Campanian terracottas as a distinct tradition from the Etrusco-Italic: Koch 1912; papers in Bonghi 1990, focused on Campania despite the title; Torelli 1999, 122; Minturnae as the boundary between the predominant distributions of the two types: Torelli 1999, 128.

[128] See also Richardson's comment at Fentress 2000b, 13 n. 14.

[129] Brown 1980, 26; Scott 1992, 92; Stambaugh 1988, 258.

[130] Iuppiter Latiaris would be appropriate for worship in a high place like the Cosan *arx*, given the location of his Latin sanctuary on Monte Cavo.

[131] Scott 1992, 95 refers to 'Hercules and Minerva/Roma'; loc. cit. for other antefix fragments possibly belonging to the first temple: Silenus, a Maenad and a satyr. Some antefixes (or at least the old moulds) reused on the new temple, others broken and used as construction make-up: Brown, Richardson and Richardson 1960, 154–7.

[132] Taylor argues that Iuppiter's paternity of both makes for 'a tenuous identification [sc. of Iuppiter as the deity of the first temple] given the promiscuous use of Hercules and Minerva imagery throughout Italy in a wide variety of contexts' (2002, 66).

[133] The excavation of the area around the 'Capitolium' seems to have recognized only two broad strata representing ancient deposition, cut by Medieval tombs (Brown, Richardson and Richardson 1960, 20–2, 206, Pl. LXX. 2); a third burnt stratum represented the supposed collapse of the temple of Iuppiter. It would seem difficult to *insist*, on such a crude stratigraphic basis, that the deposition in level I of terracottas originally from the first temple (Brown, Richardson and Richardson 1960, 151–7) represents material which had collapsed from a secondary installation as functioning antefixes for the 'Capitolium'; see Scott 1992, 94 and Taylor 2002, 65, 73–7 for problems with the excavators' stratification of the deposits on the *arx*.

[134] Brown, Richardson and Richardson 1960, 19 f., 208 f.; Brown 1980, 55; cf. Strazzulla 1985, 98, 99, who also talks (99) of 'una tendenza…tipica della situazione cosana, alla conservatività' ('a tendency…typical of the Cosan situation, toward conservatism'); and Taylor 2002, 65.

[135] On the phenomenon, see Glinister 2000.

[136] Brown, Richardson and Richardson 1960, 208 f., note that two types of clay fabric are found in Hercules and Minerva antefixes associated with re-use on the 'Capitolium': B seems to be associated with new production from old moulds, and A is 'similar' to, but therefore, importantly, not the same as, those of antefixes from the third-century temple.

[137] Strazzulla 1985, 100, seems to think in terms of ideological continuity between the two temples.

[138] For earlier estimates of the date see Brown 1980, 47; Scott 1985b, 95, cf. Strazzulla 1985, 99. The porch and *pronaos* of the temple may have been remodelled shortly after the 'Capitolium' was completed (Scott 1992, 97 f.), but see the doubts of Taylor, 2002,

67 f., lowering the construction date to 170–160 BC, and arguing for a reconstruction in the first quarter of the first century BC Scott, 1992, 94 f. suggests that both temples D and B (in the *forum*) date to the first quarter of the second century, and are almost contemporary with each other.

[139]   Brown 1980, 48 (especially the plaques above the columns; for him the antefixes, *sima* and cresting have more affinity to 'Etruscan' types already used in the colony); Scott 1992, 94 f.: the decoration of temple D and temple B is stylistically related.

[140]   Brown 1980, 47–9: a frieze with dolphins and sea monsters, cf. Scott 1985b, 95: the sea view, and three inscribed statuette bases from the *arx*; Torelli 1999, 62. The terracotta pedimental decoration would allow Mater Matuta, but anatomical terracottas also discovered are neutral. See Scott 1988, 76; Brown 1980, 49. Strazzulla, 1985, 98, characterizes the attribution to Mater Matuta as made 'sulla base di indizi piuttosto tenui' ('on the basis of rather slender indications'); cf. Torelli 1999, 39 f.: alternatives of Fortuna and Victoria (Torelli 1988b, 141, offered Iuno; ibid. for a Brownian summary of the Cosan temples). On the cult of Mater Matuta, especially in Latium, Smith 2000.

[141]   Portunus: Brown, Richardson and Richardson 1960, 142–7, 204 f., 330–2. Dated *c.* 170 BC: Brown 1980, 49; cf. Brown and Scott 1985, 101; Stambaugh 1988, 258.

[142]   On the date see Scott, 1992, 96, discussing the evidence of coins sealed in various construction phases of the building, suggesting that it was finished after 175 BC, but before 150; cf. ibid. 97 (pedimental decoration may belong to the first half of the century); Brown 1980, 51; Scott 1985b, 95, 1988, 76 (finished *c.* 160 BC); Strazzulla 1985, 98: mid-century, cf. now Taylor 2002, 61, 68. On the building itself see Brown, Richardson and Richardson 1960, 48–109, 126–40; Brown 1980, 52–6; Taylor 2002, 68–77. Strazzulla, 1985, 98 f. stresses the temple's size: it is one of the most significant religious structures in the region.

[143]   At times Scott refers to the 'Capitolium' (1988, 75, 76, 77), but elsewhere to the 'Capitolium-type' (76). Torelli too (1999, 39) calls it both 'most likely the Capitolium', and (1999, 56 n. 81) the 'so-called Capitolium'; cf. Stambaugh 1988, 258 f. Taylor (2002) refers to the Capitolium throughout.

[144]   e.g. Gargola 1995, 83; Barton 1995, 70, in a standard text-book, writes 'the Capitolium…has the expected triple *cella*'.

[145]   Brown cites Shoe 1965 in support of his argument on the mouldings: Shoe, 1965, 134, does indeed talk of the evocation of the Roman Capitolium by the podium mouldings from the Cosan 'Capitolium', but this is nonsensical. Shoe herself (1965, 22) notes that we have no evidence for the appearance of the former. More significant, but ignored by Brown, is her assertion that the Cosan mouldings recall those from the Casalinaccio temple at the Latin colony of Ardea (1965, 83, 88).

[146]   A fragment showing a *ferculum*, a stretcher for a religious procession, has been generally associated with this temple rather than temple D. Torelli 1999, 132 f., reconstructs the pedimental group as showing a sacrifice in front of a divinity (Jupiter or Mars) celebrated at the end of the triumph, the *ferculum* being consistent with a *pompa triumphalis* ('triumphal procession'). For him this is an example of Latin 'triumphal art', celebrating victories won by Latin allies in Rome's wars (celebrated in local *pompae*). This is rather speculative, although the unusual triple arch, monumentalizing one entrance to the forum, with its modern concrete construction, looks very much to Roman models and may be significant (Brown 1980, 42 f., 44; for the date (*c.* 170 BC): Scott 1985c, 96); compare the representations of military success in Asia reproduced in an elite *domus* at

Fregellae (Coarelli 1987, 130).

[147] On the terracottas associated with this temple, see also Brown, Richardson and Richardson 1960, 89 f., 206–84, 332–69, figs. 25–32; Strazzulla 1977, 41 f. More recently discovered terracotta fragments compatible with this temple include a female figure, the heads of a young man, and a bearded older man, and a female head: Scott 1992, 96 f., Tavv. VIIb, VIII, IXa and b. For the terracottas ascribed to this temple (old-fashioned antefixes apart) as attuned to innovative second-century stylistic developments in Latium and in other colonial contexts, and the possible use of Roman craftsmen: Brown, Richardson and Richardson 1960, 206–31, 332–69; Strazzulla 1985, 98 f.

[148] Brown himself noted, 1980, 56, the abnormality of a Capitolium in a Latin context, but sought to explain it in the light of Rome's recent reinforcement of the colony: as we shall see this date and context are significant.

[149] Colonna 1989, 428 f., suggesting that this form of temple design is rather old, and that its ultimate origins should be sought not in religious architecture, but in the earliest *atrium*-houses. The Capitoline heresy runs deep and wide: the principal temple on the main *arx* at Brundisium has been thought to be to the Capitoline cult (Lippolis and Baldini Lippolis 1997, 314); the only reason for this seems to be a dedication on the base of an imperial column on the waterfront to Iuppiter Optimus Maximus. Ardea and Cosa: Shoe 1965, 83, 88.

[150] Brown, Richardson and Richardson 1960, 369–72; CB 679/680, CB 482/CC 877 on Argive Hercules. See also Scott 1988, 75, 1992, 93 on the Portus Herculis below Monte Argentario; cf. Brown 1980, 56. Brown and Scott 1985, 101, suggest that the early colony used the Portus Herculis with the Portus Cosanus coming into use only later.

[151] Scott 1988, 76.

[152] The identification as Ganymede is not certain, however. Note also the three-*cella* temple of Iuno Curitis at Falerii Veteres (Potter 1979, 100).

[153] Despite Brown, Richardson and Richardson 1960, 22. Scott 1992, 93, notes the presence of Minerva on third-century Roman coins, adding the possibility that the Cosan Minerva might even be Roma. For him, the pairing of Minerva and Hercules symbolizes the fusion of Roman and Latin.

[154] Terracotta fragments of sows from temple B in the Forum used to be thought of as deriving from copies of the Latin *scrofa Laurentina* ('Laurentine sow'), and thus to symbolize the Latin identity of the colony (Brown 1980, 31; Torelli 1999, 41). It has, however, recently been suggested that the pigs belong to a different iconographic scheme (see below). Torelli's idea that the Latinity of Cosa was stressed as a counterpoint to resentful Etruscan populations nearby is interesting.

[155] See von Vaccano and von Freytag-Löringhoff 1982, 61–3, figs. 62–5; the Minerva in fig. 63 has a torc, but in fig. 64 (a repair?) does not. The Hercules and Minerva antefixes seem to have been replaced in *c.* 150 BC with new ones representing Bacchus and Ariadne (von Vaccano and von Freytag-Löringhoff 1982, 67 f.).

[156] Massa-Pairault 1985a, 119, 1985b, 139; *contra* von Freytag-Löringhoff 1992, 73. On the dating and interpretation of the various phases of terracottas see now von Freytag-Löringhoff 1992, esp. 71 f.

[157] 1992. Minerva may have relevant Etruscan connections, and thus facilitate integration between colonists and indigenous inhabitants in this part of Italy: Group C of the pedimental terracottas from the 'Grande Tempio' (large temple) at Luna has a female

figure with an aegis across one shoulder, a torc around the neck, and the right breast bare (Strazzulla 1992, 172, 174, Tav. IVa). Strazzulla herself suggests that the female figure may be the wife of Telephus (1992, 178 f.); although Minerva is never bare-breasted, and the aegis is not unique to her (appearing on images of Alexander on the early coin issues of the Diadochoi), I find this interpretation less persuasive than the view that this may be a local, Lunese, Minerva (1992, 174 f., 181). Telephus may be a vehicle for integration at Luna: Strazzulla 1992, 181–3, notes that he was in some versions the ancestor of both Romans and Etruscans (Plut. *Rom.* 2, Lykophron *Alex.* 1242–5); she also draws attention to the depiction of the Etruscan demon Vanth in a pedimental group from the 'Grande Tempio', and argues that the temple's decoration offered a shared language open to Etruscan interlocutors, stressing the common descent and common enemies of Romans and Etruscans, using 'toni profondamente radicati nella più antica tradizione locale' ('tones deeply rooted in the most ancient local tradition'). Terrenato 2001b, 61 (cf. 65) concludes from funerary epigraphy from Luna that there was a 'massive and early appearance of foreign elements, which should undoubtedly be linked with the creation of the colony'.

[158] On Hercle, the Etruscan counterpart of Herakles: Bayet 1926; Mastrocinque 1993. Mastroncinque notes the labour of Hercle which appears in the fictile decoration of the Minerva temple at Portonaccio at Veii (1993, 58).

[159] Colonna 1985.

[160] For the new temple on the eastern height, see Fentress 2000b, 14, with bibliography; Taylor 2002, 80, cautious about the identification as a temple.

[161] Proposed dates: early second century, finished towards 175 BC: Brown 1980, 38 f.; Scott 1985c, 97: 150 BC; 1992, 95: first quarter of the century, not necessarily later than Temple D; Taylor 2002, *c.* 175 BC.

[162] On the terracottas from this temple, see also Strazzulla 1985, 99.

[163] Torelli 1999, 39 f. (unconvincing on Camillus and the Cosan *curia*). See also Brown 1980, 31.

[164] See Taylor 2002, 61 for the limited number of certain third-century structures at Cosa; 2002, 69 for a pessimistic assessment of the early urban centre.

[165] Scott 1988, 76 and n. 23.

[166] Scott 1988, 76.

[167] Torelli 1983, 243–5; the technique first used at Cosa from the middle of the second century: ibid. 247.

[168] Note that her figs. 100 and 96 should be reversed.

[169] The name may have Latin overtones, recalling the Mons Albanus and Alba Longa in Latium (Fucens being an epichoric adjective, distinguishing the two Albae). Torelli, noting this (1999, 32 n. 142, 34 f., cf. Torelli 1988b, 135), suggests that 'Albsi patre' on a bronze lamina found at Alba (*ILLRP* 42) refers to Iuppiter Latiaris, and is an example of the Latinity of the cult activity of the colony; the parallels cited by Degrassi ad loc. seem against such an interpretation, although it is impossible to exclude categorically such ideological intertexts. It then becomes important to ask whether Pater Albensis was not a local deity.

[170] The pre-colonial wall trace: Mertens 1988, 101, cf. Liberatore 2001, 189; the walls of the colony are its oldest feature, certainly post 300 BC. Third-century structures: the *comitium* (perhaps very early in its first phase: Liberatore 2001, 190, 192, cf. Torelli 1988b, 136), an unpaved *forum*, a sacred area, as well as the orthogonal plan of the

settlement and its internal terracing (and possibly the sewers). Commercial and artisan activity can be postulated for the same period: note fourth- and third- century domestic ceramics from wells and other deposits under the *basilica* (walls there may also be from domestic structures): Liberatore 2001, 190 (although with the dangerous suggestion of *atria publica* in this area). See generally Mertens 1988, 95 f. (note late fourth- or early third-century Romano-Campanian coin), also 87, 90, 91, 101; Liberatore 2001, 190, 194–6. A cut across an internal terrace wall produced *petites estampilles* ceramics, suggesting a date in the first half of the third century: Mertens 1988, 91–3; a coin of Canusium dating to *c.* 300 was found in levelling material (brought from elsewhere) in the *forum* (Mertens 1988, 94) pointing to the same conclusion; note the volume of redeposited material from the first half of the third century: Mertens 1988, 101.

[171] Note especially the antefix fragments found in the fill behind the polygonal terracing wall under the *basilica*: Mertens 1988, 95 f.

[172] Mertens 1988, 91.

[173] Mertens 1988, 90; Livy 9.45.17. As Mertens points out, it is unlikely that the Romans were the first to recognize the strategic potential of the site; see now Liberatore 2001, 186 f., 196 no. 9. *Contra* Torelli 1999, 32.

[174] An indigenous temple might have stood on the highest of the three summits around the plateau of Alba, now occupied by the abandoned village of Alba Vecchia. Since this remains unexplored archaeologically, an important component of the colony's religious topography is lost to us. Mertens 1988, 97, suggests that this part of Alba, as the *arx*, had its own wall circuit. Torelli (1999, 34 f.) argues that the temple of Pater Albensis stood here; on the identification of this god, see n. 169 above.

[175] Mertens 1988, 101.

[176] The hilltop sanctuaries seem to be later; the preponderance of religious sites on high ground, as against down in the centre of the colony, is striking (Torelli 1999, 35, noting that there seems to have been no sacred building in the *forum*, a phenomenon which he compares with the situation at Cosa and Paestum in the third century).

[177] Mertens 1988, 104.

[178] Early evidence from area of Hercules *sacellum*: Mertens 1988, 95; Liberatore 2001, 192. Torelli 1999, 35 mentions a bronze club as well. Note also two cups bearing dedications to Hercules from foundation horizons at Porta di Massa (Liberatore 2001, 189 and fig. 8).

[179] Now thought more likely to belong firmly to the third century, rather than being late-third or early-second century: Mertens 1988, 95.

[180] Mertens 1988, 98. The *temple* of S. Pietro faces out over the southern entrance to the city and the Fucine basin.

[181] Note, however, that Hercules seems rarely, if at all, to have shared his own sanctuaries with other deities, while he is often found in theirs: van Wonterghem 1992, 325.

[182] It was, unlike the *arx* at Cosa, most unsuited to augural activity owing to the obstructed lines of sight imposed by the topography of the site. This is not to say that there was not some sort of augural platform in Alba Vecchia.

[183] Mertens, 1988, 104, noting also (100) the presence of material suggesting commercial relations with Campania and Apulia, especially in the first half of the third century. On transhumance: van Wonterghem 1973; Corbier 1991; van Wonterghem 1992, 321 f., 327 f., 330 f. (on Hercules at Alba Fucens and its territory); Torelli 1993, 105–17; Torelli 1999, 35 f. Torelli 1999, 35–9, links the *forum pecuarium* to the transhumance

system running from Marsic territory to Latium along the Via Valeria, with interesting comparisons with Samnium.

[184] On salt, and the vital circulation of coastal salt in upland central Italy, see Torelli 1993, 1999, 36 n. 164; Bispham 2000, 160.

[185] S. Pietro seems to be a third-century construction (Mertens 1969; Mertens, 1988, 98 f.; for the architectural terracottas, including plaques and *potnia theron* antefixes from an as yet unlocated third temple: Barreca 1952, 234–6, Strazzulla 1981, 206, no. 28; Torelli 1999, 126. Torelli (1999, 32 f., cf. Torelli 1988b, 135, Susini 1965, 148), plausibly identifies the deity of S. Pietro as an Apollo similar to the Roman Apollo Medicus, on the basis of a *graffito* reading 'Apollinar' from the temple, dating S. Pietro and Pettorino to the first years of the third century. The pairs advanced by Torelli as possible occupants of the Pettorino temple (1999, 34, cf. Torelli 1998b, 135) are speculative. The rare double *cella* might lead us to suspect that an indigenous cult was being perpetuated here, in one or both cases, under a Roman or Latin guise.

[186] Susini 1965, 146 f. on Vesuinus, a possible theonym on a third-century BG *poculum*.

[187] Morel 1988, 57–60.

[188] Morel 1988, 57 and n. 85, 58 f.; see Mangani 1973, 70 and Tav. XIII; also Stanco 1994, 24 and Tav. 6, 24–7, dating the type to *c.* 240–220 BC.

[189] Morel 1988, 58.

[190] Spanish example: Principal-Ponce 1998.

[191] Morel 1988, 58 for initial characterization; for more recent work Pedroni 1992, Principal-Ponce 1998; for the connection of this group, which enjoyed a limited distribution, with cultic dedications to Hercules, see Pedroni 1992, 584–8, Principal-Ponce 1998, 235, 237 f.

[192] For the Ariminate material see Susini 1965, 147 and fig. 3; also Fontemaggi and Piolanti 2000, 510 f., fig. 180 a–c, for discussion and images of some fragments of these vessels. On the more unusual abbreviations, see Morel 1988, 58 f., suggesting that 'HC' at Ariminum may stand for Hercules Custos (for other possible resolutions see Susini 1965, 147, Franchi De Bellis 1995, 373), while at Paestum 'HP' and 'HPA' may stand for HPH, i.e. Hera.

[193] Morel 1988, 58 f., cf. Principal-Ponce 1998, 237–9, amplifying Morel's argument.

[194] See further Susini 1965, 146; and 151 f. on Feronia's popularity in NE Roman Italy, linked to Apollo but also to *liberti*.

[195] 'C. Manlios son of Ac[----]? / consul / on behalf of / the people / of Ariminum'. See Cicala 1995; her relation of the text to the Gallic incursion of 236 BC is very attractive; while she is correct to stress the communal aspect of the dedication, I am not sure that a strong military sense can be read into the stress on the Ariminate *populus* in this text (1995, 362 f.).

[196] Diana is, of course, not named in the text, but one other example from the 'Diana assemblage' from Nemi (*ILLRP* 75) is a dedication without a named dedicatee, which nevertheless, made as it was by C. Aurelius, *cos.* 200, during his second praetorship (201), is surely to the chief divinity of the place, Diana. For activity by a colonial consul on behalf of the colony, compare *ILLRP* 169, from Beneventum, a dedication by C. Falcilius L. f. 'consol', to (the significantly-named) Iuno Quiritis.

[197] The nature and origin of this text, now lost, are obscure: Cicala 1995, 359. Susini 1965, 148, adds *CIL* XIV 4269 to the Diana dossier; see above, section 1, for *CIL* XI 361.

[198] Cicala goes further, and argues that it was Diana's wild, extra-urban, aspect at Nemi which gave her an inter-cultural value, and made her a suitable deity (along with Feronia) for colonists dealing with non-Latin – indeed wild, non-Italian – peoples, in a strange landscape, one which they were trying to transform, cultivate and civilize (1995, 358–63; note esp. 361 n. 19, citing the work of Brizzi). For Deana Divina in another mid-Republican colony, Placentia, see *CIL* XI 1211 (Susini 1965, 148; the inscription is pre-triumviral: Bandelli 1988, 111).

[199] Susini 1965, 148 and 161 f.

[200] Cf. Guidobaldi 2001, 90 for the cult of Apollo introduced by Roman settlers in the *ager Praetuttianus*.

[201] See Torelli 1993, 101, for the possible presence of Feronia at Narnia, a Latin colony liminally situated, at the time of its foundation, on the borders of Umbrian and Roman territory; she was also worshipped at Ariminum; and at Pietrasanta in the territory of Luna (Coarelli 1987, 134 f., connecting her presence with the immigration of colonists originating in Tarracina).

[202] See on the sanctuary, where the sequence of votive deposition seems to be broken during the second century BC, Mingazzini 1938, 684 f.; Guidobaldi 1988, 126; Arthur 1991, 46; Trota 1989, 11 f.; Torelli 1993, 102 f.

[203] Torelli 1999, 42. Note the stamp impressed on a votive vase found at the sanctuary, and suggestive of the ties between Marica and Hercules: *CIL* I² 2880, 7.

[204] It was, together with the *tabernae* round the *forum*, struck again in 191 BC (Livy 36.37.3). The *bidental* and *fulgur* inscription found between the temple of Iuppiter and Temple A may be associated with the later strike (Guidobaldi 1988, 128 f.). Guidobaldi and Pesando (1989, 41) note the interesting synchronism between the two prodigies at Minturnae and the two attempts by a number of colonies, especially Ostia, to defend their claims to freedom from military service (Bispham 2000, 165 f., 172 f.): it is tempting to see the prodigies as reported in the context of a shared colonial politics of resistance to Roman demands. If so the striking of the temple of Iuppiter is doubly significant.

[205] Lippolis and Baldini Lippolis 1997, 311–13; and 314 for the possible third-century cult building on the *arx*, perhaps the same building whose Corinthian capitals show clear Tarentine influence, another instance of Torellian *duttilità* (1997, 317).

[206] Bispham 2000, 162, 175 n. 142, with reference to earlier discussions; for the archaic period Torelli 1993, 91–108, on Hercules' presence at a number of coastal sites, together with a nexus of female deities, presiding over international exchange, as well as that of salt and livestock at the termini of transhumance routes; Plácido 1993, 73–80, for analogous manifestations of Hercules in south-west Spain.

[207] Note the temple of Diana at the Latin colony of Norba (Torelli 1988b, 134, insists this is Aventine Diana, just as Iuno Lucina and Iuno Moneta on other eminences of the city evoke the Roman *arx* and Esquiline). At the Roman colony of Luna, Apollo was one of the deities to whom the 'Grande Tempio' was dedicated (Strazzulla 1992, 167 f.). Finally, is it too fanciful to draw any inference from the name of the island of Dianium off Cosa (Brown 1980, 5)?

[208] Note Susini 1965, 147 f., on the importance of the cult of Hercules in Latin colonies (noting the archaic dedications from Hatria – *CIL* IX 5052–4, and Spoletium – *CIL* XI 7867), as perhaps the only 'exemple d'une correspondance de cultes répétée' ('example of a repeated correspondance of cults') within the Latin colonial pantheon

(1965, 147), also suggesting that Hercules' popularity shows the central Italian origins of many colonists; Morel 1988, 59 f., and bibliography cited there.

[209] Giangiulio 1983, and more speculatively, Giangiulio 1993; Leigh 2000, 126 f.; for Herakles' cult as an integrative force in colonial contexts across the Mediterranean, see Plácido 1993, 70 f., 79 f.

[210] Connected with Roman colonization by Coarelli, 1987, 126, Cicala, 1995, 361 and n. 19 – this is very plausible at least as far as the transformation of the rural landscape by colonization is concerned.

[211] See Susini 1965, 146, where, as well as the postulation of a pre-Roman cult stratum, a possible pre-colonial date is suggested for the beginnings of the sanctuary (cf. Bandelli 1988, 111); Torelli 1999, 29, Coarelli 2000. The existence of a *lucus* at Pisaurum is pertinently questioned by Betts, 2003, 138–44.

[212] Guidobaldi and Pesando (1989, 40) suggest that these *cippi* were originally set up together in a single area.

[213] Note also that Strazzulla (1992, 170) suggests that his presence at Luna may be explained by the 'frontier' location of that colony.

[214] See further Biondo 1988.

[215] Morel 1988, 59; Principal-Ponce 1998, 238 f., for the intersection of colonization with the interests of recently-empowered commercial interests as expressed through the cult of Hercules and associated vase production, including amphorae with 'HERC' or similar stamped on the handles (e.g. *CIL* I² 3507).

[216] D.H. 1.40–4. Scott 1988, 75, 1992, 93, draws attention to this passage. The general context of Dionysios' narrative, the literary parallels for, and variants of, Herakles' journey with the cattle of Geryon, can all be seen as paradeigmatic for colonial *movements* and their 'prehistory': Plácido 1993, 76–8 (in Italy and Sicily). Note also Leigh 2000, 126 f., esp. 126 n. 10: Herakles 'marching *along the coast* encodes the specific experience of the colonist'; better, it encodes the experience of one axis of movement for colonist and native alike.

[217] This is an old story, cf. *Prometheus Unbound* fr. 199 Nauck.

[218] Capedeville, 1995, 97–146; see Thucydides 6.2.2 on the Ligues and displacement of populations.

[219] On roads and colonization, see Coarelli 1988.

[220] On the importance of the cult of Hercules in central Apennine Italy, see (a well-known example among many) the Agnone tables (Vetter 1953, no. 147); Salmon 1967, 170 f.; van Wonterghem 1973; Di Niro 1977; Mattiocco and van Wonterghem 1989; van Wonterghem 1992; Torelli 1993, 105–17; Leigh 2000; Guidobaldi 2001, 89 on the Praetuttii. Of the 296 'Sabellic' bronzes listed in Colonna 1970, some 207 on my reckoning are certainly of the 'Ercole in assalto' (Hercules attacking) type, to say nothing of other Hercules figures. On the Ligurians in Samnium see Patterson 1988. For Hercules as 'imported' into the central Apennines from Etruria, see Devoto 1967, 198, Torelli 1993, 108 f.; for a Roman origin, Susini 1965, 147; and for an Italiote derivation via Italic mercenaries, Salmon 1967, 65, Torelli 1993, 109; a sensible overview in van Wonterghem 1992, 321–3.

[221] Speculation about the identity of Dionysos' source is probably futile, but the Euhemerizing tinge of the narrative (Plácido 1993, 78), and the date of the intensification of Roman interest in Liguria (the majority of Ligurian triumphs fall between 181 and 155 BC) make Cassius Hemina an interesting possibility (Beck and Walter 2001,

243 f. for his Euhemerizing interests).

[222] See van Wonterghem 1992, 323, 335, for Hercules as a polyvalent deity.

[223] As Nicholas Purcell points out to me, my analysis is limited in that my focus on Iuppiter is made at the expense of a discussion of the roles played by Iuno and Minerva in colonization, consideration of which might inform us, among other things, of colonial gender relations. I have said a little about Minerva above; as for Iuno, she seems a relatively common presence in Latin colonies, but not in a Capitoline context (where she is Iuno Regina, Barton 1982, 260): note the Temple of Iuno Moneta at Signia, dating from the fifth century, as its terracottas show (Coarelli 1982, 177 f., Torelli 1988b, 132); the temples of Iuno Lucina and Moneta at Norba: Torelli 1988b, 132, and n. 196 above, for Iuno Quiritis at Beneventum.

[224] Note that when first excavated in the nineteenth century, the 'Grande Tempio' on the edge of Luna, which has three *cellae*, was thought to be the Capitolium, an identification which persisted for much of the twentieth century; it is probably dedicated to the goddess Luna (Strazzulla 1992, 162 f., with bibliography); Apollo figures centrally in the main pedimental group, and was probably worshipped there too. On the terracottas from the Capitolium see Forte 1992; and on those from the 'Grande Tempio' Strazzulla 1992 (ibid. 162 for the context).

[225] Cf. Curti 2001, 20, writing of a change between the third and second centuries from a 'situation based on local communities (*and reinvented local identities*), in favour of movement towards a national status' (my italics), referring specifically to the eclipse of Latin colonies by Roman. For a rather different picture of the relationship between Rome and her allies, and the value of the Roman citizenship, see Mouritsen 1998, 87–108.

[226] Torelli 1983, 243–5, 247. Nevertheless, where influences were felt and acted upon, they often come directly from the Hellenistic East, and were not mediated through Rome.

[227] Torelli 1983, 244.

[228] On the need for Roman economic aid as well as architectural models in Roman colonies: Guidobaldi 1988, 131 f.

[229] Guidobaldi 1988, 132. In the next year Livy records a debate about whether to found at Aquileia a Latin or a Roman colony (like the large Roman colonies voted for Mutina, Parma and Saturnia that year): Livy 39.55.5, 7–9. A Latin colony was founded in the end, but it was possibly the last of its kind (see Vell. Pat. 1.15.2, and above n. 87, on Luca).

[230] Torelli 1983, 246 f., stresses the often very traditional form of these building programmes in Italy as a whole, with little concession to Hellenistic fashions: the new projects perpetuated older civic mentalities and structures.

[231] Torelli 1983, 244, 246 f., noting especially the *tituli Mummiani* (Mummius inscriptions), which show the duration of this process: some places were still being assisted in the 140s, through manubial money deriving from the sack of Corinth in 146; Livy *Ep. Oxy.* 53 (143/1 BC): '[S]igna statu<a>s tabulas Corinth[ias L. M]ummius / distribuit circa oppida et Rom[am ornavit]' ('L. Mummius distributed statues of men and gods and paintings from Corinth around the towns, and decorated Rome'). *ILLRP* 321–2 are earlier examples. These benefactions were obviously important parts of communal identity: at Parma the *titulus Mummianus* (*CIL* I² 629) seems to have been re-inscribed in the late first century BC.

[232] Cosa's *basilica* is the oldest outside Rome, built *c.* 150 (cf. Brown 1980, 56–8). The triple arch, leading into the *forum*, is later than the Roman arches (of Stertinius and Scipio Africanus): Torelli 1983, 245.

[233] Torelli 1983, 244; Torelli 1988b, 130, 136, 142, 151 f.; Guidobaldi 1988, 129. Torelli further claims (1999, 128, following Andrén 1940, 483–95 and Strazzulla 1981, 197, no. 30) that while Etrusco-Latin models are followed in the terracottas of the urban temples, those of the extra-mural sanctuary of Marica show Campanian influence.

[234] Sherwin-White 1973, 85, who also (ibid.) notes earlier censorial *locationes* affecting colonies and *municipia*: Livy 39.44.6, 40.51.1–3.

[235] On the passage, and possible supplements or emendations see Torelli 1983, 243 f., Guidobaldi 1988, 129–32, Guidobaldi and Pesando 1989, 40–5 (following Jal's Budé text); contrast Liv. 40.5.7.

[236] (5) *censores vias sternendas silice in urbe, glarea extra urbem substruendas marginandasque primi omnium locaverunt, pontesque multis locis faciendos;* (6) *et scaenam aedilibus praetoribus praebendam;* <et> *carceres in circo, et ova ad no*<ta.> *curriculis numerand*<…>*dam et metas trans*<…*das*> *et caveas ferreas pe*<*r quas bestiae*> *intromitterentur* <…> *feriis in monte Albano consulibus.* (7) *et clivum Capitolium silice sternendum curaverunt, et porticum ab aede Saturni in Capitolium ad senaculum ac super id curiam,* (8) *et extra portam Trigeminam emporium lapide straverunt stipitibusque saepserunt, et porticum Aemiliam reficiendam curarunt, gradibusque ascensum ab Tiberi in emporium fecerunt.* (9) *et intra eandem portam in Auentinum porticum silice straverunt, et* + *eo publico* + *ab aede Veneris fecerunt.* (10) *iidem Calatiae et Auximi muros faciendos locaverunt; venditisque ibi publicis locis, pecuniam quae redacta erat tabernis utrique foro circumdandis consumpserunt.* (11) *et alter ex iis Fulvius Flaccus – nam Postumius nihil nisi senatus Romani populive iussu se locaturum* <…> – *ipsorum pecunia Iovis aedem Pisauri et Fundis et Po*<t>*entiae etiam aquam adducen*<d>*am, et Pisauri viam silice ster*<n>*e*<ndam>, (12) *et Sinuessae* + *mac*<…> *aviariae* +, *in his et clo*<*acas et mur*>*um circumducen*<*dum*…> *et forum porticibus tabernisque claudendum et Ianos tres faciendos.* (13) *haec ab uno censore opera locata cum magna gratia colonorum.*

[237] Cf. Scott 1985c, 96; Strazzulla 1985, 99; Zanker 2000, 36, on the modernity of the Cosan basilica; for Zanker this is a very Roman form of building – it was also highly adaptable.

[238] In 171 the Latin colony of Aquileia had to *ask* for the Senate's help in building its city walls, and that in a zone of doubtful security: Liv, 43. 1. 5.

[239] See generally Torelli 1988b, 151. The three arches may recall the three in the Forum Romanum, the *ianus summus*, *medius* and *imus* ('highest, middle and lowest arch'), see Guidobaldi and Pesando 1989, 42 n. 34; alternatively, a triple arch like that leading into the *forum* at Cosa may be meant.

[240] See Guidobaldi 1988, 132 f., Guidobaldi and Pesando 1989, 43–6, on Cato *Agr.* 135, and other indications of Minturnian prosperity in the second century. I do not agree with the minimalist view of Torelli (1983, 246 f., 249) who sees Roman intervention in the colonies as not modernizing them within a Hellenistic idiom to any great degree, but manifesting itself in traditional forms and techniques, with Cosa the exception proving the rule.

[241] See on this theme in Roman literature Edwards 1996, chap. 3. esp. 82–8. Note the swearing of oaths by Iuppiter Capitolinus: Plautus *Curc.* 268 f., and cf. also *Trin.* 83–7.

[242] Cf. Bourgeaud 1987, but placing the origin of the stories earlier, in the fourth to

third centuries.

²⁴³ See Purcell 1990 and Williams 2001b, 94–7, on the uniformity of patterning of the landscape of the Cisalpina in the second century, and the shared traditions and outlook which allowed different Roman magistrates to engineer such similar outcomes; colonization was a key part of this process. Standardization of colonies, both physically and conceptually, from the beginning of the second century: Torelli 1988b, 146–8.

²⁴⁴ Torelli (1999, 39 f., 56) sees a shift from the sole predominance of Iuppiter to a Capitoline model as coming later, following the supposed grant of Roman citizenship to magistrates of Latin colonies. The brilliant, but unproven, theory of Tibiletti (1953) places this concession after the suppression of the revolt of Fregellae in 125; from this moment, argues Torelli, we see religious change reflecting new political ideologies; against Tibiletti's argument, see now Mouritsen 1998, 99–108.

²⁴⁵ See Salmon 1969, 71–4, recognizing but brushing aside the evidential problem; Sherwin-White 1973, 76, 78, and 82 n. 3, 84, noting the peculiarity of the size; Guidobaldi and Pesando 1989, 36, 43, Gargola 1995, 56, Zanker 2000, 27 etc.; Galsterer 1976, 43–4, 59–61 on Ostia; Torelli 1988b, 128, notes that 300 is the figure 'in the cases known to us', but then (cf. 131, 148) throws caution to the winds by deriving this from a traditional 'Romulean' population structure based on three tribes (300 divisible by 3).

²⁴⁶ The creation of the canonical list of thirty Latin colonies (as seen in the passage of Livy discussed in section 2 above) must be connected to the story of the thirty colonies of Alba Longa; but at what era this story was elaborated is unclear: see De Cazanove 2000, 74 f. In any event, there is no evidence for a date before the late third century; see also Bispham 2000, 165 f. for the existence of an 'official', geographically organized, list of Roman citizen colonies by 207 BC.

²⁴⁷ A more balanced view of the Velleian evidence: Sherwin-White 1973, 293.

²⁴⁸ Carter 1995, 40, 'Almost as important in the history of Roman architecture is the function performed by the capital in providing models for the 'little Romes' which the newly founded colonies like Cosa and Alba Fucens constituted' (referring primarily to the *curia-comitium* complex).

²⁴⁹ Carafa 1998; Humm 1999; Fentress 2000b, 22 f.; Patterson 2000, 7, 14 f.; Liberatore 2001, 192.

²⁵⁰ On Latin colonial *comitia* see on Aquileia: Bertacchi 1989, 99 f.; Alba Fucens: Liberatore 2001, 192 f.; Cosa: Brown 1980, 22–4; Paestum: Greco 1988, 83; all except Aquileia have third-century phases. Note also the *lex Osca* from Bantia (Crawford 1996 I, no. 13, l. 21); this law, thought to derive from a (perhaps third-century) prototype from the Latin colony of Venusia, allows for the flogging of the *incensus* (the man who has avoided the census) in the *comitium*. Note also Zanker (2000, 36): *comitia*, apparently ubiquitous in mid-republican Latin colonies, became obsolete by the end of the Republic (also on the marginal long-term position of the *curia* in the development of colonial urban form). Note finally the imperial Marsyas statue from Alba Fucens.

²⁵¹ Ortalli 1995, 475–80; 2000, 501; see also Robert 1993, a dog sacrifice beneath a gate of the Latin colony of Paestum.

²⁵² Liberatore 2001, 189 f. A bovine statuette from Porta di Massa might comfort the Romulists.

²⁵³ M. Antonius at Casilinum, 44 BC: Cic. *Att.* 14.20, 21, *Phil.* 2.100–4 (a colony in an existing town); Imp. Caesar 40 and 29–7 BC: Crawford 1974 I, 529 f., no. 525; Grueber

1910, II, 17, no. 4363; the *lex Ursonensis* (Crawford 1996 I, no. 26) chap. 73, also refers to the plough having been drawn around the site.

[254] See Salmon 1969, 13, for Roman colonization as state-organized.

[255] See Fentress 2000b, 19, on Megara Hyblaia and Olynthos.

[256] Such a view finds some points of engagement with the plea for giving of due weight to *negotiation* (a very woolly term unless carefully used) between Roman and Italian elites, made by Terrenato 2001a. Nevertheless, I find myself, when the chips are down, in great sympathy with the position of Curti (2001, 24) : 'it would be interesting to see if modern colonized peoples would accept the term "debate" as a description of their relationship with colonial powers'.

Bibliography

Amat-Seguin, B.

1986   'Ariminum et Flaminius', *RSA* 16, 79–109.

Andrén, A.

1940   *Architectural Terracottas from Etrusco-Italic Sanctuaries*, Acta Instituti Romani Regni Sueciae VI, Lund.

Arthur, P.

1991   *Romans in Northern Campania*, Archaeological Monographs of the British School at Rome, London.

Austin, M.M.

1981   *The Hellenistic World from Alexander to the Roman Conquest*, Cambridge.

Bandelli, G.

1988   'Le prime fasi della colonizzazione cisalpina (295–190 a.C.)', *DdA* ser. 3, 6.2, 105–16.

Barker, G.

1995   *A Mediterranean Valley. Landscape archaeology and* Annales *History in the Biferno Valley*, Leicester.

Barreca, F.

1952   'Alba Fucense – elenco descrittivo del materiale rinvenuto nelle campagne di scavo, 1949–50', *NSA*, 233–46.

Barton, I.M.

1982   'Capitoline temples in Italy and the provinces (especially Africa)', in *ANRW* II, 12.1, Berlin and New York, 259–342.

1995   'Religious buildings', in I.M. Barton (ed.) *Roman Public Buildings*, Exeter, 67–96.

Bayet, J.

1926   *Herclé*, Paris.

Beard, M., North, J.A. and Price, S.R.F.

1998   *Religions of Rome*, 2 vols., Cambridge.

Beck, H. and Walter, U.

2001   *Die frühen römischen Historiker* I. *Von Fabius Pictor bis Cn. Gellius*. Texte zur Forschung 76, Darmstadt.

Bernardi, A.

1946   'Incremento demografico e colonizzazione latina dal 338 a.C. all'età dei Gracchi', *Nuova Rivista Storica* 30, 272–89.

1973   *Nomen Latinum*, Studia Ghisleriana, Pavia.

Bertacchi, L.

1989   'Il foro romano di Aquileia, gli interventi e le principali scoperte fino al marzo 1989', *Aquileia Nostra* 9, cols. 34–111.

Betts, E.

2003   *From Sacred Site to Monumental Sanctuary: How the perception and manipulation of the landscape affected religious experience in Iron Age central Adriatic Italy*, D.Phil thesis, Oxford.

Biondo, B.

1988   'I Potizi, i Pinari e la statizzazione del culto di Ercole', in F. Franciosi (ed.) *Ricerche sulla organizzazione gentilizia romana* II, Naples, 197–210.

Biordi, M.

1995   'I materiali numismatici di età romano-repubblicana conservati nel museo della città di Rimini', in A. Calbi and G. Susini (eds.) *Pro poplo arimenese (Rimini 1993)*, Faenza, 95–109.

Bispham, E.

2000   'Mimic? A case study in early Roman colonization', in E. Herring and K. Lomas (eds.) *The Emergence of State Identities in Italy in the First Millennium BC*, Accordia Specialist Studies on Italy 8, London, 157–86.

Forthcoming   *From Asculum to Actium: The municipalization of Italy after the Social War*, Oxford.

Bonghi, M. (ed.)

1990   *Artigiani e botteghe nell'Italia preromana*, Rome.

Bourgeaud, P.

1987   'Du mythe à l'idéologie: la tête du Capitole', *Museum Helveticum* 44, 86–100.

Bradley, G.J.

2000a   *Ancient Umbria. State, culture, and identity in Central Italy from the Iron Age to the Augustan era*, Oxford.

2000b   'The colonization of Interamna Nahars', in A.E. Cooley (ed.) *The Epigraphic Landscape of Roman Italy*, BICS Supplement 73, London, 3–18.

Braudel, F.

1972   *The Mediterranean and the Mediterranean World in the Age of Philip II*, 2 vols., London and New York.

Brizzi, G.

1995   'Da Roma ad *Ariminum*: per un approccio strategico alle regioni nordorientali d'Italia', in A. Calbi and G. Susini (eds) *Pro poplo arimenese* (Rimini 1993), Faenza, 95–109.

Brown, F.E.

1980   *Cosa. The making of a Roman town*, Ann Arbor.

Brown, F.E., Richardson, E.H. and Richardson Jr, L.

1960   *Cosa II. The temples of the Arx*, MAAR 26, Rome.

Brown, F.E. and Scott, R.T.

1985   'Cosa e il suo territorio. Il porto', in A. Carandini (ed.) *La romanizzazione dell' Etruria: il territorio di Vulci*, Milan, 100–2.

Cambi, F. and Celuzza, M.G.

1985   'La centuriazione, la viabilità e gli insediamenti', in A. Carandini (ed.) *La romanizzazione dell'Etruria: il territorio di Vulci*, Milan, 104–6.

Capedeville, G.
1995   *Volcanus. Recherches comparatistes sur les origines du culte de Vulcain.* BEFAR 288, Rome.

Carafa, P.
1998   *Il comizio di Roma dalle origini all'età di Augusto*, Rome.

Carter, J.
1995   'Civic and other buildings', in I.M. Barton (ed.) *Roman Public Buildings*, Exeter, 31–65.

Cicala, V.
1995   'Diana Ariminense: tracce di religiosità politica', in A. Calbi and G. Susini, *Pro poplo arimenese* (Rimini 1993), Faenza, 355–65.

Clarke, K.J.
1999   *Between Geography and History. Hellenistic constructions of the Roman world*, Oxford.

Coarelli, F.
1982   *Lazio* (Guida archeologica Laterza), Bari and Rome.
1984   'Abruzzo', in F. Coarelli and A. La Regina, *Abruzzo–Molise* (Guide Archeologiche Laterza), Bari and Rome.
1985–7   'La fondazione di Luni: problemi storici e archeologici', in *Luni e l'Occidente romano. Atti del Convegno, Lerici 22–24 settembre 1985.* Centro Studi Lunensi. Quaderni 10–12, 17–36.
1987   *I santuari del Lazio in età repubblicana*, Studi 'Nuova Italia Scientifica' Archeologia 7, Rome.
1988   'Colonizzazione romana e viabilità', *DdA* ser. 3, 6.2, 35–48.
1992   'Colonizzazione e municipalizzazione: tempi e modi', *DdA* ser. 3, 10, 21–30.
2000   'Il *Lucus Pisaurensis* e la romanizzazione dell'*ager Gallicus*', in C. Bruun (ed.) *The Roman Middle Republic: Politics, religion, and historiography c. 400–133 BC*, Acta Instituti Romani Finlandiae 23, Rome, 195–205.

Coarelli, F. and Morel, J.-P.
1973   'Pocola', in *Roma medio repubblicana. Aspetti culturali di Roma e del Lazio nei secoli IV e III a.C.*, Rome, 1973, 57–66.

Colonna, G.
1970   *Bronzi votivi umbro-sabellici a figura umana* I: *periodo 'arcaico'*, Florence.
1989   'Note preliminare sui culti del santuario di Portonaccio a Veio', *Scienze di Antichità* 1, 419–46.

Colonna, G. (ed.)
1985   *Santuari d'Etruria*, Milan.

Comella, A.M.
1981   'Complessi votivi in Italia in epoca medio – e tardo-repubblicana', *MEFRA* 93, 717–803.

Coppola, M.R.
1984   'Il foro emiliano di Terracina: rilievo, analisi tecnica, vicende storiche del monumento', *MEFRA* 96 (1), 325–77.

Corbier, M.
1991   'La transhumance entre le Samnium et l'Apulie: continuités entre l'époque

républicaine et l'époque impériale', in *La romanisation du Samnium aux II*^e *et I*^{er} *siècles av. J.-C.*, Naples, 149–76.

Crawford, M.H.

1974   *Roman Republican Coinage*, 2 vols., Cambridge.

1995   'La storia della colonizzazione romana secondo i romani', in A. Storchi Marino (ed.) *L' incidenza dell' antico. Studi in memoria di Ettore Lepore I. Atti del Convegno Internazionale, Anacapri 24–28 marzo 1991*, Naples, 187–92.

Crawford, M.H. (ed.)

1996   *Roman Statutes* I, BICS Supplement 64, London.

Curti, E.

2001   'Toynbee's legacy: discussing aspects of the Romanization of Italy', in S. Keay and N. Terrenato (eds.) *Italy and the West. Comparative issues in Romanization*, Oxford, 17–26.

D'Ercole, M.C.

1990   *La stipe votiva del Belvedere di Lucera. Corpus delle stipi votivi in Italia*, II:2, Rome.

De Caro, S. and Greco, E.

1981   *Campania* (Guide archeologica Laterza), Bari and Rome.

De Cazanove, O.

2000   'Some thoughts on the "religious Romanisation" of Italy before the Social War', in E.H. Bispham and C.J. Smith (eds.) *Religion in Archaic and Republican Rome and Italy. Evidence and experience*, Edinburgh, 71–6.

De Martino, F.

1972–5 *Storia della costituzione romana*, 3 vols., Naples.

Devoto, G.

1967   *Gli antichi Italici*, Florence.

Di Niro, A.

1977   *Il culto di Ercole tra i Sanniti, Pentri e Frentani*, Documenti di antichità italiche e romane 9, Campobasso.

Donati, A.

1995   'Il più antico monumento ariminense: semiologia e scrittura', in A. Calbi and G. Susini (eds.) *Pro poplo arimenese (Rimini 1993)*, Faenza, 393–8.

Drummond, A.

1989   'Rome in the Fifth Century, I: The social and economic framework', in F.W. Walbank, A.E. Astin, M.W. Frederiksen and R.M. Ogilvie (eds.) *CAH*² VII 2, *The Rise of Rome to 220 BC*, Cambridge, 113–71.

Edwards, C.

1996   *Writing Rome: Textual approaches to the city*, Cambridge.

Erskine, A.

2001   *Troy Between Greece and Rome: Local tradition and imperial power*, Oxford.

Fentress, E.W.B. (ed.)

2000a   *Romanization and the City: Creation, transformations and failures*. JRA Supplement 38, R.I.

Fentress, E.W.B.

2000b   'Frank Brown, Cosa and the idea of a Roman city', in Fentress (ed.)

Romanization and the City, 11–24.

Fontemaggi, A. and Piolanti, O.
2000   'Scheda no. 180', in M. Marini Calvani (ed.) *Aemilia: La cultura romana in Emilia Romagna dal III secolo a.C. all'età costantiniana*, Venice, 510–11.

Forte, M.
1992   'Le terrecotte architettoniche di Luni: la ricomposizione del rivestimento fittile del grande tempio e del Capitolium', in *La coroplastica templare etrusca fra il IV e il II secolo a.C. Atti del XVI convegno di studi etruschi e italici, Orbetello 25–9 aprile 1988*. Istituto Nazionale di Studi Etruschi e Italici, Florence, 185–223.

Franchi de Bellis, A.
1995   'I pocola riminesi', in A. Calbi and G. Susini (eds.) *Pro poplo arimenese (Rimini 1993)*, Faenza, 367–91.

Freytag-Löringhoff, B. von.
1992   'Annotazioni al frontone dei Sette a Tebe', in *La coroplastica templare etrusca fra il IV e il II secolo a.C. Atti del XVI convegno di studi etruschi e italici, Orbetello 25–9 aprile 1988*. Istituto Nazionale di Studi Etruschi e Italici, Florence, 69–76.

Gabba, E.
1958   'L'elogio di Brindisi', *Athenaeum* n.s. 36, 90–105.
1988   'Aspetti militari e agrari', *DdA* ser. 3, 6.2, 19–22.

Galsterer, H.
1976   *Herrschaft und Verwaltung im republikanischen Italien: die Beziehungen Roms zu den italischen Gemeinden vom Lateinerfrieden 338 v. Chr. bis zum Bundesgenossenkrieg 91 v. Chr.*, Munich.
1995   'La trasformazione delle antiche colonie latine e il nuovo "ius Latii"', in A. Calbi and G. Susini (eds.) *Pro poplo arimenese (Rimini 1993)*, Faenza, 79–94.

Gargola, D.J.
1995   *Lands, Laws and Gods: Magistrates and ceremony in the regulation of public lands in Republican Rome*, Chapel Hill.

Giampaola, D.
1991   'Benevento', in *La romanisation du Samnium aux IIᵉ et Iᵉʳ siècles av J.-C. Actes du Colloque...Naples, 4–5 novembre 1988*. Bibliothèque de l'Institut Français de Naples, IIᵉ ser., vol. IX, Naples, 123–31.
2000   'Benevento: dal centro indigeno alla colonia latina', in R. Cappelli (ed.) *Studi sull'Italia dei Sanniti*, Milan, 36–46.

Giangiulio, M.
1983   'Greci e non-Greci in Sicilia alla luce dei culti e delle leggende di Eracle', in *Forme di contatto e processi di trasformazione nelle società antiche. Atti del convegno di Cortona (24–30 maggio 1981)*, Pisa and Rome, 785–845.
1993   'La dedica ad Eracle di Nicomaco (*IG XIV* 652). Un'iscrizione arcaica di Lucania ed i rapporti fra greci ed indigeni nell'entroterra di Metaponto', in A. Mastrocinque (ed.) *Ercole in Occidente. Atti del Colloquio Internazionale, Trento, 7 marzo 1990. Labirinti 2. Collana del Dipartimento di Scienze Filologiche e Storiche, Università degli Studi di Trento*, Trento, 29–48.

Giovagnetti, A.
   1995   'La ceramica di Rimini repubblicana. La vernice nera di produzione locale',
           in A. Calbi and G. Susini (eds.) *Pro poplo arimenese (Rimini 1993)*, Faenza,
           437–68.
Glinister, F.N.
   2000   'Sacred rubbish', in E.H. Bispham and C.J. Smith (eds.) *Religion in Archaic
           and Republican Rome and Italy. Evidence and experience*, Edinburgh, 54–70.
Greco, E.
   1988   'Archeologia della colonia latina di Paestum', *DdA* ser. 3, 6.2, 79–86.
Grueber, H.A.
   1910   *Coins of the Roman Republic in the British Museum*, London.
Gruen, E.S.
   1992   *Culture and Identity in Republican Rome*, London.
Guidobaldi, M.P.
   1988   'La *colonia civium Romanorum* di Minturnae', *DdA* ser. 3, 6.2, 125–33.
   2001   'Transformations and continuities in a conquered territory: the case of the
           Ager Praetuttianus', in S. Keay and N. Terrenato (eds.) *Italy and the West.
           Comparative issues in Romanization*, Oxford, 85–90.
Guidobaldi, M.P. and Pesando, F.
   1989   'La *colonia civium Romanorum*', in F. Coarelli (ed.) *Minturnae*, Rome,
           35–66.
Harris, W.V.
   1989   'Roman expansion in the West', in *CAH*² VIII, Cambridge, 107–62.
Hayes, J.W.
   1997   *Handbook of Mediterranean Roman Pottery*, London.
Horden, P. and Purcell, N.
   2000   *The Corrupting Sea. A study of Mediterranean history*, Oxford.
Humm, M.
   1999   'Le comitium du forum romain et la réforme des tribus d'Appius Claudius
           Caecus', *MEFRA* 111, 625–94.
Keay, S. and Terrenato, N. (eds.)
   2001   *Italy and the West. Comparative issues in Romanization*, Oxford.
Koch, H.
   1912   *Dachterrakotten aus Campania mit Ausschluss von Pompeii*, Berlin.
Lambrechts, R.
   1996   *Artena 3. Un 'mundus' sur le Piano della Cività*, Brussels and Rome.
Laurence, R.
   1999   *The Roads of Roman Italy. Mobility and cultural change*, London and New
           York.
Leigh, M.
   2000   'Hercules', *Journal of Mediterranean Studies* 10, 125–38.
Liberatore, D.
   2001   'Alba Fucens', in A. Campanelli (ed.) *Il tesoro del lago. L'archeologia del Fucino
           e la collezione Torlonia*, Pescara, 186–209.
Lippolis, E., Baldini Lippolis, I.
   1997   'La formazione e lo sviluppo del centro urbano di *Brundisium*: aspetti e
           problemi della ricerca', *Taras* 17, 2, 305–53.

MacMullen, R.
    2000   *Romanization in the Time of Augustus*, New Haven and London.
Malkin, I.
    1987   *Religion and Colonization in Ancient Greece*, Leiden.
    1994   'Inside and outside: colonisation and the formation of the mother-city', in
            *APOIKIA. Scritti in onore di Giorgio Buchner. Annali di Archeologia e Storia
            antica* n.s. 1, 1–10.
Mangani, E.
    1973   'Herklesschalen', in *Roma medio repubblicana. Aspetti culturali di Roma e del
            Lazio nei secoli IV e III a.C.*, Rome, 70.
Massa Pairault, F.-H.
    1985a   'Talamone e l'area costiera. Il tempio e il frontone', in A. Carandini (ed.) *La
            romanizzazione dell'Etruria: il territorio di Vulci*, Milan, 119–21.
    1985b   *Recherches sur l'art et l'artisanat étrusco-italiques à l'époque héllenistique*,
            Rome.
Mastrocinque, A.
    1993   'Eracle "iperboreo" in Etruria', in A. Mastrocinque (ed.) *Ercole in Occidente.
            Atti del Colloquio Internazionale, Trento, 7 marzo 1990. Labirinti 2. Collana
            del Dipartimento di Scienze Filologiche e Storiche, Università degli Studi di
            Trento*, Trento, 49–61.
    1998   'Roma Quadrata', *MEFRA* 100, 2, 681–97.
Mattingly, D.J. (ed.)
    1997   *Dialogues in Roman Imperialism.* JRA Supplement 23, Providence, R.I.
Mattiocco, E. and van Wonterghem, F.
    1989   'La fortuna di Ercole tra i Peligni', in E. Mattiocco (ed.) *Dalla Villa di Ovidio
            al Santuario di Ercole*, Sulmona, 47–70.
Mertens, J.
    1969   'Deux temples italiques à Alba Fucens', in J. Mertens (ed.) *Alba Fucens* II.
            Rapports et Études, Brussels, 7–22.
    1988   'Alba Fucens', *DdA* ser. 3, 6.2, 87–104.
Mingazzini, P.
    1938   'Il santuario della dea Marica alle foci del Garigliano', *MonAL* 37, 49–61.
    1958   'Tre brevi note di ceramica ellenistica', *Arch. Class.* 10, 225–6.
Mommsen, Th.
    1887   *Römisches Staatsrecht* III, Leipzig.
Morel, J.-P.
    1981   *Céramique campanienne: les formes*, 2 vols., Rome.
    1983   'Les producteurs de biens artisanaux en Italie à la fin de la république', in M.
            Cébeillac-Gervasoni (ed.) *Les 'bourgeoisies' municipales italiennes aux IIe et Ier
            siècles av. J.-C.* Centre J. Bérard. Institut Français de Naples, 7–10 décembre
            1981. Colloques internationaux du CNRS n. 609, Paris and Naples, 21–
            39.
    1988   'Artisanat et colonisation dans l'Italie romaine aux IVe et IIIe siècles av. J.-C.',
            DdA ser. 3, 6.2, 49–63.
    1991   'Artisanat, importations et romanisation dans le Samnium aux IIe et Ier siècles
            av. J.-C.', in *La romanisation du Samnium aux IIe et Ier siècles av J.-C. Actes du
            Colloque... Naples, 4–5 novembre 1988.* Bibliothèque de l'Institut Français

de Naples, II^c ser., vol. IX, Naples, 187–203.

1999   'Un *mundus* à Artena?', *JRA* 12, 483–4.

Morris, I.

1992   *Death Ritual and Social Structure in Classical Antiquity*, Cambridge.

1998   'Archaeology and archaic Greek history', in N. Fisher and H. van Wees (eds.) *Archaic Greece: New approaches and new evidence*, London, 1–91.

Mouritsen, H.

1998   *Italian Unification: A study in ancient and modern historiography*. BICS Supplement 70, London.

2004   'Pits and politics: interpreting colonial fora in republican Italy', *PBSR* 72, 37–67.

Nicolet, C.

1985   'Centralisation d'état et problèmes du recensement dans le monde gréco-romain', in *Culture et idéologie dans la genèse de l'Etat moderne: actes de la table ronde organisée par le CNRS et EFR, Rome 15–17 octobre 1984*, Collection EFR 82, Rome, 9–24.

Oebel, L.

1993   *C. Flaminius und die Anfänge der römischen Kolonisation im Ager Gallicus*. Europäische Hochschulschriften, 3.555, Geschichte und ihre Hilfswissenschaften, Frankfurt am Main.

Ortalli, J.

1995   'Nuove fonti archeologiche per *Ariminum*; monumenti, opere publiche e assetto urbanistico tra la fondazione coloniale e il principato augusteo', in A. Calbi and G. Susini (eds.) *Pro poplo arimenese (Rimini 1993)*, Faenza, 469–529.

2000   'Rimini: la città', in M. Marini Calvani (ed.) *Aemilia. La cultura romana in Emilia Romagna dal III secolo a.C. all'età costantiniana*, Venice, 501–6.

Osborne, R.

1998   'Early Greek colonization? The nature of Greek settlement in the West', in N. Fisher and H. van Wees (eds.) *Archaic Greece: New approaches and new evidence*, London, 251–69.

Pagenstecher, R.

1909   *Die kalenische Reliefkeramik. Jahrb. Arch. Inst.*, Ergänzungheft 8, Berlin.

Patterson, J.R.

1988   *Sanniti, Liguri e Romani / Samnites Ligurians and Romans*, Circello.

2000   *Political Life in the City of Rome*, Bristol.

Pedroni, L.

1992   'Il gruppo degli stampigli erculei nella ceramica a vernice nera di Cales', *MEFRA* 104, 573–95.

Plácido, D.

1993   'Le vie di Eracle nell'estremo Occidente', in A. Mastrocinque (ed.) *Ercole in Occidente. Atti del Colloquio Internazionale, Trento, 7 marzo 1990. Labirinti 2. Collana del Dipartimento di Scienze Filologiche e Storiche, Università degli Studi di Trento*, Trento, 63–80.

Potter, T.W.

1979   *The Changing Landscape of South Etruria*, Oxford.

Principal-Ponce, J.
1998   '*Tarraco*, las cerámicas del Gruppo Hercúleo y el comercio romano-itálico anterior a la segunda Guerra Púnica', *JRA* 11, 233–44.

Purcell, N.
1990   'The creation of a provincial landscape', in T.F.C. Blagg and M. Millett (eds.) *The Early Roman Empire in the West*, Oxford, 7–29.

Robert, R.
1993   'Rites de protection et de défense. A propos des ossements d'un chien découverts au pied du rempart de Paestum', *AIONArch*. 15, 119–42.

Rocco, A.
1953   *Corpus Vasorum Antiquorum. Italia* fasc. 22, *Napoli, Museo Nazionale. Fasc. 2, Ceramiche delle fabbriche tarde*, Rome.

Rossignani, M.P.
1985   'L'area al nord del Foro', in A. Frova (ed.) *Luni. Guida archeologica*, Sarzana, 55–63.

Rüpke, J.
2001   *Die Religion der Römer*, Munich.

Salmon, E.T.
1954   'Roman expansion and Roman colonization in Italy', *Phoenix* 8, 63–75.
1967   *Samnium and the Samnites*, Cambridge.
1969   *Roman Colonization under the Republic*, Harmondsworth.

Sanesi, L.
1978   'Sulla firma di una ceramista caleno e sulla questione dei *vici*', *PdP* 39, 74–7.

Scott, R.T.
1985a   'Cosa e il suo territorio. La città', in A. Carandini (ed.) *La romanizzazione dell'Etruria: il territorio di Vulci*, Milan, 95.
1985b   'Cosa e il suo territorio. L'arx', in A. Carandini (ed.) *La romanizzazione dell'Etruria: il territorio di Vulci*, Milan, 95–6.
1985c   'Cosa e il suo territorio. Il foro', in A. Carandini (ed.) *La romanizzazione dell'Etruria: il territorio di Vulci*, Milan, 96–7.
1985d   'Cosa e il suo territorio. Le case', in A. Carandini (ed.) *La romanizzazione dell'Etruria: il territorio di Vulci*, Milan, 97.
1988   'The Latin colony of Cosa', *DdA* ser. 3, 6.2, 73–7.
1992   'The decorations from the temples of Cosa', in *La coroplastica templare etrusca fra il IV e il II secolo a.C. Atti del XVI convegno di studi etruschi e italici, Orbetello 25–9 aprile 1988*. Istituto Nazionale di Studi Etruschi e Italici, Florence, 91–8.

Sherk, R.K.
1969   *Roman Documents from the Greek East. Senatus Consulta and* Epistulae *to the Age of Augustus*, Baltimore.
1984   *Rome and the Greek East to the Death of Augustus*, Translated documents of Greece and Rome 4, Cambridge.

Sherwin-White, A.N.
1973   *The Roman Citizenship*, 2nd edn, Oxford.

Shoe, L.
1965   *Etruscan and Republican Roman Mouldings*, *MAAR* 28.

Skutsch, O.
   1968   *Studia* Enniana, London.
Smith, C.J.
   2000   'Worshipping Mater Matuta: ritual and context', in E.H. Bispham and C.J.
            Smith (eds.) *Religion in Archaic and Republican Rome and Italy: Evidence and
            experience*, Edinburgh, 136–55.
Sordi, M.
   1984   'Il Campidoglio e l'invasione gallica del 386 a.C.', in M. Sordi (ed.) *I santuari
            e la guerra nel mondo classico*. Contributi dell'Instituto di Storia Antica 10,
            Milan, 82–91.
Stambaugh, J.E.
   1988   *The Ancient Roman City*, Baltimore.
Stanco, E.A.
   1994   'Ceramica a vernice nera', in M. Balzano and A. Camilli (eds.) *Ceramica
            romana. Guida allo studio* I, Rome, 19–90.
Starr, R.J.
   1981   'The scope and genre of Velleius' History', *CQ* 31, 162–74.
Strazzulla, M.J.
   1977   'Le terrecotte architettoniche nell'Italia centrale', in *Caratteri dell'ellenismo
            nelle urne etrusche*, Florence, 41–9.
   1981   'Le terrecotte architettoniche. Le produzioni dal IV al I sec. a.C.', in A. Gia-
            rdina and A. Schiavone (eds.) *Società romana e produzione schiavistica* II,
            Rome and Bari, 187–207.
   1985   'Le terrecotte architettoniche', in A. Carandini (ed.) *La romanizzazione
            dell'Etruria: il territorio di Vulci*, Milan, 97–100.
   1992   'Le terrecotte architettoniche frontonali di Luni nel problema della coroplas-
            tica templare nelle colonie in territorio etrusco', in *La coroplastica templare
            etrusca fra il IV e il II secolo a.C. Atti del XVI convegno di studi etruschi e italici,
            Orbetello 25–9 aprile 1988*. Istituto Nazionale di Studi Etruschi e Italici,
            Florence, 161–83.
Susini, G.
   1965   'Aspects de la romanisation de la Gaule Cisalpine, chute et survivance des
            Celtes', *CRAI*, 143–63.
Taylor, D.M.
   1957   'Cosa: Black-glaze pottery', *MAAR* 25, 65–193.
Taylor, R.
   2002   'Temples and terracottas at Cosa', *AJA* 106, 59–83.
Terrenato, N.
   2001a   'Introduction', in S. Keay and N. Terrenato (eds.) *Italy and the West. Compar-
            ative issues in Romanization*, Oxford, 1–6.
   2001b   'A tale of three cities: the Romanization of Northern Coastal Etruria', in
            S. Keay and N. Terrenato (eds.) *Italy and the West: Comparative issues in
            Romanization*, Oxford, 54–67.
Tibiletti, G.
   1953   'La politica delle colonie e delle città latine nella guerra sociale', *RIL* 86,
            45–53.

Torelli, M.

1973 'Stipi votive', in *Roma medio repubblicana*, Catalogo di Mostra, Rome, 138–9.

1982 'Colonizzazione etrusche e latine d'epoca arcaica: un esempio', in *Gli Etruschi a Roma. Incontro di studio in onore di M. Pallotino. Roma 11–13 dicembre 1979*, Rome, 71–83.

1983 'Edilizia pubblica in Italia centrale tra guerra sociale ed età augustea: ideologia e classi sociali', in M. Cébeillac-Gervasoni (ed.) *Les 'bourgeoisies' municipales italiennes aux IIe et Ier siècles av. J.-C.* Centre J. Bérard. Institut Français de Naples, 7–10 décembre 1981. Colloques internationaux du CNRS n. 609, Paris and Naples, 241–50.

1988a 'Aspetti ideologici della colonizzazione romana più antica', *DdA* ser. 3, 6.2, 65–72.

1988b 'L'età regia e repubblicana', in P. Gros and M. Torelli, *Storia dell'urbanistica. Il mondo romano*, Bari and Rome, 3–164.

1993 'Gli aromi e il sale. Afrodite e Eracle nell'*emporia* arcaica dell'Italia', in A. Mastrocinque (ed.) *Ercole in Occidente. Atti del Colloquio Internazionale, Trento, 7 marzo 1990. Labirinti 2. Collana del Dipartimento di Scienze Filologiche e Storiche, Università degli Studi di Trento*, Trento, 91–117.

1999 *Tota Italia: Essays in the cultural formation of Roman Italy*, Oxford.

Tramonti, S.

1995 'L'Adriatico a Roma: la deduzione di Ariminum, una colonia sul mare', in A. Calbi and G. Susini (eds.) *Pro poplo arimenese (Rimini 1993)*, Faenza, 227–52.

Tréziny, H.

1997 'On the equality of lot division at Megara Hyblaia in the eighth century BC', *AJA* 101, 381.

Trota, F.

1989 'Minturnae preromana e il culto di Marica', in F. Coarelli (ed.) *Minturnae*, Rome, 11–28.

Vaccano, O.W. von.

1992 'Osservazioni riguardanti la storia edilizia del tempio di Talamonaccio', in *La coroplastica templare etrusca fra il IV e il II secolo a.C. Atti del XVI convegno di studi etruschi e italici, Orbetello 25–9 aprile 1988*. Istituto Nazionale di Studi Etruschi e Italici, Florence, 57–68.

Vaccano, O.W. von and Freytag-Löringhoff, B. von.

1982 *Talamone, il mito dei Sette a Tebe. Catalogo della Mostra, Firenze, 14 febbraio–3 ottobre 1982*, Florence.

van Wonterghem, F.

1973 'Le culte d'Hercule chez les Paeligni. Documents anciens et nouveaux', *Antiquité Classique* 42, 36–48.

1992 'Il culto di Ercole fra i popoli osco-sabellici', in C. Bonnet and C. Jourdain-Annequin (eds.) *Héraclès. D'une rive à l'autre de la Méditerranée. Bilan et perspectives*. Actes de la Table Ronde de Rome, Academia Belgica-École Française de Rome, 15–16 septembre 1989, Brussels and Rome, 319–51.

Vetter, E.

1953 *Handbuch der italischen Dialekte*, Heidelberg.

Webster, J. and Cooper, N. (eds.)

1996   *Roman Imperialism: Post-colonial perspectives*, Leicester.

Williams, J.H.C.

2001a   *Beyond the Rubicon. Romans and Gauls in Republican Italy*, Oxford.

2001b   'Roman intentions and Romanization: Republican northern Italy, *c.* 200–100
         BC', in S. Keay and N. Terrenato (eds.) *Italy and the West. Comparative issues
         in Romanization*, Oxford, 91–101.

Wilson, J.-P.

2000   'Ethnic and state identities in Greek settlements in Southern Italy in the
        eighth and seventh centuries BC', in E. Herring and K. Lomas (eds.) *The
        Emergence of State Identities in Italy in the First Millennium BC*. Accordia
        Specialist Studies on Italy 8, London, 31–43.

Wiseman, T.P.

1986   'Monuments and the Roman annalists', in I.S. Moxon, J.D. Smart and A.J.
        Woodman (eds.) *Past Perspectives: Studies in Greek and Roman historical
        writing*, Cambridge, 87–100.

1995   *Remus. A Roman myth*, Cambridge.

Woolf, G.

1998   *Becoming Roman*, Cambridge.

Zanker, P.

1998   *Pompeii. Public and private life*. Revealing Antiquity 11, Cambridge, Mass.

2000   'The city as symbol: Rome and the creation of an urban image', in E.W.B.
        Fentress (ed.) *Romanization and the City: Creation, transformations and
        failures*. JRA Supplement 38, Providence, R.I., 25–41.

Zuffa, M.

1962   'Studi archeologici riminesi', *Studi Romagnoli* 13, 59–70.

5

COLONIZATION AND IDENTITY
IN REPUBLICAN ITALY

Guy Bradley

Introduction

This chapter investigates the role ethnic identity played in Roman Republican colonization. It is written in the belief that our understanding of colonization procedures should take account of recent studies showing the complexity of identity in early Rome. If such studies are right to suggest that Rome was an 'open city' in the archaic period with a polyethnic make-up, how did this affect Rome's treatment of conquered ethnic groups involved in colonization schemes?

Our focus is on the Latin colonies founded in areas of Italy conquered by the Roman state. The importance of the role that colonization played in the creation of the Roman empire has long been appreciated. It made possible the demographic expansion of the Roman state; it was a way for Rome to dominate conquered territory; and it was also incidentally a process that spread Roman influence in colonized areas, as these cities used Latin as their language and formed models of Roman culture.[1] There is an established scholarly consensus on many aspects of colonization in the Republican period. Salmon, in the standard work on the subject in English, argued that in the mid-Republic colonies were essentially military in function.[2] The predominantly Roman origin of the settlers in earlier colonies was a vital element in their success: they acted as bastions of Roman control in hostile territory. Only with the second century did their primary purpose become the resettlement of landless Roman citizens.

However, recent scholarship has begun to recognize the extent to which many of our images of Republican colonization were constructed by later Roman authors. A central text is a speech of Hadrian related by Aulus Gellius (*NA* 16.13.8–9), describing colonies as copies and images of the Roman people.[3] The archaeology of colonies has frequently been interpreted in this light. Frank Brown suggested that the layout of the Latin colony at Cosa in Etruria (established in 273) was created using a foundation ritual reputedly employed by Romulus in planning Rome.[4] The city was then equipped within a few decades of the foundation with a temple of Jupiter on its Arx, a forum and a *comitium*, all in the image of the mother city. But re-examination of the evidence has caused much of this to be questioned. Torelli pointed out the late and antiquarian nature of the sources for Roman foundation rites.[5] Brown's interpretation of the archaeology of Cosa has been reassessed by Fentress, who suggests that the street plan actually dates to the town's refoundation in 197.[6] The new layout incorporated larger houses for the town's elite. Brown's desire to see the original settlement as egalitarian, which may have been influenced by the ideals of modern American colonization movements, had led him to interpret the large aristocratic houses that dominated the forum as public buildings. In fact, most of the city's public buildings, such as the Capitolium, were not built until after 197, and the whole creation of the urban infrastructure seems linked to the reinforcement of the colony at this point.

Recent work on ancient Greece has also illuminated the anachronistic nature of the literary evidence for colonization in the archaic period (eighth to sixth century).[7] Scholars have argued that the literary record was substantially constructed and reworked in the classical period. The archaeology of early colonization has shown that the first foundations exemplified by (but not restricted to) Pithecusae were of a very different nature to the elaborate cities of the classical period. Most early colonies show the same sort of mixed material culture that occurs at Pithecusae, and so show no firm evidence for the intervention or interest of *poleis* from mainland Greece (if we can talk of *poleis* as early as the eighth century). The archaeological evidence points to a more gradual process of settlement than later myths of individual 'founders' might suggest, and such myths are now understood to tell us more about the societies in which they were recounted than those to which they supposedly relate. The growth of sites like Pithecusae in the eighth century must be closely linked to trade and migration, part of a highly interconnected Mediterranean situation where individuals and groups were continually on the move.[8] These early Greek settlements abroad had much more profound and complex relationships with the indigenous populations than was once thought, and also prove to be much more diverse than the 'standardized' foundations of the classical period. Osborne regards only the colonies of the fifth and fourth centuries as comparable to those founded by Rome,[9] and the establishment of Latin colonies in Italy was not on the whole closely connected to maritime communications. But his method has a lot to offer studies of Roman colonization, especially in the archaic period, where there is evidence that many Roman 'colonies' were not the state-controlled exercises that the Romans later believed them to be.

Sources

Ancient literary records of colonization, even in the early Republic, often have a strong imprint of reliability, given by Livy in bald notices that are likely to have derived from official records.[10] For instance at Livy 2.21.7 the refoundation of Signia in 495 is listed along with the establishment of twenty-one voting tribes and the dedication of the temple of Mercury. Our sources also sometimes provide the names of the *triumviri* responsible for the setting up of a colony, as at Antium in 467 (discussed below) or at Saticula in Samnium in 313 (Festus 458). Oakley states, rightly in my opinion, that 'there is no reason to reject these notices'.[11] Festus' detailed reference to the foundation of a colony at Saticula also shows that some details and records of foundations were omitted by Livy (to say nothing of the sections of his work known only through epitomes). There are some disagreements between the accounts of Livy and Velleius Paterculus, who inserted an excursus on colonization in his brief history of Rome (1.14–15), but the substantial correlation between these two and other sources helps to reinforce the impression that there was a consistent record kept by the state of colonies founded.[12]

But alongside the general reliability of records of colonial foundations (where we have them), there are the problems imposed by the consistently anachronistic outlook of the sources.[13] Late Republican and imperial sources show a very poor understanding of early colonial situations. Their conceptions led them wherever possible to see colonization movements in terms of the organized sending-out of self-contained units of settlers orientated around an urban centre, the model that was most familiar to them.[14] An example is the supposed colonization of Fidene at the time of Romulus: Dionysius of Halicarnassus (2.53.4) describes it as a garrison of 300 men, presumably modelling it on mid-Republican citizen colonies, whereas Plutarch (*Life of Romulus* 23.6) records that it had 2500 settlers, typical of later Latin colonies, and even provides a foundation date (the Ides of April).[15] By the late Republic a developed ideology of colonization had arisen, in which colonization was seen as an ordered, state-controlled process which played a vital part in the success of the Roman empire. Our sources are inevitably influenced by this type of hindsight. Cicero, for instance, famously saw colonies as *propugnacula imperii*, bulwarks of empire, but was the function of colonies the same when this empire did not exist, and when Rome was one of many competing towns in Latium?[16] We often have to rely on Livy and other writers conveying information about early forms of colonization that they did not understand. Here, one of the strengths of Livy in comparison with Dionysius of Halicarnassus is that he tends to alter material less, and often simply tacks his own rationalizing interpretation onto events.

We need therefore to take care above all to avoid seeing colonies in an anachronistic light, and to distinguish between types of report. Whilst it is reasonable to accept most notices of colonial foundations (at least from the beginning of the Republic), it is necessary to be much more cautious about ancient interpretations and preconceptions. This is a position much easier to describe in theory than to apply in practice, as ideology and preconceptions to some extent inform everything that our sources wrote. It is particularly a problem with views of indigenous populations, where there is a danger that Roman liberalism with citizenship in early colonies was anachronistically retrojected by late Republican and imperial sources to the archaic period.[17]

Archaeological, epigraphic and numismatic material provides a different perspective from the often tendentious or confused picture of the literary sources. This material must be handled with care, and caution adopted when using one type of material to interpret another. We have seen above the dangers of interpreting the archaeological evidence from Cosa in the light of literary evidence, in this case opinions expressed in the speech of a non-contemporary (Hadrian). But used as evidence in their own right, these non-literary sources can provide a much more neutral perspective.

Roman identity and citizenship

I want to begin by looking at what we can discern about Roman identity and citizenship in the early periods of Roman history. This is necessary to understand the context within which early Roman colonization took place. It is well known that the myths of Roman origins stress the openness of the city.[18] For instance, it is said that Romulus built up a body of citizens through the creation of an asylum on the Capitol, where fugitives from surrounding territories were welcomed (Livy 1.8.5–6). The Rape of the Sabine women provided these citizens with wives, but provoked a war with the Sabines. The war between the two groups ended with their agreement to live together in peace, under the dual leadership of Romulus and Titus Tatius (Livy 1.9–13). Many of Rome's kings were reputedly outsiders. Numa was invited from Sabinum to rule the city; Tarquinius Priscus was of half-Greek parentage, had an Etruscan wife and migrated to Rome from Tarquinii. In one version, Servius Tullius was a slave born in the palace to a Latin woman captured in war (Livy 1.38.5). Such stories must have played a role in the Roman construction of their own self-image, which stressed the mixed origins of many early Roman heroes, and the Roman people as a whole.

For the late monarchic and early Republican period there is evidence of a more historical nature for inter-community movement.[19] We can point to early Republican figures like Coriolanus, who left Rome to command a Volscian army against his mother country.[20] The founder of the Claudian gens, Attus Clausus, reputedly fled the Sabine town of Regillum in 504 with a large number of dependents (Livy 2.16.3–5). He was made a patrician by the new regime at Rome, and secured grants of land for his clients.[21] Such stories are difficult to dismiss as fabrications and receive support from other types of source material. The inscription known as the *Lapis Satricanus*, found in the wall of a temple at Satricum in southern Latium, records a dedication to Mars by the *suodales*, the followers of Poplios Valesios around 500.[22] This is of interest both because the group define themselves in terms of their relationship with a leader figure rather than membership of a state, and because the name might be that of Publius Valerius, a prominent figure in the early Republic, who would therefore seem to be operating well outside the confines of Roman territory.[23]

Other evidence shows that this phenomenon was common to Etruria and other neighbouring districts as well. The Etruscan hero Mastarna, whom the Emperor Claudius identified as moving from Etruria to Rome where he took up the kingship as Servius Tullius (*ILS* 212), also features in the frescoes of the François Tomb in Vulci. He is portrayed in an adventure with the Vibennae brothers from Vulci, where they are overcoming various opponents, one of whom is Roman. Livy has several interesting records of armies in opposition to Rome being led by commanders from different communities, just as Coriolanus was supposed to have led the Volsci. These include an Aequian called Cluilius in charge of the Volsci at Ardea in 443 (4.9.12) and a Fundanian called Vitruvius Vaccus leading resistance at Privernum in 330 (8.19.4). The latter is said to have been a 'man of distinction (*vir clarus*) not only in his home city, but in Rome as well', where he owned a house on the Palatine.[24] Epigraphic evidence from Etruscan cities records the presence of names that must belong to assimilated, high-status immigrants, such as *rutile hipukrate* (Rutilus Hippokrates – a Latin *praenomen* added to a Greek gentilial) at Tarquinii and *tite latine* (Titus Latinius) at Veii.[25]

Such transfers and operations of individuals away from their place of origin are strange and confusing to our late Republican sources, who as a result often try to rationalize. So Tarquinius Priscus is characterized as unable to succeed at Tarquinii because of his background, and yet when he moved to Rome could aspire to the kingship. Obviously it is not in itself surprising that individuals could move from place to place in the archaic period. The important feature is that these individuals are able to preserve their social status in their new communities. Apparently unhindered by any ethnic baggage, they merged with the elite and might obtain high office: Coriolanus led the Volscian army; Attus Clausus joined the Roman senate. Similar stories may lie behind the early consuls listed in the Fasti with Etruscan names or with ethnic *cognomina* such as Sabinus or Tuscus (Etruscan).[26]

This horizontal social mobility has been identified by Ampolo as characteristic of Etruscan and Roman societies in the archaic period (seventh to fifth centuries).[27] Together with the image of an open society propagated by later Romans, it suggests that a situation existed where individual ethnic identities were not central to behaviour, and where state barriers were underdeveloped by later standards.[28] This must be related to another peculiar feature of Roman society, the apparent openness of the citizenship.[29] Greek observers remarked on the extraordinary tendency of the Romans to grant freed slaves Roman citizenship.[30] The origins of such a practice seem likely to lie in a period when movement between highly stratified societies was easy for the elite, but the lower orders of society gained little protection from being citizens of a state. Freedmen are mentioned in the Twelve Tables of 450 (V, 8), and the principle of manumission was presumably well established by this date. Only with the rise of the plebeian movement, and the assertion of citizen rights associated with the outlawing of debt-bondage in the fourth century, did Roman citizenship begin to be a valuable commodity.

Livy suggests that the extension of Roman citizenship to other peoples was not welcomed in the late fourth century, and in the Hannibalic War the offer of citizenship might even be rejected.[31] It is not until the expansion of Roman power in the second century that the attractiveness of Roman citizenship seems to have increased.[32] Conquered Italian peoples, such as the Campanians of Capua, were frequently incorporated into the citizen body in the fourth and third centuries, through the imposition of *civitas sine suffragio*. This practice continues until at least the first few decades of the third century when the eastern Sabine area was conquered by M.' Curius Dentatus and partially enfranchised. The porous and inexclusive nature of Roman citizenship contrasts strongly with the tight restrictions on access to citizenship imposed in many classical Greek states. In archaic Rome political and social authority was monopolized by the Patricians, and social status seems to have been of far more importance than citizenship. It is therefore unsurprising that the comparatively valueless commodity of Roman citizenship could be extended to slaves and conquered enemies.

This feature of Roman society was also reflected in religious practice: Roman religion had ancient institutions for incorporating foreign deities into its pantheon, such as the Sybilline Oracles, books of religious advice, or the practice of *evocatio*, the calling out of a foreign deity from a besieged city.[33] This wide range of evidence for the openness to outsiders of Roman society is symptomatic of a distinctive Roman mentality. It is tempting to call it 'archaic', but there are signs that it persists throughout Roman history. In some periods, such as the second century BC, political concerns about the consequences of such policies arose, and there may always to some extent have been a tension between those favouring expansion of the state and those resisting it: famous episodes of debate include the disputes leading up to the Social War, and Claudius' successful attempt to persuade the Senate to allow Gauls from Gallia Comata to join its ranks. Like earlier Roman politicians promoting the extension of citizenship, Claudius explicitly claimed to be acting in accordance with traditional practice (*ILS* 212), and the precedents of earlier mythical and historical incorporations provided a model to which he could appeal.

The character of early Roman colonization

Early Roman colonization in Latium should be seen in the context of a developing state identity at Rome, and perhaps a fairly loose conception of ethnic difference. What is immediately apparent is the diversity of colonization activities that are recorded in our literary sources. Roman colonies are often said to have involved indigenous populations, such as the Rutilians at Ardea (4.11).[34] Colonies established by Rome are frequently portrayed as turning against it: Antium is probably the best-known example, which I will discuss in more detail, but it is also the case for Circeii and Velitrae.[35] Oakley has noted that this is often surprising to Livy: for instance, at 8.14.5 he details the particularly harsh punishment of Velitrae in 338, because it had often rebelled despite being made up of Roman citizens. It is also interesting that the opponents of the Romans are presented as founding colonies of their own: the Aequi colonise Bola (4.49), the Antiates re-establish Satricum (7.27), a city which had for a time been a Roman colony.[36]

The history of Antium, on the coast of Latium to the south of Rome, combines many of these interesting features. We are told its colonization was first suggested in 467 by the consul Quintus Fabius, who aimed to settle the strife between the plebeians and patricians that had arisen in that year (Livy 3.1.5–7, D.H. 9.59.1–2). The territory had been conquered the year before under the leadership of Titus Quinctius, and he became the leader of the colonial triumvirs. That the triumvirs were all Roman shows that foundation initiatives were not, as Salmon thought, the preserve of the Latin League.[37] The composition of the colony, like that reported for many others in this era, included the conquered population, in this case Volscians: our sources add what looks like an unnecessary rationalising interpretation, that this was undertaken because there were insufficient Romans.[38] Antium is presented as the Volscian capital by the 380s in book six of Livy. In 385 a large Volscian force gathered in the Pomptine district, who were aided by Latins, Hernici, and Roman colonists from Circeii and Velitrae (Livy 6.12.6). On being taken prisoner by the Romans these men were forced to admit the full involvement of their respective states, which suggests that it was also possible for them to operate outside their city's jurisdiction. In 347 or 346 Livy records the Antiates sending out a Volscian colony to Satricum (7.27.2). After the Latin defeat in 338, a Roman colony was again sent to Antium, with the extraordinary qualification that the Antiates might again enroll themselves as colonists (Livy 8.14.8: *ut Antiatibus permitteretur, si et ipsi adscribi coloni vellent*). This surprising episode cannot have been an annalistic invention, and is supported by the reference to a complaint in 317 from unspecified Antiates, probably the unincorporated part of the indigenous population, that they were living without a fixed constitution or magistrates (Livy 9.20.10). The Senate appointed patrons from the colony to draw up the required laws, who probably incorporated the complainants into the colony, or arranged for them to be administered from it.[39] This example, to which others could be added, strongly suggests that the Romans had not developed a set policy of excluding natives from colonies.

Alternative types of 'colonization', not firmly under state control, also seem to have existed in the archaic period.[40] Colonization was closely connected to warfare. Land usually had to be conquered before being settled. Much warfare seemed to have taken place outside the control of archaic state authorities. Prominent individuals such as Appius Herdonius, the brothers Vibennae, Mastarna, and Publius Valerius are attested as undertaking military operations independently, with their own war bands.[41] They have been described as *condotierri*, drawing an analogy with mediaeval warlords, who were sometimes successful in establishing themselves as dynastic leaders of Italian communes. Private military operations in the archaic period might also be undertaken by *gentes*, supra-family groups. This is clear from the war waged by the *gens Fabia* on Veii in 477 (Livy 2.48–50). The story of Attus Clausus, referred to above, shows how whole gentile groups might move and resettle.

The nature of the Roman state in the archaic period makes it worth asking under whose control early colonization operations were undertaken. Our sources describe the kings founding colonies, such as Ostia by Ancus Marcius (Livy 1.33.9). But the considerable power of the Senate over mid-Republican colonization must be a later development. The Senate *per se* may not have been a particularly influential body until the *lex Ovinia* was passed in the late fourth century.[42] In the early Republic the situation seems more akin to the monarchy, with the initiative resting with powerful individuals. Colonial triumvirs, some of whose names seem to have been genuinely remembered from this period, must have been in a very powerful position, given the absence of guiding senatorial power. It seems to have been the right of the men who conquered the land to settle it, and the right of the successful general to be responsible for its distribution. He could expect to occupy the foremost position on the triumviral commission: Titus Quinctius, for example, led the triumvirate founding the colony at Antium in 467.[43] There is not a great deal of difference between this type of state-sanctioned operation and the activities of powerful *condotierri* such as Publius Valerius, who, if correctly identified as Publius Valerius Publicola, reputedly founded a colony at Sigliuria, probably Signia.[44]

Thus in the archaic period colonization could be a private operation, a *coniuratio* in the term used by Càssola, in which a war band might seize land as well as cattle, slaves and other types of booty. A different type of private land siezure is attested in the mid-Republic, what Bayet termed 'armed secession'.[45] He noted that the Roman army stationed in Capua in 342 reputedly hatched a plot to capture the city in the same way that Samnites had some 80 years earlier (Livy 7.38). In 282 just such a plot was carried out by the Roman legion sent to garrison Rhegion; the city was not recaptured until 270, and the Campanian garrison gained a dominant position like that of the Mamertini who took over Messana on Sicily. Bayet offers two interesting observations on these episodes. The Capua sedition develops into a secession, which is ultimately said by some writers to have won privileges for the plebs: Livy dutifully records these at 7.42.1–2, and expresses some surprise that this was possible. In addition, Servius (*ad Aen.* 1.12) records that colonies could be founded by secession (*ex secessione*), which were to be distinguished from those founded by public agreement (*ex consensu publico*). There would thus seem to be some justification in seeing this as another unofficial way of establishing a colony, which like the archaic *coniuratio*, left its traces in the historical record.

Anthropologists often focus on the tendency of early state societies to undergo fission, perhaps what we are seeing with Bayet's 'secession'.[46] It is only with the establishment of durable state structures that this tendency is controlled, and perhaps channelled into a form for the benefit of the state. As well as the Roman cases, some distant reflection of this may be found in the Italic myths of the 'Sacred Spring', where part of the population (those born in a designated year) migrated to form their own community elsewhere. Whilst these myths serve as ethnic foundation stories, and must be fictionalized, ideas of such practices may stem from the regular fission of pre-state social groups.[47]

Social and economic aspects of early colonization

The historical tradition frequently portrays colonization in the fifth and early fourth century as the result of plebeian agitation.[48] Salmon completely denied the historicity of these episodes, seeing them as a result of the contamination of the annalistic record in the period after the Gracchi, when discussion of land distributions became hugely controversial.[49] Although admitting that priestly records were likely to have preserved reports of colonial foundations, he rejected the idea that they could include traces of the controversies that led to these actions. He instead argued that early- and mid-Republican foundations should be seen as primarily of military importance.[50]

The difficulties of asserting the value of the annalistic record for this type of information are formidable. But the problem with Salmon's approach is not just that it involves the wholesale rejection of a central element of the annalistic account for the early Republic, but also that it substitutes for it a version dictated at best by the hindsight of Roman authors of the late Republic such as Cicero, who saw colonies as *propugnacula imperii* (at least when it suited his legal argument).[51] This version may indeed be substantially correct, but we should also take account of other indications in our sources.

The link between colonization and the Struggle of the Orders is made explicit even for quite late periods in the literary accounts. Livy records, for instance, that the foundation of Cales in 334 was designed to anticipate the desires of the plebs (8.16.13). Cales was the first Latin colony to be founded outside Latium, and it inaugurated what is often seen as the golden age of Latin colonization. This period corresponds with the end of debt-bondage (*nexum*), a form of labour which Finley suggested was at the heart of the Struggle of the Orders.[52] *Nexum* was abolished in 326, but was probably already on the wane by this period. Several notices in Livy suggest that chattel slavery, which must have provided a more convenient alternative labour source for the rich, substantially increased in the fourth century.[53] Livy reports that all the population of the great Etruscan city of Veii was enslaved in 396 on its capture (5.22.1): there was presumably a market for the captives. In 357 manumissions reached a high enough level to make it worth imposing a 5% tax on the value of manumitted slaves (Livy 7.16.7–8).[54] In 296 the availability of freedmen encouraged the authorities to recruit them into the army as an emergency measure (Livy 10.21.3–4).

These developments have an interesting relationship with the ideal of the small citizen farmer, of which the story of the Roman general Cincinnatus, called from the plough to save the state in 458 (Livy 3.26.7–12), is perhaps the best example. The success of the plebeian movement in establishing the illegality of using citizens as debt-bondsmen may have played a part in the creation of this ideology, and it was presumably this sort of ideal that the colonization schemes were putting into practice.[55]

Livy records agitation for land distribution far less often in the mid-Republic as the cause of colonization. This could be due to the increasing availability of dry notices of colonial schemes, and the decline in annalistic speculation; but perhaps there is also no longer the same desire amongst the plebs to be assigned new land. Livy (10.21.10) reports difficulties in finding settlers for Minturnae and Sinuessa in 296. The plebs reputedly feared they would have to be a perpetual outpost in hostile territory rather than settlers on the land (*quia in stationem se prope perpetuam infestae regionis, non in agros mitti rebantur*).[56] Brunt asserted that any record of the feelings of the plebs at this time must be seen as annalistic interpretation.[57] But I think it entirely possible that difficulties with recruitment for colonies at this time may have been authentically remembered.[58] The links between social conflict and colonization recorded by Livy and Dionysius in the fifth and early fourth century genuinely reflect the situation in this period. It may therefore be misleading to emphasize the military role of colonization at the expense of its socio-economic function. As well as changing in function over time, colonies probably meant different things to different sectors of Roman society.

Indigenous populations in mid-Republican colonies

The late fourth century in many ways sees the end of these unusual colonization practices.[59] The process of colonization changed after 338 with the crushing of the Latin revolt against Rome and the reorganization of Latium under Roman control. Much of Latium and Campania was now part of the Roman state. Colonies began to be founded much further afield in Italy, in conjunction with the expansion of Roman territory. The colonists in Latin colonies were given Latin status, which now ceased to have a direct connection with Latium. As befits strongholds in recently conquered territory, Latin colonies were self-governing cities who could organize their own defence. Their independence is also apparent from the coinage they emitted. The break with earlier practice has been emphasized by Salmon, who sees 338 as a crucial turning point when Rome took on the responsibility of founding colonies alone, unlike the previous foundations by the Latin League. Rome had, in Salmon's view, become 'wary of this communal kind of colonization' as the new Latin colonies created tended to side with the existing Latin states, and led the revolt in 340.[60] But Cornell has shown that we need not assume that earlier colonial foundations were solely the responsibility of the Latin league and that the decisions were perhaps mainly taken by Rome.[61] Whatever the earlier role of the Latin League, Rome became the only authority founding colonies from 338.[62]

Did the conquest of Italy outside of Latium from 338 to the 260s greatly accentuate ethnic hostility, prohibiting mixtures of colonists and indigenous populations? Brunt affirmed that colonial populations in the mid-Republic were predominantly Roman or Latin: 'for reasons of security natives were not generally admitted to local citizenship or to residence within the walls of the early colonies'.[63] Furthermore, he claimed that the details of early Republican colonial foundations are unreliable, and Livy and Dionysius were probably influenced by the enfranchisement of Italy after the Social War and the colonization practices of Caesar and Augustus;[64] this led them to retroject liberality with the citizenship into the past. Brunt suggested that although the record is poor for the mid-Republic, we can look to 'intrinsic probabilities'.[65] The surveyor Hyginus (178–9L) says that the 'ancients' often placed the city on high ground because of the fear of attack. Instances of strong indigenous resistance to the establishment of Latin colonies are known, such as that by the Aequi against Alba Fucens and by the Marsi against Carseoli (Livy 10.1.7, 10.3.2). Livy also sometimes attests the genocidal slaughter of the earlier occupants of a colonial area, such as that at Luceria in 318 (Livy 9.26.1–5).[66] Brunt added 'No doubt these annalistic reports are as suspect as those [on plebeian agitation], but at least they correspond to natural expectations. The mutual hatred which characterized the relations of Sullan colonists and the Italians whose lands they had taken over might well have been exceeded in earlier times, when the colonists were men of alien race and language.'

There is certainly evidence for hostility between colonists and indigenous populations. Land had to be confiscated from defeated Italian populations to be redistributed to the new settlers. The literary evidence cited by Brunt also receives independent support from the archaeological survey of the *ager Cosanus* and the Albegna valley in Etruria. In the territory where the Latin colony of Cosa was founded in 273 BC few fourth-century sites seem to have survived the Roman conquest. Survey evidence does not reveal the ethnic identity of farm owners, and it was difficult for the surveyors to date sites accurately to the third century BC.[67] But there does seem to be a real contrast between the territory of the colony and more distant areas, such as that around Telamon to the north and in the upper Albegna valley, where there was much more continuity of pre-existing settlement. Celuzza has suggested that new sites appearing outside the immediate hinterland of the colony, on the left bank of the middle Albegna valley, may be the result of the forced displacement of the indigenous population from the colonial territory.[68] Whether this amounts to 'ethnic cleansing' could be questioned when we have such a poor idea of the motivation or makeup of the colony, which could technically include other Etruscans (e.g. from Veii or Caere) as Romans.[69] Nevertheless the evidence does suggest that the foundation of the colony led to the displacement of most of the pre-existing population in its territory.

But this is not necessarily a typical case. Torelli has already pointed out the great contrast between the situation at Cosa and that at Paestum, both founded in 273.[70] The colony at Cosa was established on an unoccupied site, whereas the colonization of Paestum involved the dispatch of colonists to a large and prosperous city (Greek Poseidonia). The trajectories of the two colonies were consequently different. At Paestum the archaeological record shows that the physical installation of the colony undoubtedly had a substantial impact on the organization of the town, increasing its size from around seventy to one hundred and twenty hectares.[71] The Roman period saw the creation of a new forum and *comitium-curia* complex, superceding the old Greek assembly place, the *ekklēsiastērion*, which had continued to be used through the Lucanian period. However, the speed and extent of the change is controversial, and elsewhere in this volume M. Crawford has argued that the reordering of the community on Roman lines was both slower and less profound than has previously been presented. The eastern part of the town may have been open before the colonization, suggesting that the Latin colony was physically added to the city, rather than directly replacing it. What is clear from the archaeological evidence is that Paestum must have continued to have a massive Lucanian and probably also Greek element to the population.[72]

Paestum has a complex earlier history, having begun as a Greek colony and then passing under the political control of the Lucanians around 400. It was alleged by Aristoxenus of Tarentum, writing around 300, that the people of Poseidonia were completely barbarized, becoming in his words 'Tyrrhenians or Romans'; they had changed their speech and other practices, and in his time reputedly celebrated only one Greek festival (Athen. 14.632a). However, it is striking that the major Greek temples of the city largely continued in use during the Lucanian and Roman periods. There is other evidence that the city's Greek character remained: unlike all other Latin colonies, and like its Greek neighbours, Paestum continued to mint coinage into the early imperial period; ambassadors from Paestum are attested by Livy (22.36.9) as presenting the Roman senate with wealth in the form of golden bowls in 216, just as an embassy from Greek Neapolis had done the year before.[73] It now seems that the city underwent a gradual change through the Greek, Lucanian and Roman periods, and it is possible that Aristoxenus was making a deliberate point about Lucanian attempts to pass themselves off as Greek.

Another interesting example is Ariminum, founded in 268 at the south eastern point of the Po valley. A pair of notices in Strabo imply that the earlier Etruscan and Umbrian populations of this area were incorporated into the Roman colonies sent to the region. He notes that 'Ariminum is a settlement of the Umbrians, just as Ravenna is, although each of them has received Roman colonists' (Strabo 5.1.11). Strabo may be following an earlier source, such as Polybius.[74] We have some other types of source material to correlate with what he says. The continuous use of the extra-urban sanctuary at Villa Ruffi in the colony's hinterland is attested by material including archaic Etruscan bronzes, red figure pottery and Roman marble statues.[75] An interesting picture also emerges from coinage. The issues of Ariminum and Hadria, another colony further south on the Adriatic coast, were based on a non-Roman weight standard of 350–400 g shared with the Italic Vestini. Both these colonies, along with Luceria and Venusia in Apulia, used decimal divisions of weight, as opposed to the duodecimal Roman system.[76] The exact significance of such standards is difficult to discern, but it seems reasonable to suppose that a substantial local element in their populations influenced the choice.[77]

It has been argued that Ariminum is a special case because the Umbrians could be relied upon to support the Romans against the alien Gauls.[78] But some Umbrians and some Gauls, perhaps Senones, had allied against Rome at Sentinum just thirty years earlier. So the Umbrians are unlikely to have seemed much more trustworthy allies than Gauls. To my mind the exceptional feature of this northern Italian situation is that we have explicit testimony on the ethnic composition of colonies, something that we largely lack for central Italy, perhaps because ethnically mixed colonies were seen as unremarkable in a central Italian context.

Other evidence directly attests the presence of non-Latin or non-Roman elements in some colonies, although it can be difficult to decide if they are remnants of the indigenous population or later migrants to the colony. In Aesernia a resident group of Samnites (*Samnites inquolae*) is recorded on an inscription of the second century.[79] They are a collegiate group with *magistri*, who oversaw a dedication to Venus. According to La Regina these Samnites must have been part of the indigenous population of the area, incorporated into the colony on its foundation with the inferior status of *incolae* (normally resident aliens). Degrassi suggested that these Samnites were of Latin status, attached to the colony by a process of *attributio*. In contrast, Coarelli has argued that they must have been more recent immigrants, part of a massive movement of peoples that took place in the second century from the Apennine uplands into Latin colonies on the fringes of Samnium such as Fregellae (Livy 41.8.6–12, cf. 32.2.6–7 for infiltrators at Narnia in Umbria). The organized nature of the group suggests that they had lived in Aesernia for some time, but it is ultimately impossible to be certain whether their presence went back to the foundation of the colony.

Nomenclature can also be of some help. The Oscan name Dasius belonged to a member of the colony at Brundisium well respected enough to be placed by the Romans in charge of a stronghold against Hannibal in northern Italy. This was in 218, some 26 years after Latin colonists had been sent to Brundisium, a Messapian city 'rich in historical traditions'.[80] Dasius must be of local, Messapian origin; yet he was serving in a position of responsibility that would only be entrusted to a member of the local elite. This strongly implies that members of the local aristocracy had been included in the colony with full status. Other non-Romans have been identified, again on the basis of their names, in the colonies of Beneventum (Oscan names), Paestum (Oscan and Etruscan), and Venusia.[81]

More evidence comes from colonies founded after the Hannibalic War. In fact, Càssola argued that it was only in the second century that Latin and Roman colonies started to include allies, and then only on a piecemeal basis. This was because joining a colony had become undesirable for Romans. Indigenous populations would, in his view, have always been treated on an inferior basis. The first example of the complete incorporation of the indigenous population was the anomalous case of Carteia in Spain, made up of Roman freedmen and indigenous women, and designated a Latin colony by the Senate in 171 (Livy 43.3.1–4). Other cases from this period include the three hundred Roman settlers added to the Greek city of Dichaearchia in 194, which in the new guise of Roman Puteoli retained its cultural character.[82] The reinforcement of Cosa in 197 drew on all Italians who had not gone over to Hannibal (Livy 39.55). And we happen to know that the poet Ennius, another Messapian from Rudiae, gained Roman citizenship from his inclusion in a Roman colony (either of Potentia or Pisaurum). This is unlikely to be a special concession to Ennius, and must mean that allies were enrolled in at least one of these colonies in 184.[83]

The presence of non-Romans in northern Italian colonies has also been widely accepted, though the evidence is not clear cut. A passage of Cicero describing the kinsmen of Piso from Placentia as 'breeches-wearing' (i.e. clothed in Gallic fashion), has been cited as evidence of their Gallic character.[84] But he is clearly not a neutral witness in this case, and is aiming to slander his opponent. Gabba notes the evidence for indigenous *accolae*, i.e. Gallic neighbours, living in close proximity to Cisalpine colonies, though references to them in Livy (21.39.5; 28.11.10; 37.46.10) are not explicit over their direct attribution to the colonies.[85]

What is more certain is that the co-existence of colonists and local inhabitants was often not on an equal basis. Colonies at least in the second century BC were founded as hierachical societies, not egalitarian communities. We know that plots of differential size were given to colonists in foundations such as Copia, where *equites* received 40 *iugera* and *pedites* 20 (Livy 35.9.7), and Aquileia, where 50 *iugera* was assigned to 3000 *pedites*, 100 to *centuriones*, and 140 to *equites* (Livy 40.34.2). Gabba argued that indigenous populations would be useful as a labour force for the ruling elite of colonies, who would not work the land themselves. Some of these populations may have been allotted land as part of the third class of the colony.[86] The classification of groups like the Samnites in Aesernia as *incolae* implies they had a distinct and undoubtedly inferior status to ordinary colonists.

175

From this evidence it seems likely that substantial numbers of the indigenous population were incorporated into Latin colonies.[87] In many cases they were in a subordinate position, at least initially, in relation to colonists from Rome and other Roman areas. But in a few documented cases, perhaps typical of a wider trend, locals entered the colonial elite.[88] So the situation seems more complex than a general exclusion of natives, despite Brunt's 'natural expectations'. The example of Dasius of Brundisium and the situation at Paestum both suggest that the practice of incorporating non-Romans into colonies went back before the Hannibalic War. Salmon makes the interesting observation that as a result of the settlement in 338, Roman territory already encompassed other peoples such as Volscians at Antium and Velitrae, and the Oscan-speaking Campanians of Capua and Cumae.[89] They would be as eligible for colonization schemes as inhabitants of Rome, implying that ethnically diverse colonial populations were possible, even if recruitment was restricted to Roman citizens. Non-Roman ethnicity does not always seem to have been a bar to incorporation, and the status of incorporated individuals may have been more important than their ethnic identity.

In fact, there is plenty of evidence that ethnic composition was no guarantee of a city's security or of loyalty to the Roman state. Our sources represent the Roman state as almost splitting apart in the Struggle of the Orders, and the secessions of the plebs as in many ways breakaway states. The early colonies of Circeii and Setia sided with the Latins in 340 (Livy 8.3–6): this needs to be explained not in terms of their ethnic make-up, but rather by their contemporary political interests. Roman legions posed threats to Capua, and carried out the seizure of Rhegion.

The most interesting cases are the rebellions of the Latin colonies of Fregellae and Venusia against Rome in 125 and in 91. Both rebellions were motivated primarily by the desire of their inhabitants for Roman citizenship. But as on neither occasion were they joined by any other Latin colonies, scholars have been tempted to connect their actions to their ethnic composition.[90] Salmon, for instance, argued that these revolts were the result of the strong 'alien influence' of local Oscan-speaking populations who had infiltrated these towns.[91] There is good evidence for the immigration of large numbers of Samnites and Paeligni into Fregellae in the second century.[92] But as Mouritsen points out, it is implausible that the inhabitants of Fregellae would have revolted in 125 without the prospect of support.[93] This was surely expected from other Latin colonies, and the Latin commentator Asconius records that the destruction of this city oppressed all the allies of the Latin name, not the Oscan peoples of the central Apennines.[94] Furthermore, the names of colonists at Fregellae testify to the mixed origins of the town's aristocracy, thought to remain substantially loyal in the revolt, and the loyal colonists subsequently settled in Fabrateria Nova include some with Oscan names.[95] Venusia may, on its foundation, have included many people from the indigenous population.[96] But its decision to join the allies in the Social War must have been largely determined by its military position, surrounded by anti-Roman forces.[97] The political and military context in which a community found itself normally played a much more decisive role in its decisions than its ethnic makeup, although the latter could contribute to the former.

Later views of colonies

How were these origins viewed in the late Republic and early Empire? We know that some colonies commemorated their foundation, probably as a way of stressing their Romanness, which other ex-allied cities were not able to do.[98] Cicero (*Pro Sestio* 131) tells us that at Brundisium the day on which the colony was created was celebrated each year. An inscription from Puteoli is dated 'ninety years after the establishment of the colony' (*CIL* X 1781) despite the original Romans in the colony having been heavily outnumbered by Greeks.[99] Livy seems to have thought of colonies as wholly Roman in composition (27.9.11).

However, this evidence has to be compared with other material which shows that the inhabitants of some colonies might trace the history of their city back beyond its colonization. This seems to be the case for Interamna Nahars in Umbria, which a local inscription records was founded in 673. Elsewhere I have argued that the city became a Latin colony in the early third century. This is the most plausible explanation of the different types of evidence for the city in the Republican period, despite the lack of literary evidence for its colonization.[100] If this interpretation is right, it would suggest that when colonies constructed their past, they might regard a colonial influx as simply one stage in their history, rather than the formative moment. The choice of this date in Interamna, whether genuine memory or invented tradition, must be a sign of local belief in the importance of the early (and perhaps pre-colonial) settlement and suggests that many of the indigenous inhabitants had been incorporated in the colonial settlement.

A similarly flexible attitude to colonial history is expressed by Strabo, who describes Magna Graecia as completely barbarized, except for Tarentum, Rhegium, and Neapolis. These are surprising choices to pick as standard-bearers of Greek culture in Italy, as Tarentum had received a Roman colony in the late second century and Rhegium was not only seized by the Roman legion which had been sent to garrison it in the early third century (and which killed most of the population in the process, according to Strabo) but had also been colonized by veterans in the late Republic. Other ancient authors stressed the integrative nature of colonies. In his famous excursus,

Velleius Paterculus weaves together extensions of Roman citizenship in Italy with colonial foundations. Appian's introduction to the *Civil Wars* (1.7) describes colonies as often being founded on the sites of existing towns, and noted that 'this was the alternative they devised to garrisons'. And in the Augustan list of the towns of Italy given by Pliny in his *Natural History*, most colonies of the third and second centuries are simply classed as *oppida*, irrespective of their different origins from indigenous Italic centres.

Conclusion

We have sought to untangle ethnicity from colonization. Modern preconceptions encourage us to view Roman colonies in an ethnic light, but Rome itself was a polyethnic state, perhaps from its earliest origins, and the diverse forms of early colonization, which were often not under state control, meant that the role played by ethnicity was much more complex than we might imagine. There seems good reason to think that the nature of colonization in the archaic period meant that the resident population was often included in colonies. In fact, the indecisive nature of ethnic conceptions in the archaic period probably meant that such inclusions were not originally the anathema they appear to us. The diversity of early colonization and its difference from later practice were very difficult for late Republican and Augustan annalists to understand, given their view, informed by hindsight, of the orderly and inevitable nature of the Roman conquest of Italy. Whilst it is important to appreciate the anachronism inherent in the sources, our response should not be a simple dismissal of their evidence. Rather, we should use the information of primary sources when it is not obviously invented along late Republican lines, or when it is supported by comparative parallels. This evidence suggests we should see colonization as a process that developed slowly over time, perhaps beginning as private aristocratic operations or as expeditions led by the king, and in the archaic period encompassing demographic migrations and armed captures of cities and land. Although the sources freely describe the settlements that resulted as *coloniae*, this will often have been an anachronistic term for them.

The different types of archaic colonization were only slowly standardized in the middle Republic, a period which probably saw the gradual creation of an ideology of colonization. This ideology affected both the nature of colonization, which began to involve the foundation of whole cities as ideal communities (hierarchical rather than egalitarian in nature), and the historiography of the process, as an idealized view of past colonization was developed. It does not seem at all apparent that every foundation from 338 was predominantly military. The situation is more complex than a simple need for bastions in the mid-Republic, and socio-economic foundations in the second century. I would suggest that demographic pressure on land, and social conflicts within Rome meant that colonization had a combination of motives from the start of the Republic.[101] The absorption of indigenous populations into colonies was not uncommon. While some colonies included few or no natives (such as Cosa), the ethnic make-up of colonies was not a consistent concern of the Roman authorities and is not therefore a decisive consideration in their foundation. Some happened to be where locals were annihilated, others where locals persisted.

The status of included indigenous populations often remains obscure, and in many cases they are likely to have occupied inferior positions. But the mental context of archaic Republican colonization suggests that full inclusion was more likely than a modern mindset would lead us to expect, and there is clearly a continuity in the archaic ethnic mentality that promoted the absorption of foreign peoples. The frequent openness of colonies should not be seen as a sign of Roman generosity, as Greek and Roman authors of the Augustan period tended to portray it, but rather of a hard-headed evaluation of self-interest.[102] This mentality is entirely compatible with, and inherent in the operation of Roman imperialism. At exactly the time that some Italians were being included in Roman colonization schemes, many others must have been working farms in the Roman *campagna* as slaves.

Acknowledgements

Thanks to Ed Bispham, Michael Crawford, Emmanuele Curti, Fay Glinister, Anton Powell, and other members of audiences at Oxford, Glasgow and London for comments and suggestions. All dates are BC unless otherwise noted.

Notes

[1] Cf. Torelli 1999 for a more active view of Roman policy in this area.

[2] 1969, 15.

[3] *Quae tamen condicio, cum sit magis obnoxia et minus libera, potior tamen et praestabilior existimatur propter amplitudinem maiestatemque populi Romani, cuius istae coloniae quasi effigies parvae simulacraque esse quaedam videntur...* ('This condition [of colonies], although it is more exposed to control and less free, is nevertheless thought preferable and superior because of the greatness and majesty of the Roman people, of whom those colonies seem to be miniatures, as it were, and in a way copies' [trans. adapted from Loeb]). Gellius' use of the present tense shows that *coloniae* of Hadrian's own day are being referred to, which were considerably different from the Latin colonies of the mid-Republic (cf. Bispham 2000, 157–8 and in this volume, *contra* Salmon 1969, 18; see also Zanker 2000, 41).

[4] Brown 1980, 16–17.

[5] Torelli 1999, 15.

[6] Fentress 2000, 17–18.

[7] Wilson 1997; Osborne 1998, rejecting the term 'colonization'; Whitley 2001, 124–7 for a more conservative approach.

[8] Horden and Purcell 2000, 399.

[9] 1998.

[10] Oakley 1997, 62.

[11] 1997, 53; *contra* Càssola 1988, 6, 16.

[12] Although the 'parlous state of Velleius' text' (Salmon 1969, 17) poses problems, and even 'archival' material might occasionally be invented (Oakley 1997, 38–9).

[13] Stressed by Càssola 1988, although to my mind he overstates the case. Cf. Cornell 1991, 58 seeing colonization itself as a process based on an anachronistic view of the past.

[14] See, for instance, Servius, *Aen* 1.12: *sane veteres colonias ita definiunt: colonia est coetus eorum hominum qui universi deducti sunt in locum certum aedificiis munitum, quem certo iure obtinerent* ('Indeed previous scholars define colonies thus: a colony is a body of those men who have been led out as a group to a fixed destination, provided with buildings, a place which they were to possess on fixed terms').

[15] Bayet 1938, 113 n. 6.

[16] Cic. *De Lege Agraria* 2.73; *Pro Font.* 13; further discussed below.

[17] Càssola 1988, 5–6; Brunt 1971, 538–9.

[18] Momigliano 1984; Cornell 1995, 60.

[19] Cornell 1995, 143–5, 157–9.

[20] Livy 2.33–40; Cornell 2003.

[21] Torelli 1999, 17 suggests the Veturii may be another *gens* who transfer to Rome, this time from Praeneste in 499.

[22] Stibbe 1980.

[23] Hermon 1999 thinks that Valerius established a military colony at Satricum with a *ver sacrum* ('a sacred spring'); cf. Torelli 1999, 16–17.

[24] Cic. *Dom.* 101; Oakley 1998, 607.

[25] Ampolo 1976–7, 337–9, 324 with other examples; Cornell 1995, 158.

[26] Ampolo 1981; Cornell 1997, 10 citing the consuls Post. Cominius Auruncus (501), Appius Claudius Sabinus (495), T. Sicinius Sabinus and C. Aquillius Tuscus (both in 487); the latter has the same gentilial name as an *Avile Acvilnas* known from archaic Etruscan inscriptions at Ischia di Castro (near Vulci) and Veii (Pallottino 1992, 7); Torelli 1999, 17.

[27] Ampolo 1976–7.

[28] See Ampolo 1976–7, 343: 'in età arcaica conta più il *ghenos* dell'*ethnos*, il *nomen gentile* più del *nomen* in senso etnico'; Cornell, 1997; Spivey 1997, 19 notes the 'transcendence of social status over ethnicity in the ancient Mediterranean'.

[29] Cornell 1991, 62–3; Giardina 1997, 5–6.

[30] *SIG* 543 (an inscription of a letter of Philip V of Macedon to the city of Larissa in 217); D.H. 1.9.4.

[31] Livy 9.43 (306), Livy 9.45 (304).

[32] This has recently been doubted by Mouritsen 1998; my view is set out in Bradley 2002.

[33] North 1976; Beard et al. 1998, 34–5, 61–3. Note, however, the interesting contrast offered by many Greek states, e.g. Sparta, where their exclusiveness of citizenship

was accompanied by submission to external religious authority (a point I owe to A. Powell).

[34] Torelli 1999, 20–2, 23–4 discusses the archaeological evidence from the colony.

[35] Oakley 1997, 508–9. He lists the following other examples (at 343): Livy 6.12.6, 17.7–8, 21.3; 8.3.9; 8.14.5.

[36] For an unusual later example, when Gauls attempted to found a town (*oppidum*) near the future site of Aquileia in 186 BC, see Livy 39.22.6, 45.6, 54.6.

[37] Oakley 1997, 343.

[38] Cornell 1995, 302, seeing this as a reinforcement of the record's historicity.

[39] For this interpretation see Oakley 1998, 565–6; on the identity of the complainants, see also Sherwin-White 1973, 81.

[40] Cornell 1995, 144, 308–9; Crawford 1995; Hermon 1999, 2001; cf. Coarelli 1990, Torelli, 1999, 16–17.

[41] Cornell 1988, 94–5; Torelli 1999, 16 for the link with colonization. The evidence for these individuals is cited in the section above.

[42] Cornell 2000 for full discussion, using the evidence of Festus 290L s.v. *Praeteriti senatores*.

[43] Càssola 1988, 15–17 for these principles. He believes the names of the triumvirate at Antium to be invented; but see above, and Oakley 1997, 52–3. Càssola also notes the case of Venusia (291), where L. Postumius Megellus was unjustly excluded from the triumviral commission (D.H. 17–18.5.1–2).

[44] Plutarch, *Publicola* 16, with Torelli 1999, 17.

[45] 1938.

[46] e.g. Service 1975.

[47] Dench 1995, 206 for fictions; Hermon 2001, 75–99, explicitly links the sacred spring with colonization movements.

[48] e.g. Livy 3.1.4–5, 4.47.6, 4.49.6, 6.21.4; D.H. 9.59.1 (colonies); Livy 4.48.1–4, 6.11.8, 6.21.4 (viritane or unspecified agrarian proposals). Cf. Oakley 1993, 21–2; Patterson in this volume.

[49] Salmon 1969, 115 (and n. 203). Cf. Brunt 1971, 538–40.

[50] Salmon 1969, 15.

[51] Cicero uses the phrase in *De Lege Agraria* 2.73, contrasting the usefulness of ancient colonies to the safety of the state with the ill-thought-out settlements that would result from Rullus' agrarian bill; and *Pro Font.* 13 on Narbo Martius, which provided witnesses in support of Fonteius' defence.

[52] Finley 1981.

[53] Cornell 1995, 333, 393.

[54] Oakley 1998, 181–2 on the historicity of this notice.

[55] Cf. Gabba and Pasquinucci 1979, 29; Cornell 1991, 58; Gabba 1988, 21.

[56] Cf. Livy 9.26.4 for similar sentiments about the unattractiveness of distant Luceria, amongst aggressive peoples (*infestas gentes*).

[57] Cf. Càssola 1988, 9–11; Patterson, this volume.

[58] Note that Luceria, Minturnae and Sinuessa were nevertheless founded.

[59] Coarelli 1992.

[60] Salmon 1969, 45.

[61] 1995, 302–4.

[62] The process of colonial foundation is examined by Gargola 1995.

[63] Brunt 1971, 540. For an opposing view, see, for example, Gabba 1988, 21. On Brunt's agenda, dictated by his interpretation of the Augustan census figures, see Broadhead 2002, 28.

[64] For further discussion of the possible influence of late Republican colonization on Roman historiography, see Patterson in this volume.

[65] Brunt 1971, 539.

[66] M. Crawford has suggested to me that the massacre of enemies was not necessarily something that the Romans would be ashamed of in this period: claims of genocide were often, to our eyes, curiously exaggerated, perhaps with the aim of securing a triumph.

[67] Fentress in Carandini et al. 2002, 62.

[68] Celuzza in Carandini et al. 2002, 108–10, including, at 109, discussion of the evidence for limited continuity of the indigenous population at nearby Orbetello.

[69] For the phrase, see Fentress 2000, 12–13.

[70] 1999, 43; cf. Celuzza in Carandini et al. 2002, 105.

[71] Greco 1988, 82.

[72] Cf. Torelli, 1999, 45.

[73] Crawford, 1985, 71–2, and this vol.

[74] Pasquinucci 1988, 56.

[75] Zuffa 1971; Fontemaggi and Piolanti 1995, 532–3.

[76] Crawford 1985, 15.

[77] Cf. Crawford 1985, 43–5.

[78] Brunt 1971, 540.

[79] La Regina 1970–1, 452, cf. Gabba 1994, 186, *CIL* I² 3201 with Degrassi's commentary; Coarelli 1991, 178–9. A dedication to Iuno Populona at Luceria indicates the presence of a similar group of *Samnites incolae* there, according to Torelli 1996, 38.

[80] Gabba 1958, 100.

[81] Beneventum: Torelli 2002, 77; Paestum: Torelli 1999, 76, Crawford, this volume; Venusia: *ILLRP* 690–2, with Salmon 1967, 316, n. 3 and 1969, n. 184.

[82] Brunt 1971, 540.

[83] Livy 39.44.10 for triumvirs; Cic. *Brut.* 20.79; Richardson 1980, 4; Càssola 1988, 12 for Ennius as indicative of the wider incorporation of allies.

[84] Cic. *In Pis.* 53; Bernardi 1973, 66 n. 2; Salmon 1969, n. 65.

[85] Gabba 1994, 52, 186; Celuzza in Carandini et al. 2002, 110.

[86] Gabba and Pasquinucci 1979, 34; 1994, 186. Note also the evidence for different sizes of urban plots at Cosa after the reinforcement of 197 (Fentress 2000, 17–18), where allies were included (Livy 33.24.8).

[87] Cf. the conclusion of Cornell (1989, 388), based on demographic arguments.

[88] The certainty of Càssola (1988, 5–6) that these populations were always of lower status is misplaced.

[89] 1969, n. 65. Note also Livy's reference to Etruscans from Caere serving in the Roman army in 302 (10.4.9).

[90] Despite this explanation featuring in no ancient source.

[91] 1969, 117; cf. Salmon 1967, 316, 343, 357.

[92] Livy 41.8.6–12, recording the migration of 4000 Samnite and Paelignian families to Fregellae before 177; cf. Livy 32.2.6–7 on Narnia, where representatives of the colony complain of the infiltration of outsiders, who passed themselves off as colonists. Coarelli 1991, outlines the archaeological evidence for changes in Fregellae in the mid-second

century, and argues (at 183) that the changing ethnic make-up of the colony did have an impact on the rebellion and its suppression.

[93] Mouritsen 1998, 118–19.

[94] Cf. Stockton 1979, 97.

[95] Rawson 1998, 72.

[96] D.H. 17–18.5.2; Torelli 1999, 94, 116; disputed by Brunt 1971, 56 and Bernardi 1973, 75 n. 65, suggesting that the number of colonists (20,000) may have been transmitted wrongly.

[97] Mouritsen 1998, 161 n. 26.

[98] Laurence 1998, 104.

[99] Foundation dates are also known for Saticula (Festus 458L), Placentia (Asconius, *Pis.* 3C) and Bononia (Livy 37.57.7); see Gargola 1995, 73.

[100] Bradley 2000b; for doubts about Interamna's colonial status, see Fora 2002.

[101] Cf. Càssola 1988, 14.

[102] Cf. Mattingly 1992, 50, on 'racially enlightened (though highly elitist) assimilation' of North African tribal elites, a policy operating on 'pragmatism, not altruism', and often 'exploitative and cynical'.

Bibliography

Ampolo, C.
    1976–7   'Demarato: osservazioni sulla mobilità sociale arcaica', *DdA* 9–10, 333–45.
    1981   'I gruppi etnici in Roma arcaica: posizione del problema e fonti', in *Gli Etruschi e Roma. Studi in onore di M. Pallottino*, Rome, 45–70.

Bayet, J.
    1938   'Tite-Live et la précolonisation romaine', *Revue de Philologie* 12, 97–119.

Beard, M., North, J.A. and Price, S.R.F.
    1998   *Religions of Rome* I, Cambridge.

Bernardi, A.
    1973   *Nomen Latinum*, Pavia.

Bispham, E.
    2000   'Mimic? A case study in early Roman colonization', in E. Herring and K. Lomas (eds.) *The Emergence of State Identities in Italy in the First Millennium BC*, London, 157–86.

Bradley, G.J.
    2000a   *Ancient Umbria: State, culture, and identity in Central Italy from the Iron Age to the Augustan era*, Oxford.
    2000b   'The colonisation of Interamna Nahars', in A. Cooley (ed.) *The Epigraphic Landscape of Roman Italy*, BICS Supplement 73, London, 3–17.
    2002   'The Romanisation of Italy', Review discussion of H. Mouritsen, *Italian Unification* (London 1998), *JRA* 15, 401–6.

Broadhead, W.
    2002   *Internal Migration and the Transformation of Republican Italy*, unpublished Ph.D thesis, London.

Brown, F.
    1980   *Cosa: The making of a Roman town*, Ann Arbor.

Brunt, P.A.

  1971   *Italian Manpower 225 BC–AD 14*, Oxford.

Carandini, A., Cambi, F., Celuzza, M. and Fentress, E. (eds.)

  2002   *Paesaggi d'Etruria. Valle dell'Albegna, Valle d'Oro, Valle del Chiarone, Valle del Tafone*, Rome.

Càssola, F.

  1988   'Aspetti sociali e politici della colonizzazione', *DdA* 3rd ser., 6.2, 5–17.

Coarelli, F.

  1990   'Roma, i Volsci e il Lazio antico', in *Crise et transformation des sociétés archaïques de l'Italie antique au Ve siècle av. J.-C.*, Rome, 135–54.

  1991   'I Sanniti a Fregellae', in *La Romanisation du Samnium aux IIᵉ et Iᵉʳ siècles av. J.-C.*, Naples, 177–85.

  1992   'Colonizzazione e municipalizzazione: tempi e modi', *DdA* 3rd ser., 10, 21–30.

Cornell, T.J.

  1988   'La guerra e lo stato in Roma arcaica (VII–V sec. a.C.)', in E. Campanile (ed.) *Alle origini di Roma*, Pisa, 89–100.

  1989   'The conquest of Italy', in F.W. Walbank et al. (eds.) *CAH²* VII 2, *The Rise of Rome to 220 BC*, Cambridge, 351–419.

  1991   'Rome: the history of an anachronism', in A. Molho et al. (eds.) *City States in Classical Antiquity and Medieval Italy*, Stuttgart, 53–69.

  1995   *The Beginnings of Rome*, London.

  1997   'Ethnicity as a factor in early Roman history', in T.J. Cornell and K. Lomas (eds.) *Gender and Ethnicity in Ancient Italy*, London, 9–21.

  2000   'The lex Ovinia and the emancipation of the Senate', in C. Bruun (ed.) *The Roman Middle Republic: Politics, religion, and historiography c. 400–133 BC*, Rome, 69–89.

  2003   'Coriolanus: Myth, history and performance', in D. Braund and C. Gill (eds.) *Myth, History and Culture in Republican Rome. Studies in honour of T.P. Wiseman*, Exeter, 73–97.

Crawford, M.H.

  1985   *Coinage and Money under the Roman Republic*, London.

  1995   'La storia della colonizzazione romana secondo i romani', in A. Storchi Marino (ed.) *L'incidenza dell'antico. Studi in memoria di Ettore Lepore* 1, Naples, 187–92.

Curti, E., Dench, E. and Patterson, J.R.

  1996   'The archaeology of central and southern Italy: recent trends and approaches', *JRS* 86, 170–89.

Dench, E.

  1995   *From Barbarians to New Men: Greek, Roman and modern perceptions of peoples of the Central Apennines*, Oxford.

Fentress, E.

  2000   'Frank Brown, Cosa, and the idea of a Roman city', in E. Fentress (ed.) *Romanization and the City*. JRA supplement 38, Portsmouth, R.I., 11–24.

Finley, M.I.

  1981   'Debt-bondage and the problem of slavery', in *Economy and Society in Ancient Greece*, London, 150–66.

Fontemaggi, A. and Piolanti, O.

1995   'Il popolamento nel territorio di Ariminum: testimonianze archeologiche', in A. Calbi and G. Susini (eds.) *Pro poplo arimenese. Epigrafia e antichità* 14, Faenza, 531–61.

Fora, M.

2002   'Regio VI: Umbria: Interamna Nahars', in *Supplementa Italica* 19, Rome, 17–40.

Gabba, E.

1958   'L'elogio di Brindisi', *Athenaeum* 46, 90–105.

1988   'La colonizzazione romana tra la guerra latina e la guerra annibalica. Aspetti militari e agrari', *DdA* 3rd ser., 6.2, 19–22.

1994   *Italia romana*, Como.

Gabba, E. and Pasquinucci, M.

1979   *Strutture agrarie e allevamento transumante nell'Italia romana (III–I sec. a.C.)*, Pisa.

Gargola, D.

1995   *Lands, Laws, and Gods*, Chapel Hill, London.

Giardina, A.

1997   'L'identità incompiuta dell'Italia romana', in *L'Italia romana. Storie di un'identità incompiuta*, Rome-Bari, 3–116. Previously published in *L'Italie d'Auguste à Dioclétian*, Rome, 1994, 1–89.

Greco, E.

1988   'Archeologia della colonia latina di Paestum', *DdA* 3rd ser., 6.2, 79–86.

Hermon, E.

1999   'Le *Lapis Satricanus* e la colonisation militaire au début de la république', *MEFRA* 111.2, 847–81.

2001   *Habiter et partager les terres avant les Gracques*, Rome.

Horden, P. and Purcell, N.

2000   *The Corrupting Sea: A study of Mediterranean history*, Oxford.

La Regina, A.

1970–1 'I territori sabellici e sannitici', *DdA* 4–5, 443–59.

Laurence, R.

1998   'Territory, ethnonyms and geography: the construction of identity in Roman Italy', in J. Berry and R. Laurence (eds.) *Cultural Identity in the Roman Empire*, London, 95–110.

Lomas, K.

2000   'The polis in Italy: ethnicity and citizenship in the western Mediterranean', in R. Brock and S. Hodkinson (eds.) *Alternatives to Athens: Varieties of political experience and community in Ancient Greece*, Oxford, 167–85.

Mattingly, D.J.

1992   'War and peace in Roman North Africa. Observations and models of state-tribe interaction', in R.B. Ferguson and N. Whitehead (eds.) *War in the Tribal Zone: Expanding states and indigenous warfare*, Santa Fe, N.M., 31–60.

Momigliano, A.

1984   'How to reconcile Greeks and Trojans', in *Settimo Contributo alla storia degli studi classici e del mondo antico*, Rome, 437–62.

Mouritsen, H.
  1998   *Italian Unification: A study in ancient and modern historiography*, London.
North, J.A.
  1976   'Conservatism and change in Roman religion', *PBSR* 44, 1–12.
Oakley, S.P.
  1993   'The Roman conquest of Italy', in J. Rich and G. Shipley (eds.) *War and Society in the Roman World*, London 9–37.
  1997   *A Commentary on Livy books VI–X,* 1, Oxford.
  1998   *A Commentary on Livy books VI–X,* 2, Oxford.
Osborne, R.
  1998   'Early Greek colonisation? The nature of Greek settlement in the West', in N. Fisher and H. Van Wees (eds.) *Archaic Greece*, London and Swansea, 251–69.
Pallottino, M.
  1992   'Vérité ou vraisemblance des données prosopographiques à la lumière des découvertes épigraphiques', in *La Rome des premiers siècles. Légende et histoire.* Actes de la Table Ronde en l'honneur de Massimo Pallottino, Florence, 3–7.
Pasquinucci, M.
  1988   'Strabone e l'Italia centrale', in G. Maddoli (ed.) *Strabone e l'Italia antica*, Perugia, 47–59.
Rawson, E.
  1998   'Fregellae: fall and survival', in F. Coarelli and P.G. Monti (eds.) *Fregellae* 1. *Le fonti, la storia, il territorio*, Rome, 71–6.
Richardson, J.S.
  1980   'The ownership of Italian land: Tiberius Gracchus and the Italians', *JRS* 70, 1–11.
Salmon, E.T.
  1967   *Samnium and the Samnites*, Cambridge.
  1969   *Roman Colonization under the Republic*, London.
Service, E.
  1975   *Origins of the State and Civilization*, New York.
Sherwin-White, A.N.
  1973   *The Roman Citizenship*, 2nd edn, Oxford.
Spivey, N.
  1997   *Etruscan Art*, London.
Stibbe, C.M.
  1980   *Lapis Satricanus: Archaeological, epigraphical, linguistic and historical aspects of the new inscription from Satricum*, Rome.
Stockton, D.
  1979   *The Gracchi*, Oxford.
Torelli, M.
  1996   'La romanizzazione del Sannio', in L. Loretta del Tutto Palma (ed.) *La tavola di Agnone nel contesto italico*, Florence, 27–44.
  1999   *Tota Italia*, Oxford.
  2002   *Benevento romano*, Rome.
Whitley, J.
  2001   *The Archaeology of Ancient Greece*, Cambridge.

Wilson, J.-P.
    1997   'The nature of Greek overseas settlements in the archaic period: *emporion* or *apoikia*?', in L. Mitchell and P.J. Rhodes (eds.) *The Development of the Polis in Archaic Greece*, London, 199–207.

Zanker, P.
    2000   'The city as symbol: Rome and the creation of an urban image', in E. Fentress (ed.) *Romanization and the City: Creation, transformations, and failures.* JRA Supplement 38, Portsmouth, R.I., 25–41.

Zuffa, M.
    1971   'Abitati e sanctuari suburbani di Rimini dalla protostoria alla romanità' in *La città etrusca e italica preromana*, Bologna, 299–315.

6

COLONIZATION AND HISTORIOGRAPHY:
THE ROMAN REPUBLIC

John R. Patterson

In the years between the 'Latin War' of 341–338 and the end of the second century BC, the Romans established some sixty colonies in Italy.[1] These varied extensively in the circumstances of their foundation, their physical location and appearance, and their constitutional status. Some were citizen or so-called 'Roman' colonies, typically small in scale and located in militarily sensitive positions, whose inhabitants maintained their Roman citizenship despite being established in a community far from Rome. Others were 'Latin' colonies, often further away still, whose occupants did not possess Roman citizenship; the grants of land they received were, however, frequently extensive in scale. The literary tradition also records about twenty colonial foundations established in the regal period or earlier in the Republic, a similar number may have been set up by Sulla, and over fifty colonies were founded (or re-founded) by Caesar, the triumvirs, and by Augustus in the early years of his principate, making a total of some 150 colonial settlements in Italy by the end of the first century.[2]

The importance of these colonies within the history of Rome – and indeed that of Italy more generally – can hardly be overestimated. They served as military strongpoints in hostile territory, helped to defend Roman rule in Italy from external enemies and internal resistance, and rewarded veterans; they acted as models for civic life, and vehicles for the spread of Roman material culture, contributing to the eventual integration of the populations of Rome and Italy; they provided an opportunity for Romans, Latins and allies in difficult circumstances to gain economic and social advancement. Their long-term demographic and cultural impact was very significant, as tens of thousands of Romans and Italians moved substantial distances to join colonies, or were evicted to make way for the colonists.[3] Furthermore, the whole issue of the establishment of colonies was in itself a major subject of contention in the political life of Rome, particularly in the late second and first centuries. Latin colonies possessed public spaces designed to reflect those of Rome, with temples, *forum*, *comitium* and senate-house;[4] under the Empire colonies were seen as having a particularly distinguished status, 'on account of the greatness and majesty of the Roman people, of which these colonies appear to be likenesses and miniature images (*quasi effigies parvae simulacraque*)'.[5] The towns were often laid out in a regular grid-plan format,[6] and their territory divided up between the settlers by means of centuriation into square or rectangular blocks, or strips known as *strigae* and *scamna*.[7] Both the urban and the rural landscapes of Italy were thus affected to a very significant extent by the establishment of colonies; some of these centres, by virtue of their strategically important locations and the natural resources of their territories, continue to be major cities even now – Piacenza, Cremona, Modena and Bologna in the north of Italy, Benevento and Brindisi in the south, for example.

Over the past half-century, our knowledge of republican colonization has increased substantially, largely due to the contribution of archaeology: important fieldwork has taken place at Cosa,[8] at Alba Fucens,[9] at Paestum,[10] at Fregellae,[11] and around Interamna,[12] to take only a few examples.[13] The archaeology of Roman and Latin colonies is indeed one of the few cases in which we can plausibly claim to be able to use archaeology to cast light on *histoire événementielle* (to use Braudel's term), given that the establishment of a colony can be dated to a specific year, and even in some cases a specific day – 5 August 244 at Brundisium,[14] 31 May 218 at Placentia,[15] and 28 December 189 at Bononia[16] – even more so when the destruction or abandonment of a colony can be securely dated, as notably in the case of the sack of Fregellae in 125.[17]

These precise chronologies of course derive from the literary record for colonization – preserved largely in Livy's *History*, which is complemented by a list of foundations provided by Velleius Paterculus and some information from Diodorus, Cicero and other writers.[18] The foundation of Saticula in 313, for example, is not mentioned in Livy but is known from a passage in Festus.[19] This evidence in turn is assumed to derive largely from the work of earlier annalists and from official records of the Roman state, while it seems likely that in antiquity there also existed histories specifically focusing on colonization, of which only tantalizing fragmentary indications now survive, for example in Asconius' account of the foundation of Placentia.[20] Putting together the literary and archaeological sources can be a particularly fruitful way of approaching colonial settlement, but in order to establish the chronology of colonial foundations without being misled into circular arguments, a careful analysis of the literary as well as the archaeological data is essential. The study of the literary record of the early and mid-Republic as a whole presents challenging methodological problems, of course,[21] and the issues surrounding colonization are no exception; a particular problem here is that the foundation of colonies was a technique employed by the Romans across a lengthy period of time, to respond to a variety of political, military and economic concerns, and the nature of the colonies themselves is bound to have varied significantly as a result.[22] All the more reason to look carefully at the historiographical contexts in which accounts of colonization occur.

Introducing his book *Roman Colonization under the Republic*, published in 1969, E.T. Salmon commented: 'So much has been said about this great Roman institution in the past that anyone who writes about it today is hardly likely to shed a blinding new light on it, much less to revolutionize traditional conceptions of it. He can, however, seek to collate what is known or guessed about the colonies, provide an up-to-date synthesis, describe their vicissitudes and men's changing attitudes towards them, appraise their varying purpose and importance, and perhaps suggest some new approaches to several old problems.'[23] His observations are still apt. This chapter aims to 'describe men's changing attitudes to the colonies', and in the process 'appraise their varied purpose and importance', by examining the different narrative contexts in which ancient authors, Livy in particular, discuss the phenomenon of colonization, and by exploring the changing ways in which colonies and colonists are portrayed in literary accounts. In particular, it will focus on two types of problem which are attested as having arisen in connection with the establishment of colonies: difficulties in recruiting colonists, and opposition and resistance to their foundation on the part of local populations.

Colonization in historiographical context

Central to ancient (and indeed many modern) depictions of colonization is the idea that the colonies formed components in a military strategy.[24] Cicero himself observed that 'our ancestors set up colonies in appropriate places in such a way as to protect them against even the suspicion of danger, so that they resembled fortifications of empire (*propugnacula imperii*) more than they did towns of Italy'.[25] In the same way, Siculus Flaccus commented that the Romans established colonies 'either to control the previous populations of the towns, or to resist the attacks of enemies'.[26] Analysis of the location and chronology of colonial foundations and their relationship with the roadbuilding projects undertaken by the Roman state in the mid-Republic does indeed seem to suggest coherent planning.[27] For example, the sequence of colonial foundations at the time of Rome's struggle with the Samnites in the second half of the fourth century BC – beginning with Cales in 334 and Fregellae in 328, and continuing with Luceria (on the eastern side of Samnite territory) in 314 and Interamna in 312 – can be seen as an attempt to surround the Samnite territory with colonies, and protect the Campanian plain. They can also be linked with the construction of the Via Appia between Rome and Capua in 312, and the earlier construction of the Via Latina, which is convincingly argued by Coarelli to have taken place in the 330s or 320s (see *Fig.* 1). To the east of the city, the building of the Via Valeria by the censor M. Valerius Maximus in 307 predates only by a few years the foundation of Alba Fucens (303) and Carseoli (298) in the territory of the Aequi. If we accept the traditional date of 241 for the construction of the Via Aurelia along the coast of Etruria, this can similarly be linked with the establishment of citizen colonies at Alsium (247) and Fregenae (245) and perhaps in broader terms to those of the preceding years at Cosa (273), Castrum Novum (264) and Pyrgi (mid-third century, perhaps also 264).[28] All these settlements can be seen to contribute to the fortification of the coast north of Rome against Carthaginian attack (see *Fig.* 2). Likewise, the establishment of Beneventum in 268 and Aesernia in 263 can be seen as a response to Samnite participation in Pyrrhus' campaigns against Rome, again contributing to the isolation of Samnium. A similar narrative and analysis can be constructed for the series of colonial foundations in northern Italy in the early second century.[29] Placentia and Cremona, originally founded in 218, were reinforced in 190, and Bononia was established in 189. The Via Aemilia, which ran along the southern edge of the Po plain, connected Placentia and Bononia

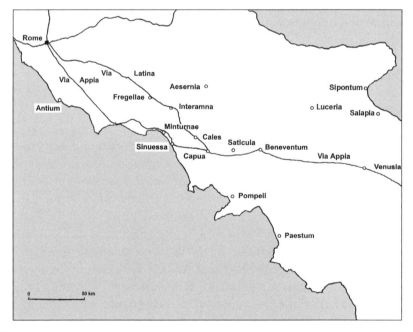

Fig. 1. Southern Italy.

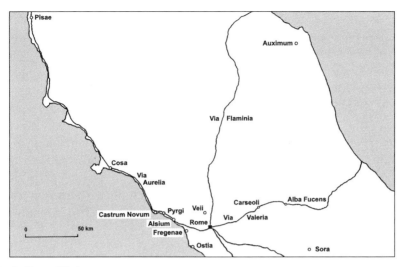

Fig. 2. Central Italy.

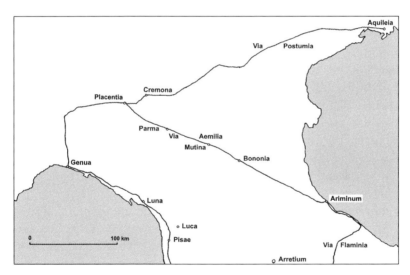

Fig. 3. Northern Italy.

with Ariminum in 187;[30] citizen colonies were established at Mutina and Parma in 183, to control access to the Apennine valleys and guard against incursions by the Ligurians who occupied them. With the defeat of the Ligures Apuani, and their mass deportation into Samnium in 180, Luna was established in 177 near the Tyrrhenian coast; over a fifteen-year period, we can see the Romans establishing their control of the region with the suppression first of the Gauls and then the Ligurians, and the building of roads and colonies was a central part of that strategy (see *Fig.* 3).

Examining the membership of the commissions responsible for founding colonies in this period also proves instructive: there appears to be a connection between the military risks associated with the location where a colony was to be established, and the seniority of the commissioners appointed to lead it out. Only consulars and ex-praetors participated in the commissions for the establishment of Cremona, Placentia and Aquileia, while more junior magistrates were involved in founding smaller colonies in the more peaceful south. We might compare the increasing use of consular commanders as the wars in Spain became a cause of concern to the Roman Senate in the latter half of the second century.[31] There also seems to have been a link between a general's role in the conquest of a territory and his participation in the commission responsible for the distribution of that land to veterans and other settlers.[32]

However, an alternative tradition about the motivation behind colonial settlement can also be detected; passages in the literary record stress the importance of colonization as a means of relieving poverty among the poor at Rome by allowing the redistribution of land. Appian, for example, while acknowledging the military importance of colonization, also alludes to the way in which conquest led to the acquisition and exploitation of land. 'The Romans, as they took control of Italy piece by piece through warfare, took part of the Italians' land and either founded new towns or recruited colonists from their own people to occupy those towns which already existed. Their intention was to use them instead of fortifications (ἀντὶ φρουρίων); the cultivated part of the land they had captured on each occasion they distributed to settlers, sold or leased out.'[33]

The idea that the establishment of colonies for military purposes could be combined with the distribution of land to settlers, and with the leasing or sale of public land, thus identifying what seems to be an economic motive and consequence for colonization, is echoed in numerous passages in Livy. One of the most interesting of these is his account of the establishment of a colony at Antium in 467. According to Livy, T. Aemilius, consul in that year, proposed to institute a bill for the distribution of land, and gained the support of the tribunes of the *plebs*, but in the process attracted the opposition of the *possessores* (occupiers) and many of the patricians, who complained that the *princeps civitatis* (leading citizen, meaning the consul) was making himself *popularis* at the expense of others. Aemilius' colleague as consul, Q. Fabius (who was also notable as the only survivor of the disastrous defeat of the Fabii by the Veientes at the battle of the Cremera) resolved the tension by proposing the establishment of a colony on land taken the previous year from the Volscians. 'In this way, the *plebs* would acquire land without the *possessores* complaining, and there would be concord within the state.'[34] Livy goes on to observe, however, that when the members of the *plebs* were invited to register for the new colony, so few persons enrolled that Volscian colonists were asked to join the community: 'the rest of the people preferred demanding land at Rome to receiving it elsewhere'.[35] Dionysius of Halicarnassus tells the story in similar terms, though he explains in a slightly different way the reluctance of the plebeians to join the colony: 'the division of the land did not please the masses and the poor at Rome who considered that they were being banished from their fatherland'.[36]

The episode of the colony at Antium effectively illustrates many of the problems involved in dealing with first-century accounts of colonial settlement in the early and mid-Republic. Scepticism about the story has been expressed by modern scholars from various angles.[37] The tradition (reported in Livy and Dionysius) that Antium revolted only a few years later suggests that if a colony was in reality established there, its impact was insignificant.[38] Salmon believes that the information provided by Livy and Dionysius may in fact relate to the establishment of the citizen colony known to have been founded at Antium in 338.[39] The leading role of Q. Fabius within the story in restoring *concordia* to the state – as other members of his *gens* had done[40] – might also arouse suspicion, fitting into an admiring view of the Fabii which may be traced back to family traditions propagated in the work of the third-century BC historian Fabius Pictor;[41] and the reference to *concordia* might also suggest that the story echoes the careers of the Gracchi. On the other hand, the fact that the names of the *triumviri* who established the colony, Ti. Quinctius, A. Verginius and P. Furius (L. Furius, according to Dionysius), are recorded in the surviving literary tradition, like those of later colonial foundations,[42] induces cautious optimism, while Cornell sees the sources' misunderstanding of the need to recruit local inhabitants for the colony as an indication that the tradition may in fact be correct.[43] In any case, we should remember that there may well have been significant differences between what was understood as a 'colony' in the second or first centuries and the reality of what was involved in the establishment of a 'colonial' settlement in the fifth century. Just as the warfare of the early Republic may typically have consisted of semi-independent initiatives by groups such as the Fabii (at the Cremera) and the '*suodales* of Poplios Valesios' attested at Satricum,[44] so it is likely that fifth-century 'colonization' may have involved the small-scale occupations of territory by individual families and their supporters rather than co-ordinated and centralized operations undertaken by the Roman state.[45]

In this context, however, the issue of whether or not a colony was established at Antium in 467 is of less importance than the way in which Livy and Dionysius choose to present the story. The linkage of colonial settlement, distribution of land, and the long-term political tensions between rich and poor at Rome which constituted the 'struggle of the orders' is one which recurs in many episodes in Livy, and not only in the earliest books, which we might imagine to have been most open to his own inventiveness or that of his annalistic predecessors. For example, in the account Livy gives of the foundation of Satricum in 385, the historian describes the Senate as a 'voluntary benefactor'(*largitor voluntarius*, perhaps with the additional sense of 'giver of bribes'), seeing the establishment of the colony as a response to popular protest after the imprisonment of Marcus Manlius, who had made himself dangerously popular with the *plebs* as a result of his campaigns on their behalf against debt and usury. As an attempt to placate the plebeians, this was however portrayed as unsuccessful: the 2.5 *iugera* of land allocated to the settlers was perceived as being too meagre, and accepting it 'seen as the reward for betraying Manlius'.[46] Likewise, the establishment of Cales in 334 is similarly described by Livy in terms of benefaction: '[the consuls] proposed that a colony be established at Cales, in order that they should anticipate the desire of the *plebs* by doing them an act of generosity (*beneficium*)'.[47]

Closely related to this tradition is the notion that colonies had a role in increasing Roman (or Italian) manpower. Livy reports that in 393, the Senate decreed that seven *iugera* of land in the territory of Veii should be allocated to each of the plebeians – not just heads of families – 'in order that with the hope of this incentive before them, they might be willing to bring up children'.[48]

Much later, when in 209, during the course of the Second Punic War, twelve of Rome's colonies complained that they were unable to provide soldiers and money for the Roman forces, Livy portrays the consuls addressing the representatives of the delinquent colonies and reminding them that they 'were not Capuans or Tarentines, but men of Rome, where they had grown up, and from where they had been sent into colonies and into land captured in war in order to increase their race'. [49] We have to see 'increasing their race' as possible only within the context of increased holdings of land allocated to colonists that made larger families viable, and the social and economic advancement which the membership of a colony could bring about.[50] Appian, sketching the background to the Gracchan land crisis, similarly explains that the motive for renting out public land was 'to increase the population of the Italian race'.[51]

Ogilvie, in his commentary on Livy's account of the foundation of Antium, rightly observed that many of the words and phrases used – *princeps civitatis* for example, and of course *popularis* – recall the language of first-century politics.[52] The repeated references to class struggle at Rome, and concerns about the problems of access to land in explaining the foundations of colonies, might simply be seen as retrojections of political conflict over colonization in the age of the Gracchi in particular, when we know that a desire to relieve the impoverishment of the Roman peasantry was a factor motivating land distribution schemes – just as so many of Livy's descriptions of political struggle in early Rome appear to recall the concerns of second- or first-century politics. The use of language recalling the late Republic does not in itself mean that the episodes recounted are invented, though – Romans of the second or first century BC would quite naturally have used the political language of their own times to conceptualize and describe events of earlier times. 'Land and debt were constant issues in political struggle in the Greco-Roman world', as Cornell justly observed.[53]

In fact, there are good reasons for taking seriously the repeated linkage, in literary accounts, of colonial foundations with attempts to improve the conditions of the *plebs* at Rome even before the later second century. Cornell and Oakley, for example, have demonstrated that during the period between the 380s and 340s when no colonial foundations are attested (presumably because of the increasingly strained relations between the Romans and their Latin allies in the period leading up to the Latin War), there is a dramatic increase in the number of Livy's references to the sufferings of the *plebs* as a result of debt-bondage and usury, and to the efforts made to alleviate that suffering. Indeed the problem of debt was a major theme of his account of the activities of M. Manlius. There is a *prima facie* case for arguing that the suspension of colonization did indeed have deleterious effects on the economic condition of the people of Rome; conversely, the abolition of debt-bondage in 326 or 313 takes place at a time when colonies were again being founded in significant numbers, and the number of chattel slaves available at Rome was increasing as a result of successful military activity in Italy.[54] Livy himself made the link: in his account of the year 300, referring to the recent establishment of Sora and Alba Fucens, to which some 10,000 colonists altogether had been sent, he observed that 'the removal of a great number to colonies quietened the *plebs* at Rome'.[55] Comparative optimism about the reliability of the account of colonial foundations in Livy is justified, at least from the fourth century onwards: the standardization of the material presented in the (usually brief) references, which frequently include mention of the number of colonists, the quantity of land allocated to the settlers, and the names of the triumvirs responsible for the creation of the colony, suggests that the material may have been taken from authoritative Roman records,[56] while it is also possible that the names of the triumvirs founding the community, like the date of its original establishment, may also have been commemorated locally, since their descendents might serve as heredi-tary patrons of the colony.[57] It has been noted that in Livy's narrative these records begin to appear more consistently in this standardized format, similar

197

to that characteristic of his later books, from the foundation of Cales in 334 onwards.[58]

The fourth form of narrative in which colonization can be contextualised, beyond those relating to military strategy, relieving poverty and increasing manpower, is that of the spread of Roman citizenship, both within and beyond the confines of Italy. Here the key text is the excursus on colonization at the end of book 1 of Velleius' *History of Rome*, which covers the period from before the Trojan War to the destruction of Corinth and Carthage in 146. The events of this year are seen by Velleius (as previously by Sallust)[59] as a significant turning point in the history of Rome, in that they removed the fear of external enemies and exposed the city to the detrimental influence of eastern *luxuria*.[60] At this point Velleius provides two excursuses, one on ancient literature and (more importantly in this context) a second on the colonies founded by the Senate from 390 onwards.[61] This account is notable not only for the fact that it omits what Velleius terms 'the military colonies' (presumably those established for the veterans of Sulla, Caesar, the triumvirs and Augustus), but also fails to draw a distinction between the Latin and citizen colonies, and combines the foundation of these colonies with discussion of other occasions on which the Roman citizenship in its various forms was extended to the peoples of Italy.[62]

As Gabba has underlined, this theme ties in well with Velleius' own personal interests and concerns. Velleius tells us himself that he was the great-great-grandson of Minatius Magius of Aeclanum, who recruited a legion among the Hirpini to help the Roman cause in the Social War, and in that conflict attacked the rebel cities of Herculaneum, Pompeii and Compsa; in recognition of this the Romans made him a special grant of their citizenship, and appointed his sons praetor. Minatius Magius' own great-grandfather, Decius Magius of Capua, had similarly remained loyal to the Roman cause when his city went over to the side of Hannibal in the Second Punic War.[63] Velleius can be seen to have a particular interest in (and sympathy for) those Italians who gained citizenship through loyalty to Rome, and it is not surprising, therefore, that his account of the Social War concentrates on the Italians' enthusiasm for acquiring the Roman citizenship, their frustration at being denied it, and the justice of their case, given that it was in this very context that Minatius Magius gained distinction and honour from the Romans. Whether or not we share Velleius' analysis of the origins of the Social War, there is clearly a coherence between his position on this issue and his highlighting of the question of citizenship in the excursus on colonization, which occurs at such a crucial point in his narrative.[64]

In this way we can see four possible explanatory frameworks in which Rome's programme of colonization can be set, relating to the different purposes to which colonies were put at different times, but also reflecting three of the main series of events around which the story of the Roman Republic can be structured by a historian – Rome's conquest of Italy, the Struggle of the Orders, and the spread of Roman citizenship to the peoples of Italy. The somewhat formulaic accounts of colonies given by Livy (and Dionysius) do, however, leave many questions unanswered, and it is clear that many important features of colonization are obscured or neglected in their narratives. For example, examination of epigraphic and prosopographical data suggests that local populations could play a significant role in the affairs of Latin colonies, as well as the Roman or Latin settlers;[65] religious and mythological associations could be exploited to consolidate the loyalty of the indigenous elites, as at Luceria, where the town's legendary associations with Diomedes, and the Romans' Trojan origins, coalesced in worship at the town's sanctuary of Athena Ilias.[66] Archaeological investigation has similarly revealed the potential for diversity even within the category of Latin colonies: the contrast between Cosa, established on a rocky outcrop in Etruria, and Paestum, within the existing urban centre of Poseidonia, both in 273, is a striking one.[67] Likewise, the substantial estates known to have been allocated to higher-status participants in Latin colonies mean that these would have had much more complex and variegated agricultural economies – and indeed urban lifestyles – than the traditional portrayals of small-scale subsistence agriculture in egalitarian colonies would suggest.[68] In creating a new Latin colony the Romans were establishing a community on the hierarchical model of their own city, which necessitated creating a wealthy elite who could serve as local senators, as well as a body of plebeians.[69]

Two particular problems connected with the establishment of colonies under the Republic do however recur in the literary sources, namely the difficulties periodically experienced by the Romans in recruiting colonists, and the hostility to colonies (and colonists) which manifests itself particularly in the first century.

Problems with colonization (1): recruitment difficulties

Livy's account of the foundation of Antium in 467 illustrates one of the central paradoxes involved in narratives of colonization. On the one hand the establishment of colonies was seen as motivated by popular enthusiasm, and by the desire of the elite to gain popular support; on the other, it was apparently not always easy to persuade people to join them. Livy in this case disapprovingly explains recruitment difficulties in terms of the plebeians' 'preference for demanding land at Rome to receiving it elsewhere'. The difficulty in finding recruits for colonies surfaces in later chronological contexts too.

In his account of the foundation of the colony at Luceria in 314, Livy describes how there was a feeling at Rome that it would be better to destroy the town (which had betrayed its Roman garrison to the enemy) rather than 'banish citizens so far from home among such hostile peoples'.[70] This feared lack of enthusiasm is manifested a few years later when the *triumviri* responsible for recruiting colonists to go to the new citizen colonies of Minturnae and Sinuessa apparently found it difficult to recruit those who would enrol 'because they thought that they were being sent not to settle in the fields, but to serve almost as a permanent garrison in a hostile district'.[71]

In Livy's narrative, then, the factor that chiefly attracts recruits to the colonies is seen as the provision of land; the dangers of living in an isolated outpost surrounded by Rome's enemies serves as a countervailing negative. The idea of the Roman People's concern for their counterparts in such isolated communities is illustrated by Livy's account of a Roman attack on Sora in 315, which 'having killed its Roman colonists had gone over to the Samnites'.[72] As has often been noticed, there is a problem here, since the establishment of a colony at Sora seems in fact to have taken place 12 years later, in 303.[73] The Romans killed in the Soran revolt are thus more likely to have been members of a garrison than formal colonists, but what is important is the fact that they are *portrayed* by Livy as colonists. In 314 the Romans defeated the Samnites and besieged Sora, which they eventually captured with the aid of a deserter. 225 individual Sorans who were deemed to be responsible for the rebellion and the massacre of the 'colonists' were taken to Rome, beaten and beheaded in the Forum 'to the great joy of the *plebs*', according to Livy, 'who were particularly concerned that wherever numbers of the people were sent into colonies they should be kept safe'.[74]

Involvement in a colonial settlement, therefore, was portrayed on the one hand as being attractive to the *plebs* (by virtue of the generous grants of land available) but on the other hazardous because of the military risks involved, especially where the location in question was a small-scale citizen colony. Brunt aptly noted in this context that 'there can have been no authentic evidence about the feelings of Roman plebeians *c.* 300 BC',[75] still less (we might add) for the mid-fifth century. Besides, this sort of information was (we may imagine) much less likely to be commemorated in the colonies themselves than more creditable aspects of their history. While it is quite comprehensible that people would have been fearful of the risks involved in joining a colony in these circumstances, it is harder to accept, given the extensive problems of debt and poverty outlined above, that there would have been widespread resistance to involvement in colonial settlement at this time. Colonization was one of the few ways in which those at Rome below the elite could participate in the rewards of conquest.[76] It is more likely that the perception of popular resistance to participating in colonization is derived from the particular circumstances of the (much better documented) early second century BC, when there are repeated references to difficulties in recruiting colonists for settlements in both northern and southern Italy. This trend emerges in the 190s in particular. In 193, for example, Livy observes that the 3000 infantry and 300 cavalry sent to establish a Latin colony at Thurii represented a small number in proportion to the extent of the land occupied; as a result one third of the territory was reserved for future recruits.[77]

Several explanations may be offered for the comparative lack of enthusiasm for colonial settlement in the early second century (though it should be kept in mind that substantial numbers of people did still take part in colonization in this period).[78] It may be that the manpower shortage in the years following the Hannibalic war may in part be behind this reluctance. Thurii could hardly be thought to be in dangerous territory militarily – it was in the territory once occupied by the famously wealthy Sybaris, and the name Copia ('abundance') given to the colony may to a certain extent have reflected reality as well as aspiration. Nevertheless, and despite the allocation of comparatively generous tracts of land to the colonists – 20 *iugera* for *pedites* and 40 for *equites* – the problem persisted. In 190 it was decided to create two new colonies as well as to send reinforcements to Cremona and Placentia, which had suffered the misfortune of being founded just before Hannibal's invasion of Italy, and had borne the brunt of attacks by his forces and those of the Gauls.[79] However, only one of these new colonies, Bononia, was actually founded (in 189), despite exceptionally generous grants of land of 70 *iugera* for *equites* and 50 each for other colonists.[80] Aquileia (perhaps the last of the Latin colonies, unless we consider Luca to have had that status)[81] was established in 181. Here too the grant for *pedites* was 50 *iugera*, while 100 *iugera* were allocated to centurions and 140 to *equites*.[82]

Evidently the generous allocation of land in these cases was thought necessary to entice colonists to take up residence in areas which had only recently been captured from the Gauls. That fear of the local populations was reasonable is illustrated not only by the sufferings of Placentia and Cremona a generation before, but also by the attacks on the territory of Bononia by the Ligurians in 187, soon after the establishment of the city,[83] and a further assault on the territory of Mutina ten years later which led to the capture of that colony.[84] It may also, however, have been intended to compensate the participants for the loss of their Roman citizenship – which, we might imagine, is likely to have been a particular concern to the more affluent members of the communities, who were best placed to exploit its advantages. That the citizenship issue was important is suggested by the fact that several colonies established in the 180s – Potentia, Pisaurum, Saturnia, Mutina and Parma – were of the citizen type, although the large numbers of settlers involved at these sites made them much more analogous to Latin colonies than to the traditional maritime citizen colonies of 300 settlers. The choice of the citizen type of colony also meant that manpower under direct Roman command would not have been reduced (as it was where substantial numbers of Romans were sent to Latin colonies).

After the establishment of Luna in 177 there seems to be a significant gap in the list of colonies, with the possible exception of Auximum, if we date the establishment of that colony to 157 rather than to the more convincing 128.[85] Why this should be is not entirely clear; presumably the end of significant levels of campaigning in the Italian peninsula, and the defeat of the Ligurians in particular, must have been one important factor. The apparent difficulties in recruiting colonists willing to leave Rome for new lives at the extreme north or south of Italy, as we have seen, will have been another. Perhaps the economic vibrancy of Rome, and the employment possibilities available as the city was enriched by the wealth brought in from conquests in the East, made staying a more attractive prospect than leaving.[86] In political terms, it is possible that traditionalist senators were concerned (however unjustifiable this may have been in reality) about the excessive influence the founders of colonies might be thought to acquire in their role as patrons of substantial new communities.[87] M. Aemilius Lepidus, for example, was founding commissioner of three northern colonies in these years, Mutina, Parma and Luna, as well as building the Via Aemilia. The later 180s was a period of heightened political competition at Rome, reflected by a clutch of laws relating to luxury, *ambitus*, and iteration of office, and so the more general political context too may provide a context for this anxiety, and help to explain the absence of colonization in the years which followed.[88]

Problems with colonization (2): resistance and opposition

Colonization reappears in the historical record in relation to the Gracchan land-distribution schemes or as an alternative to these, and in the context of provision of land for veterans from the armies of Marius, Sulla, Caesar or the triumvirs. The portrayal of the procedure and impact of these later colonization schemes is substantially different from that of early and mid-Republican colonization. The focus of attention in accounts of the colonization of this earlier period had been on the military expansion of Rome, popular demands for land distribution, efforts to increase manpower, and the extension of the Roman citizenship. Now the emphasis in literary accounts of later colonization is very much on the destructive effect of the colonial process, and its disruptive impact on existing landowners and the neighbours of the colonists. Henceforth the main political problem was not so much an unwillingness to join colonies, but resistance and opposition to their establishment, both locally and in Rome. Indeed, colonization in first century Italy arguably provides one of the few cases from classical antiquity where the voice of the dispossessed emerges more clearly than that of the colonists.[89]

A sense of the disruptiveness involved in colonial settlement is echoed in Livy's accounts of the colonization process in Italy of the early and mid-Republic, and it is clear that he would have been aware of it from personal experience. Around 30 BC, Ateste, a town whose territory lay adjacent to that of Livy's own home town of Patavium, received a substantial contingent of Octavian's veterans, and the fact that many commemorate themselves as *Actiaci* suggests that these had served in the victorious army at the battle of Actium.[90] Although it seems that the tombstone of Salvius Sempronius of *Legio XI*, one of these *Actiaci*, which was found at Padova, was brought to that city at some point after his death,[91] it is highly likely that numerous refugees displaced by the colonization process would have migrated from Ateste to Patavium, the nearest major city.

Livy frequently refers to the way in which the establishment of colonies was perceived by Rome's neighbours and rivals as an aggressive act – for example, the Samnites are presented as regarding the foundation of Fregellae in the valley of the Liri as not only an injury but an insult: in addition to being established in territory they viewed as theirs, it had been given the name of a settlement they themselves had destroyed.[92] Similarly in 303 the Aequi, 'outraged that a colony (i.e. Alba Fucens) had been established like a citadel within their lands attacked it with all their force.'[93] Livy reports that the following year, the Marsi also used force to resist the establishment of Carseoli (though there is evidently some confusion here, since Carseoli was founded in 298).[94] These attacks by Rome's enemies on colonial settlements could of course then be used to help justify Rome's continuing aggression. Livy also refers on several occasions to the earlier status of territories taken over as colonies in Livy's narrative. The location of Fregellae, for example, is (implausibly) described as 'formerly the territory of the people of Signia, and subsequently of the Volsci';[95] the territory of Vibo, established in what is now Calabria, in 192, was referred to as 'land most recently belonging to the Bruttii; the Bruttii had taken it from the Greeks'.[96] Likewise, the territory in which Bononia was founded in 189 was described as 'formerly belonging to the Boii'.[97] These descriptions might possibly be taken as intended to play down the disruptive impact of the new colonies, in that the areas in question had already changed hands several times, and in the case of Fregellae to imply an (invented) historical claim on its territory, but the formulaic nature of the references is such that Livy may rather simply have intended to inform his reader about the geographical and ethnographical background to the establishment of the colonies.[98]

In the second century, the impact of new colonies on their neighbours, Rome's allies, became a matter of increasing concern. Livy reports that in 180 the people of Pisa offered land to Rome in order to establish a colony (which may have been Luca or Luna), presumably to help protect them from the depredations of the Ligurians just to the north,[99] with whom they had a history of hostility.[100] Only a few years later, in 168, however, we hear of a dispute between Pisa and Luna over the status of land which had been allocated to the (citizen) colony at Luna, but which the Pisans claimed was theirs. The Senate responded by establishing a commission of five to review the evidence and come to a decision.[101]

The two episodes illustrate the problematic nature of colonial settlement not only for the would-be settlers, but for their neighbours too. While the Ligurians were considered a threat, the Pisans were happy to welcome colonists into their territory; with the advent of peace in this part of Italy, however, disputes over land and resources became a more important concern. Furthermore, since the Italian allies now contributed over half of the forces under Roman command, and sometimes substantially more, their political and military importance was substantial; alienating them was risky for the Romans, as the events of the Social War were eventually to prove.[102] Concern about the impact of colonial settlement thus increased in direct proportion to the political influence and military importance of those most affected by it.

Negative portrayals can be seen increasingly to characterize the depiction of colonies and colonists from the latter part of the second century onwards. This is particularly true in the case of the land-reforms of Ti. Gracchus in 133 BC, which had the primary aim of reviving the peasantry and increasing the number of men available for military service, by redistributing illegally occupied public land across Italy. Although it appears that the main beneficiaries were landless Romans, it is likely that as with earlier colonization schemes some Italians received land too: it would have been in the interest of the Romans to reinforce allied as well as Roman military manpower.[103] Agrarian legislation was perennially controversial,[104] and Gracchus' initiative predictably attracted strong opposition within the political class at Rome, in particular due to the strategy he adopted to achieve the success of his proposal. Appian comments that by this measure Gracchus alienated not only wealthy Romans, but also allies. The latter complained of the disruption caused by the re-surveying and re-allocation of land, and enlisted the help of Scipio Aemilianus to draw attention to their grievances.[105] It is striking that the efforts of Tiberius' brother Gaius to solve the land problem some ten years later involved the creation of colonies – at Tarentum, Scolacium and even overseas at Carthage – as well as the more widespread individual settlements on the model Tiberius had initiated.[106] Presumably one perceived advantage of Gaius' solution would be that it would alienate only the residents of a few communities (some of which were overseas), rather than causing the more general resentment to which Appian refers as a consequence of Tiberius' initiatives.[107]

It is with the establishment of colonies for veterans of the dictator Sulla that the most hostile picture of colonization begins to appear. Cicero, in 63, speaks of 'the land distributed by Sulla, further extended by certain individuals, which aroused such hostility that it cannot withstand the protest raised by one single true and brave tribune of the people',[108] while in his account of the year 46 Appian describes how Julius Caesar sought to purchase land for distribution to his soldiers and to use public land 'not like Sulla who took land away from the owners and by settling those who were given it alongside those who were evicted, made them eternal enemies of each other'.[109] Much of this enmity seems to have been associated with the high-handed way in which confiscated land was taken from previous owners for distribution to Sulla's soldiers: serious long-term problems were caused by the establishment of these colonies.[110]

At Pompeii, for example, the years following Sulla's dictatorship were characterized by severe antagonism between the colonists and the original inhabitants of the town.[111] Likewise, we know of long-term divisions in Etruscan towns where Sullan settlement took place: Pliny records that the people of Arretium were divided into Veteres and Fidentiores (i.e. the original inhabitants and the colonists), and those of nearby Clusium into Veteres and Novi; both of these towns are known to have received Sullan colonies.[112] The upheavals caused by the Sullan colonial settlements also appear to have contributed to the widespread unrest in Etruria in the 70s and 60s which culminated in Manlius' uprising in collaboration with Catiline in 63 – both colonists and the dispossessed were said to have supported Catiline's rebellion.[113] In the years that followed Sulla's death, the colonist became seen as a problematic and ambiguous figure, tarnished by association with the dictator.[114] Cicero, who wanted to avoid offending the Sullan colonists, but at the same time sought to discourage the Roman *plebs* from sympathizing with Catiline and his associates, observed that 'from colonies which Sulla founded, which I know to be entirely composed of excellent citizens and extremely brave men, there are however some settlers who have behaved arrogantly and extravagantly as a result of their unexpected and sudden acquisition of wealth'.[115]

In the same way, when Cicero addressed the People on the subject of Rullus' land bill early in 63, he had to tread delicately. Before the popular

assembly he wanted to play down the attraction of the colonial settlements which could be available if the bill were passed, and from which the
Roman *plebs* might potentially benefit, instead listing the attractions of life
at Rome.[116] 'Romans, if you listen to me, hold on to your influence, your
freedom, your votes, your dignity, your city, your forum, your games, your
festival days, and all your other advantages, unless of course you prefer to
leave these benefits and the splendour of the state behind, and be settled in
the deserts of Sipontum or the unhealthy swamps of Salapia with Rullus as
your leader.'[117] Both towns mentioned were located on the coast of Daunia.
The former, established as a citizen colony in 194, had to be reinforced only
a few years later, after it was discovered to be in a state of abandonment;[118]
while the latter was originally founded in a notoriously pestilential district
and had to be moved to a more salubrious location with the approval of the
Senate and People of Rome.[119]

At the same time, there are indications that those who participated in
colonies were not held in high esteem. Seeking to excite opposition against
him in the popular assembly, Cicero claims that Rullus told the Senate that
the population of Rome should be 'drained off', and so, he suggests, equates
them with *sentina* ('dregs'). His own speech in the Senate on the subject,
however, refers to Rullus' colonists as *egentes atque improbi* (destitute and
delinquent).[120] A similar idea emerges in Cicero's *Pro Caecina*, when he
discusses the question of how Roman citizens can give up their citizenship
in order to join Latin colonies, and argues that this is done either of the
individual's free will 'or in order to avoid a legal penalty',[121] again suggesting
that colonists could be seen (in some quarters anyway) as disreputable or
even criminal.

Negative views of colonization can be identified most clearly in the case
of the narratives of triumviral colonies, which were implemented with
particular brutality and little regard for local sensibilities. In 43, eighteen of
the most prosperous towns in Italy were selected for veteran settlement by the
triumvirs, and colonies were set up there following the battle of Philippi.[122]
Their establishment frequently involved not only the allocation of substantial
quantities of land within an urban territory to legionary veterans, but also the
transfer of extensive tracts of property in adjacent territories to the control of
the new colony, as happened for example at Beneventum (which took land
from the neighbouring towns of Ligures Baebiani and Caudium)[123] and at
Cremona, where the territory was extended at the expense of neighbouring
Brixia and Mantua.[124] Numerous accounts survive, both in historical narratives and in the poetry of the 30s, of the disruption that resulted from the
arrival of the new colonists. Dio describes how fighting broke out across Italy
between the newly arrived veterans and the existing landowners: 'one side

was superior by virtue of its military equipment and its experience in war, the other was stronger in terms of numbers and the tactic of throwing objects down from the roofs'.[125]

Such scenes happened all over Italy. Vergil's first *Eclogue*, like the ninth, paints a pathetic picture of peasants being forced to leave their farms to make way for incoming soldiers; the way the countryside is described seems to suggest a dramatic setting in southern Italy. 'Shall an impious soldier hold these well-cultivated fallow fields? What barbarian these crops?'[126] Vergil is said to have lost his family estate when part of the territory of Mantua was assigned to the colonists at Cremona, hence 'Mantua, alas too close to unhappy Cremona'.[127] Likewise, Propertius refers to the loss of his estates to the 'grim surveying-rod',[128] while Horace depicts the sad lot of Ofellus, who has lost his land to Umbrenus, a colonist, and become a tenant on his former farm.[129] Horace too seems to have lost family property at this time.[130] The protests even reached the city of Rome itself: 'young men, old men, and women with their children came together to Rome, to the Forum and the temples, lamenting that they had committed no crime for which they, who were Italians, should be removed from their lands and hearths like those conquered in war'.[131] An indirect indication of the disruptiveness and unpopularity of the triumviral settlements is the care taken by Augustus as *princeps* with his own settlement schemes, which appear to have been more limited in scale than those of the triumvirs. In the *Res Gestae* he stresses that lands allocated to veterans were paid for, rather than confiscated.[132]

Colonies of the early and mid-Republic were no doubt also extremely unpopular with the local populations – the impact of Roman conquest in the territory of Vulci and the establishment of Cosa were evidently disastrous for the indigenous communities, for example[133] – but their voice was (and is) largely silent. A speech which Appian puts into the mouth of Brutus after the murder of Caesar neatly illustrates the Roman view. 'When our ancestors defeated their enemies, they did not take all their land from them, but divided it up and settled former soldiers on part of it, who would act as guards over those that had been defeated. If the captured land was not sufficient they added public land or bought more. In this way the People established you in colonies without causing grief to anyone (ἀλύπως ἅπασι).'[134] Opposition to the colonial schemes of the first century was, however, much more vocal and influential. The way in which colonization was conceptualized changed, too: as we have seen, Velleius ends his account of colonization at the end of the second century, with the advent of what he terms *coloniae militares* (military colonies) which he clearly regards as different in nature to traditional colonies, though it is likely that many of the colonies established in the mid-Republic were also in fact largely populated by men who had been serving as soldiers. Veteran colonies attracted fierce opposition both locally and at Rome. Earlier colonial settlements, as Appian notes, had tended to be located on conquered land, or that which had been acquired by the Roman state as *ager publicus*; problems arose when this public land had for many years been farmed and informally or illegally occupied, whether as part of large estates or as common lands exploited by the local peasantry. By the beginning of the first century, however, it is unlikely that there was much public land left for allocation, so if colonies were to be established in Italy, this would largely have to be at the expense of the current occupants. From the point of view of the founders of the colonies, however, it was important that the veterans were settled in the peninsula, so that they could provide political support – and, if the need arose, physical support – for those who had set up their community.[135] The confiscation of land was only the beginning of the troubles for those who lived in communities designated for colonization. Tensions tended to persist for years afterwards; as the colonists were settled together, and were frequently members of the same military unit, they had a strong collective identity, and we can easily envisage how they might intimidate the other local inhabitants. Horace recalls from his youth the bullying behaviour of the sons of centurions in his home town of Venusia: as this was a town which did not have colonial status in the mid-first century BC, the impact of the veterans on communities which did become colonies must have been correspondingly more significant.[136]

In Rome, too, the establishment of colonies was unpopular, for a variety of reasons, with a broad sweep of political opinion. The wealthy feared the disruption to landed property that would result, and the risks posed to political stability by veterans loyal to their former commander; the urban *plebs* might support colonial schemes which might benefit themselves, but the more affluent elements in the popular assemblies were unlikely to be enthusiastic. Those who had most to gain, the veterans themselves, were in this period largely marginalized from political life at Rome – recruited in the main from the Italian countryside and spending many years serving overseas, they participated only infrequently in assemblies or political meetings (though when they did present themselves in Rome their impact could be substantial).[137] It was only when the state was in the control of a powerful individual or individuals – Sulla, Caesar, the triumvirs – that large-scale colonial settlement could effectively be implemented in Italy. Colonization in the peninsula thus came to be associated with the evils of dictatorship and one-man rule, a perception Augustus and his successors were naturally keen to play down.

Conclusion

The colonial process, like the image of the colonist himself, was thus ambiguous and complex in terms of the way it was presented both by politicians and by historians. Colonies could be portrayed as agrarian initiatives, if those proposing them wished to be seen as helping the *plebs*; alternatively they could be presented as predominantly military in character. Colonists themselves could be seen as heroic individuals whose contribution to the *propugnacula imperii* served to defend the Roman state and expand its frontiers; at the same time colonies could be considered as a means for allowing the poor of the city and its environs to escape from poverty, and exchange debt and oppression for social and economic advancement elsewhere. Given that either or both justifications could be used for the establishment of a colony depending whether the proposer or historian wanted to be seen as a supporter of the *plebs* or an adherent of traditional militaristic expansionism, it is often difficult for us to decide which motivation predominated on a particular occasion, but we can be sure that both agrarian and military consequences resulted from colonial initiatives.

The colonies of the mid-Republic had a significant social and political role, in that although they allowed economic advancement for the participants, this was at the cost of their political rights either in theory (when they joined Latin colonies) or in practice (when they joined the more distant citizen communities). The arrangement had the benefit for the Roman state of allowing social mobility while at the same time avoiding any disruption of the political order at Rome, since although the beneficiaries of colonial schemes became wealthier as a result, the hierarchies in the city were unlikely to be affected to any significant extent.[138] New citizen colonies would potentially increase the numbers of *assidui* available to serve in the Roman army; new Latin colonies would also provide contingents to serve with Rome's forces, with the additional benefit that these would be self-financing. The importance of colonization in contributing to political stability at Rome can be illustrated by the close conjunction between problems of debt and the absence of colonization in the fourth century, and also in the second half of the second, when the absence of colonial settlement, together with more general economic and political tensions, can be seen as a contributory factor in the destabilizing of Roman society which led to the upheavals of the Gracchan era.

With the revival of colonization in the 120s, however, colonies came to be seen as contributing to Rome's problems rather than as a solution to them. Colonial settlements began increasingly to impinge on communities or individuals with varying degrees of influence within the Roman political system. While it was clearly unproblematic to establish colonies in territory under the control of Rome's enemies (and this could even be helpful if it provoked a violent reaction from them), settlement which impinged on Rome's Italian allies posed problems even in the second century, as we have seen in the case of Pisa and Luna. The more the Italian peninsula was politically and militarily integrated, the more problematic the creation of colonies in Italy became; this was especially the case after the Social War, when the whole of Italy acquired the franchise. In practice, the extent to which different areas of Italy were effectively integrated into Rome's political structures – formal and informal – in the years which followed varied considerably, and this had the effect that those places with close links to the Roman elite – Volaterra for instance, as Terrenato has recently illustrated[139] – were able to ward off the damaging effects of colonization more effectively than those without such privileged access to the powerful; the sense of grievance this generated was a major factor behind the widespread upheavals in Italy during the 60s.[140] Violence was another way in which the less fortunate could make their voices heard. In the process, the figure of the colonist became more ambiguous still – an upstanding soldier on the one hand, a threat to civic order on the other. The process was to culminate with the atrocities of the triumviral period and Augustus' eventual abolition of colonial settlement for veterans in favour of cash donatives. Thereafter colonization in Italy was largely seen as a means of responding to urban crisis, reversing demographic decline, and demonstrating imperial favour and generosity.[141] The main impetus of colonial settlement was now transferred to the provinces, where the combination of romanized lifestyles and high-handed behaviour towards local populations continued to alienate and attract the peoples of the empire in equal measure.[142]

Acknowledgements:

A version of this paper was delivered at a seminar in Oxford in May 2000 and it also owes much to ideas put forward in discussion at the conference on colonization held at the Institute of Classical Studies in June 1998. I am very grateful to John-Paul Wilson and Guy Bradley, and to Ed Bispham, Fergus Millar and Mark Pobjoy for the invitations to speak in London and Oxford respectively, and to members of the audience on both occasions. Thanks are due in particular to Andrew Lintott for guidance on colonial foundation dates, to Michael Crawford, Guy Bradley, and Anton Powell for comments on earlier drafts of the paper, and to Jason Lucas for help with the maps.

Notes

[1] All dates are BC unless otherwise noted; references to ancient authors follow the conventions used in the third edition of the *Oxford Classical Dictionary* (1996). For useful handlists of Roman and Latin colonies, see Salmon 1969 at 110 and 158–64,

and Coarelli 1992, 27.

[2] For the phenomenon of colonization under the Republic in general see Salmon 1969; Sherwin-White 1973, 76–80; Galsterer 1976, 41–64; Brunt 1987, esp. 190–8, 294–344, 538–44; Coarelli 1992; and the articles collected in *Dialoghi di Archeologia* 3.6.2 (1988). For the Caesarian, triumviral and Augustan colonies, see Keppie 1983. Gargola 1995 focuses in particular on the procedures involved in the setting up of a colony.

[3] Crawford 1996; Torelli 1999, 123–7; Scheidel 2004.

[4] Richardson, L. 1957; Gros and Torelli 1988, 134–44; Mouritsen 2004, 37–40.

[5] Gell. *NA* 16.13.8–9.

[6] Castagnoli 1956, 81–103; Ward-Perkins 1974, 27–9; Gros and Torelli 1988, 127–47; Owens 1991, 94–120; Zanker 2000, 25–7.

[7] Bradford 1957, 145–216; Dilke 1971, 142–9; *Misurare la terra* 1983; Chouquer et al. 1987; Campbell 2000.

[8] For a synthetic account of the excavations, see Brown 1980, and for a recent overview of the republican phases at the site (with a full bibliography) Fentress 2000.

[9] For a synthesis, see Mertens 1981.

[10] For an overview of the Roman phases of the site, see Pedley 1990; Torelli 1988; Torelli 1999, 43–88.

[11] See Crawford and Keppie 1984; Crawford, Keppie and Vercnocke 1985; Coarelli 1986; Coarelli and Monti 1998.

[12] Hayes and Wightman 1984.

[13] For further discussion of the archaeology of colonization in Italy, with further bibliographical detail, see Curti, Dench and Patterson 1996, 173–5.

[14] Cic. *Att.* 4.1.4; Vell. Pat. 1.14.8.

[15] Asc. *Pis.* 2–3C.

[16] Livy 37.57.7. On foundation rituals see Gargola 1995, 72–82.

[17] Crawford and Keppie 1984, 23–4.

[18] Salmon 1969, 17.

[19] Festus *Gloss. Lat.* 458L.

[20] Asc. *Pis.* 2–3C, with Crawford 1995.

[21] The methodological issues are valuably laid out in a series of publications by T.J. Cornell and T.P. Wiseman: Wiseman 1979; Cornell 1982; Wiseman 1983; Cornell 1995, 16–18; Wiseman 1996.

[22] Càssola 1988, 5.

[23] Salmon 1969, 11.

[24] e.g. Salmon 1969, 15.

[25] *Leg. Agr.* 2.73.

[26] *De Cond. Agr.* 135L.

[27] Salmon 1969, 84; Coarelli 1988.

[28] Harris 1971, 148–9.

[29] Salmon 1969, 101–9.

[30] Wiseman 1970, 126–8.

[31] Gargola 1995, 63; Richardson, J.S. 1986, 149–55.

[32] Càssola 1988, 15–17.

[33] App. *B. Civ.* 1.7.

[34] Livy 3.1.5.

35 Livy 3.1.7.
36 D.H. *Ant. Rom.* 9.59.2.
37 Càssola 1988, 6.
38 Livy 3.23, D.H. *Ant. Rom.* 10.21; see Coarelli 1982, 292.
39 Salmon 1969, 42, and n. 115; for the colony in 338, see Livy 8.14.8.
40 e.g. Livy 2.48.1 where Kaeso Fabius, cos. 479, brings about *concordia* between patricians and plebeians.
41 Ogilvie 1965, 359; Wiseman 1979, 24–5; Oakley 1997, 29–30.
42 Ogilvie 1965, 393; see also Càssola 1988, 16.
43 Cornell 1995, 302.
44 For the activities of such 'condottieri', see Cornell 1995, 143–5.
45 Càssola 1988, 17; Torelli 1999, 16–18; Bispham 2000, 161.
46 Livy 6.16.7.
47 Livy 8.16.13.
48 Livy 5.30.8.
49 Livy 27.9.11.
50 Brunt 1987, 142.
51 App. *B. Civ.* 1.7.
52 Ogilvie 1965, 392.
53 Cornell 1989, 324.
54 Oakley 1993, 18–22; Cornell 1989, 323–4; 1995, 330–3; 393–4.
55 Livy 10.6.2.
56 Oakley 1997, 52–3, 62.
57 Badian 1958, 162–3.
58 Oakley 1998, 586–7.
59 Sall. *Cat.* 10–11.
60 Lintott 1972, 627.
61 Vell. Pat. 1.14–18.
62 Gabba 1973, 347–60; see also Woodman 1975, 9.
63 Vell. Pat. 2.16.2–3 with Livy 23.7.4–10.13; on Velleius' ancestors see Sumner 1970, 257–61.
64 Mouritsen 1998, 10.
65 La Regina 1970–1, 453 discusses the *Samnites inquolae* ('resident Samnites') at Aesernia; see also Torelli 1999, 2–4 on the involvement of local elites more generally.
66 Torelli 1999, 94–7.
67 Curti et al. 1996, 173; Torelli 1999, 43.
68 Gabba and Pasquinucci 1979, 19–21; Fentress 2000, 17–20.
69 Gabba 1988.
70 Livy 9.26.4.
71 Livy 10.21.10: see Guidobaldi 1988; 1989, 36.
72 Livy 9.23.2.
73 Livy 10.1.2. See Salmon 1967, 235; Oakley 1984, ad loc.; Càssola 1988, 6.
74 Livy 9.24. On whether colonies and garrisons can meaningfully be distinguished in the Mid-Republic, see Crawford 1995, 191.
75 Brunt 1987, 192.
76 Gabba 1988, 19; Cassola 1988, 9–11.
77 Livy 35.9.7–9.

[78] Hopkins 1978, 57.

[79] Livy 37.46.9–11; 47.1–2.

[80] Livy 37.57.7–8.

[81] Toynbee 1965, 2, 533–40; Coarelli 1985–7.

[82] Livy 40.34.2.

[83] Livy 39.2.5.

[84] Livy 41.14.2.

[85] Vell. Pat. 1.15.3 with Salmon 1963, 3–13. Some caution is appropriate, however, since the apparent gap in colonization largely coincides with that between the breaking off of Livy's text and the beginning of Appian's *B. Civ.* See Tibiletti 1950, 232–4, Coarelli 1977, 2.

[86] See Coarelli 1977 for an account of the exceptionally high level of public building in the city of Rome in this period.

[87] Badian 1958, 162–3; Salmon 1969, 112–13.

[88] Patterson 2000, 48–51.

[89] I am grateful to Guy Bradley for this observation.

[90] Keppie 1971; 1983, 111–12, 195–201.

[91] *CIL* V 2839; see Bassignano 1997, 118.

[92] Livy 8.23.7.

[93] Livy 10.1.7.

[94] Livy 10.3.2.

[95] Livy 8.22.2.

[96] Livy 35.40.6.

[97] Livy 37.57.8.

[98] See Oakley 1998, 624–5; compare Clarke 1999, 269–70 on similar passages in Strabo's account of Italy.

[99] Livy 40.43.1.

[100] Strabo 5.2.5.

[101] Livy 45.13.10. See Gargola 1995, 98–9.

[102] Ilari 1974, 171–3; Brunt 1987, 677–86; Mouritsen 1998, 44–5.

[103] Richardson, J.S. 1980. For a recent summary of the debate, with further bibliography, see Mouritsen 1998, 15–17.

[104] Livy 2.41.3.

[105] App. *B. Civ.* 1.18–19.

[106] App. *B. Civ.* 1.24; Plut. *C. Gracch.* 5–6.

[107] Gargola 1995, 148, 165.

[108] Cic. *Leg. Agr.* 2.70.

[109] App. *B. Civ.* 2.94.

[110] On Sullan colonies in general, see Brunt 1987, 300–12.

[111] Cic. *Sull.* 60–2 with Berry 1996, 250–7; see also Wiseman 1977.

[112] Plin. *HN* 3.52; see Harris 1971, 259–67 on Sulla's colonies in Etruria, and Keppie 1983, 102.

[113] Sall. *Cat.* 28; Cic. *Mur.* 49 with Harris 1971, 289–92.

[114] Harris 1971, 269.

[115] Cic. *Cat.* 2.20; see also Sall. *Cat.* 28.4.

[116] Millar 1998, 101–5.

[117] *Leg. Agr.* 2.71.

[118] Livy 34.45.3, 39.23.3.
[119] Vitr. *De Arch.* 1.4.12; see Gabba 1994, 119–22.
[120] *Leg. Agr.* 1.22.
[121] *Caecin.* 98.
[122] App. *B. Civ.* 4.3; see Keppie 1983, 60–1.
[123] Keppie 1983, 158–9.
[124] Keppie 1983, 190–2.
[125] Dio Cass. 48.9.4.
[126] *Ecl.* 1.70–1; see Keppie 1981; DuQuesnay 1981, 38.
[127] *Ecl.* 9.28; see Serv. *Life of Virgil*, 22H.
[128] Prop. 4.1.130.
[129] Hor. *Sat.* 2.2.112–36.
[130] Hor. *Epist.* 2.2.50–2.
[131] App. *B. Civ.* 5.12.
[132] *RG* 16 with Chouquer et al. 1987, 255 and Keppie 1983, 82, who however notes the limitations placed on our knowledge by the nature of the evidence available for the Augustan period.
[133] Fentress 2000, 12–13.
[134] App. *B. Civ.* 2.140.
[135] Hopkins 1971, 70; Brunt 1987, 301.
[136] *Sat.* 1.6.72–3 with Keppie 1983, 104.
[137] Astin 1989, 174–85; Patterson 2000, 70.
[138] The role of colonization as a route to social mobility is discussed in Càssola 1988; Patterson 1993.
[139] Terrenato 1998, 106.
[140] Stewart 1995.
[141] Keppie 1984, 105–7.
[142] Levick 1967, 1–6; Millett 1999. See especially Tac. *Ann.* 14.31 for provincial resentment of the colonists at Camulodunum.

Bibliography

Astin, A.E.
    1989   'Roman government and politics, 200–134 BC', in A.E. Astin, F.W. Walbank, M.W. Frederiksen, and R.M. Ogilvie (eds.) *CAH²* VIII, 163–96.

Badian, E.
    1958   *Foreign Clientelae*, Oxford.

Bassignano, M.S.
    1997   'Ateste', in *Supplementa Italica* 15, 11–376.

Berry, D.H.
    1996   *Cicero,* Pro P. Sulla Oratio*: Edited with introduction and commentary*, Cambridge.

Bispham, E.
    2000   'Mimic? A case study in early Roman colonization', in E. Herring and K. Lomas (eds.) *The Emergence of State Identities in Italy in the First Millennium BC*, London, 157–86.

Bradford, J.
 1957   *Ancient Landscapes: Studies in field archaeology*, London.
Brown, F.
 1980   *Cosa: The making of a Roman town*, Ann Arbor.
Brunt, P.A.
 1987   *Italian Manpower*, reissued with a postscript, Oxford.
Campbell, B.
 2000   *The Writings of the Roman Land Surveyors: Introduction, text, translation and commentary* = JRS Monograph 9, London.
Càssola, F.
 1988   'Aspetti sociali e politici della colonizzazione', *DdA* 3.6.2, 5–18.
Castagnoli, F.
 1956   *Ippodamo di Mileto e l'urbanistica a pianta ortogonale*, Rome.
Chouquer, G., Clavel-Lévêque, M., Favory, F. and Vallat, J.-P.
 1987   *Structures agraires en Italie centro-méridionale: cadastres et paysages ruraux* = *Collection de l'École française de Rome* 100, Rome.
Clarke, K.
 1999   *Between Geography and History: Hellenistic constructions of the Roman World*, Oxford.
Coarelli, F.
 1977   'Public building in Rome between the Second Punic War and Sulla', *PBSR* 45, 1–23.
 1982   *Guida archeologica Laterza: Lazio*, Rome and Bari.
 1985–7 'La fondazione di Luni', *Quaderni del centro di studi Lunensi* 10–12, 17–25.
 1986   *Fregellae 2: il santuario di Esculapio*, Rome.
 1988   'Colonizzazione romana e viabilità', *DdA* 3.6.2, 35–48.
 1992   'Colonizzazione e municipalizzazione: tempi e modi', *DdA* 3.10: 21–30.
Coarelli, F. and Monti, P.G.
 1998   *Fregellae 1: le fonti, la storia, il territorio,* Rome.
Cornell, T.J.
 1982   Review of T.P. Wiseman, *Clio's Cosmetics. Three studies in Greco-Roman literature,* in *JRS* 72, 203–6.
 1989   'The recovery of Rome', in F.W. Walbank, A.E. Astin, M.W. Frederiksen, R.M. Ogilvie and A. Drummond (eds.) *CAH*[2] VII 2, 309–50.
 1995   *The Beginnings of Rome*, London.
Crawford, M.H.
 1995   'La storia della colonizzazione romana secondo i Romani', in A. Storchi Marino (ed.) *L'incidenza dell'antico: studi in memoria di Ettore Lepore. Atti del convegno internazionale, Anacapri 24–28 marzo 1991*, Naples, 1: 187–92.
 1996   'Italy and Rome from Sulla to Augustus', in A.K. Bowman, E. Champlin, A. Lintott (eds.)*CAH*[2] X, 414–33.
Crawford, M.H. and Keppie, L.
 1984   'Excavations at Fregellae, 1978–1984: an interim report on the work of the British team', *PBSR* 52, 21–35.

Crawford, M.H., Keppie, L. and Vercnocke M.
    1985   'Excavations at Fregellae, 1978–1984: an interim report on the work of the British team, Part II', *PBSR* 53, 72–96.

Curti, E., Dench, E. and Patterson, J.R.
    1996   'The archaeology of central and southern Roman Italy: recent trends and approaches', *JRS* 86, 170–89.

Dilke, O.A.W.
    1971   *The Roman Land-surveyors: An introduction to the Agrimensores*, Newton Abbot.

DuQuesnay, I.
    1981   'Vergil's First Eclogue', in *Papers of the Liverpool Latin Seminar* 3, 29–182.

Fentress, E.
    2000   'Introduction: Frank Brown, Cosa and the idea of a Roman city', in E. Fentress (ed.) *Romanization and the city: Creation, transformation and failures* = JRA supplement 38, Portsmouth, R.I., 9–24.

Gabba, E.
    1973   *Esercito e società nella tarda repubblica romana*, Florence.
    1994   *Italia Romana*, Como.
    1988   'Aspetti militari e agrari', *DdA* 3.6.2, 19–22.

Gabba, E. and Pasquinucci, M.
    1979   *Strutture agrarie e allevamento transumante nell'Italia romana*, Pisa.

Galsterer, H.
    1976   *Herrschaft und Verwaltung im republikanischen Italien*, Munich.

Gargola, D.J.
    1995   *Laws, Lands and Gods: Magistrates and ceremony in the regulation of public lands in Republican Rome*, Chapel Hill.

Gros, P. and Torelli, M.
    1988   *Storia dell'urbanistica: il mondo romano*, Rome and Bari.

Guidobaldi, M.P.
    1988   'La colonia civium romanorum di Minturnae', *DdA* 3.6.2, 125–33.

Guidobaldi, M.P. and Pesando, F.
    1989   'La colonia civium romanorum' in F. Coarelli (ed.) *Minturnae*, Rome, 35–66.

Harris, W.V.
    1971   *Rome in Etruria and Umbria*, Oxford.
    1985   *War and Imperialism in Republican Rome, 327–70 BC* (revised edn), Oxford.

Hopkins, K.
    1978   *Conquerors and Slaves*, Cambridge.

Ilari, V.
    1974   *Gli italici nelle strutture militari romane*, Milan.

Keppie, L.J.F.
    1971   'A note on the title "Actiacus"', *CR* n.s. 21, 329–30.
    1981   'Vergil, the confiscations, and Caesar's tenth legion', *CQ* 31, 367–70.
    1983   *Colonisation and Veteran Settlement in Italy 47–14 BC*, London.
    1984   'Colonisation and veteran settlement in Italy in the first century AD', *PBSR* 52, 77–114.

La Regina, A.
   1970–1 'Contributo dell'archeologia alla storia sociale: territori sabellici e sannitici', *DdA* 4–5, 443–59.
Levick, B.M.
   1967 *Roman Colonies in Southern Asia Minor*, Oxford.
Lintott, A.
   1972 'Imperial expansion and moral decline in the Roman Republic', *Historia* 21, 626–38.
Mertens, J.
   1981 *Alba Fucens*, Brussels.
Millett, M.
   1999 'Coloniae and Romano-British studies' in H. Hurst (ed.) *The Coloniae of Roman Britain: New studies and a review* = JRA Supplement 36, Portsmouth, R.I., 191–6.
Misurare la terra
   1983 *Misurare la terra: centuriazione e coloni nel mondo romano*, Modena.
Mouritsen, H.
   1998 *Italian Unification: A study in ancient and modern historiography*, London.
   2004 'Pits and politics: interpreting colonial fora in Republican Italy', *PBSR* 72, 37–67.
Oakley, S.P.
   1984 *A Commentary on Livy Book Nine, Chapters One to Twenty-eight*, unpublished Cambridge Ph.D dissertation.
   1993 'The Roman conquest of Italy', in J. Rich and G. Shipley (eds.) *War and Society in the Roman World*, London, 9–37.
   1997 *A Commentary on Livy Books VI–X*, vol. 1, Oxford.
   1998 *A Commentary on Livy Books VI–X*, vol. 2, Oxford.
Ogilvie, R.M.
   1965 *A Commentary on Livy Books 1–5*, Oxford.
Owens, E.J.
   1991 *The City in the Greek and Roman World,* London.,
Patterson, J.R.
   1993 'Military organization and social change in the late Roman Republic', in J. Rich and G. Shipley (eds.) *War and Society in the Roman World*, London, 92–112.
   2000 *Political Life in the City of Rome*, Bristol.
Pedley, J.G.
   1990 *Paestum*, London.
Richardson, J.S.
   1980 'The ownership of Roman land: Tiberius Gracchus and the Italians', *JRS* 70, 1–11.
   1986 *Hispaniae: Spain and the development of Roman imperialism 218–82 BC*, Cambridge.
Richardson, L., Jr
   1957 'Cosa and Rome: comitium and curia', *Archaeology* 10, 49–55.
Salmon, E.T.
   1963 'The *coloniae maritimae*', *Athenaeum* 41, 3–38.

1967   *Samnium and the Samnites,* Cambridge.

1998   *Roman Colonization under the Republic*, London.

Scheidel, W.

2004   'Human mobility in Roman Italy, 1: the free population', *JRS* 94, 1–26.

Sherwin-White, A.N.

1973   *The Roman Citizenship*, 2nd edn, Oxford.

Stewart, R.

1995   'Catiline and the crisis of 63–60 BC: the Italian perspective', *Latomus* 54, 62–78.

Sumner, G.V.

1970   'The truth about Velleius Paterculus: prolegomena', *HSCP* 74, 257–97.

Terrenato, N.

1998   '*Tam firmum municipium*: the romanization of Volaterrae and its cultural implications', *JRS* 88, 94–114.

Tibiletti, G.

1950   'Ricerche di storia agraria romana', *Athenaeum* 28, 183–266.

Torelli, M.

1988   'Paestum romana', in *Poseidonia-Paestum. Atti del ventisettesimo convegno di studi sulla Magna Grecia (Taranto-Paestum, 9–15 ottobre 1987)*, Taranto, 33–115.

1999   *Tota Italia: Essays in the cultural formation of Roman Italy*, Oxford.

Toynbee, A.J.

1965   *Hannibal's Legacy*, 2 vols., London.

Ward-Perkins, J.B.

1974   *Cities of Ancient Greece and Italy: Planning in classical antiquity*, New York.

Wiseman, T.P.

1970   'Roman Republican road-building', *PBSR* 38, 122–52 = *Roman Studies, literary and historical*, Liverpool, 1987, 126–56.

1977   'Cicero, *Pro Sulla* 60–1', *Liverpool Classical Monthly* 2.2, 21–2.

1979   *Clio's Cosmetics. Three studies in Greco-Roman literature*, Leicester.

1983   'The credibility of the Roman annalists', *Liverpool Classical Monthly* 8.2, 20–2 = *Roman Studies, literary and historical*, Liverpool, 1987, 293–6.

1996   'What do we know about early Rome?', *JRA* 9, 310–15.

Woodman, A.J.

1975   'Velleius Paterculus', in T.A. Dorey (ed.) *Empire and Aftermath: Silver Latin II*, London, 1–25.

Zanker, P.

2000   'The city as symbol: Rome and the creation of an urban image', in E. Fentress (ed.) *Romanization and the city: Creation, transformation and failures* = JRA supplement 38, Portsmouth, R.I., 25–42.

INDEX

Modern town names are in brackets. Numbers in italics refer to illustrations.